Documents of Contemporary Art

In recent decades artists have progressively expanded the boundaries of art as they have sought to engage with an increasingly pluralistic environment. Teaching, curating and understanding of art and visual culture are likewise no longer grounded in traditional aesthetics but centred on significant ideas, topics and themes ranging from the everyday to the uncanny, the psychoanalytical to the political.

The Documents of Contemporary Art series emerges from this context. Each volume focuses on a specific subject or body of writing that has been of key influence in contemporary art internationally. Edited and introduced by a scholar, artist, critic or curator, each of these source books provides access to a plurality of voices and perspectives defining a significant theme or tendency.

For over a century the Whitechapel Gallery has offered a public platform for art and ideas. In the same spirit, each guest editor represents a distinct yet diverse approach – rather than one institutional position or school of thought – and has conceived each volume to address not only a professional audience but all interested readers.

Series Editor: Iwona Blazwick; Commissioning Editor: Anthony Iles; Project Editor: Francesca Vinter; Editorial Advisory Board: Erika Balsom, Sean Cubitt, Neil Cummings, Sven Spieker, Sofia Victorino, Thomas Weaver

that small, naif, Charlie Chaplin-like, luxuriously-indulged, sharp-witted, passionately snobbish, figure, a model for many variations bred thickly everywhere.

Theodor Adorno//Peggy Ahwesh//Sasha Archibald//
Negar Azimi//Roland Barthes//Lauren Berlant//
Nayland Blake//Ian Bogost//Julia Bryan-Wilson//
Norman Bryson//Mary Ann Doane//Jennifer Doyle//
Lee Edelman//Adrienne Edwards//Alex Fialho//
Rosemarie Garland-Thomson//Goutam Ghosh//
Lewis Gordon//Johanna Gosse//Stephen Jay Gould//
Catherine Grenier//Daniel Harris//Jason Havneraas//
Friedrich Wolfram Heubach//Hsuan L. Hsu//Marilyn
Ivy//Mike Kelley//Sharon Kinsella//Christopher
Knight//Leigh Claire La Berge//Elizabeth Legge//
Wyndham Lewis//Lori Merish//William Ian Miller//
Michael Moon//John Morreall//Sianne Ngai//Juliane
Rebentisch//Frances Richard//Carrie Rickey//David
Robbins//John Roberts//Mika Rottenberg//Friedrich
Schiller//Peter Schjeldahl//Kanako Shiokawa//Kristian
Skylstad//Angelik Vizcarrondo-Laboy//Elizabeth Honor
Wilder//Kevin Young

The Cute

Whitechapel Gallery
London
The MIT Press
Cambridge, Massachusetts

Edited by Sianne Ngai

THE CUT

Documents of Contemporary Art

Co-published by Whitechapel Gallery and The MIT Press

First published 2022
© 2022 Whitechapel Gallery Ventures Limited
All texts © the authors or the estates of the authors, unless otherwise stated

ISBN 978-0-85488-298-4 (Whitechapel Gallery)
ISBN 978-0-85488-303-5 (Whitechapel Gallery e-book)
ISBN 978-0-262-54465-8 (The MIT Press)
ISBN 978-0-262-37225-1 (The MIT Press retail e-book)
ISBN 978-0-262-37224-4 (The MIT Press library e-book)

A catalogue record for this book is available from the British Library

Library of Congress Cataloging-in-Publication Data is available

Whitechapel Gallery   10 9 8 7 6 5 4 3 2 1
The MIT Press   10 9 8 7 6 5 4 3 2 1

Series Editor: Iwona Blazwick
Commissioning Editor: Anthony Iles
Project Editor: Francesca Vinter
Design by SMITH
Gemma Gerhard, Justine Hucker, Allon Kaye, Claudia Paladini
Printed and bound in China

Cover, Cosima von Bonin, *SCALLOPS (DARK VERSION), ROCKING*, 2014. Courtesy the artist and Petzel, New York. Photo: Stephan Wyckoff.

Whitechapel Gallery Ventures Limited
77–82 Whitechapel High Street
London, E1 7QX
whitechapelgallery.org

Distributed to the book trade (UK and Europe only) by Thames & Hudson
181a High Holborn
London, WC1V 7QX
+44 (0) 20 7845 5000
sales@thameshudson.co.uk

The MIT Press
Cambridge, MA 02142
mitpress.mit.edu

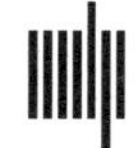

THE MACHINE AND THE COMMODITY

The cute transforms us (and our objects of attention) into both literal and metaphorical vessels of babbling baby-speak

Sianne Ngai
Introduction

This survey tracks the massive impact of a 'minor' aesthetic category on contemporary art, and on the expanding range of cultural practices and discourses upon which artists draw. Given the enormity and potential boundlessness of the archive, the task is more challenging than it first appears. Because the cute is an everyday aesthetic, and not an institutionally codified artistic style, its manifestation in artistic activity is not securely fixed in space or time, or by nation or period, in the way that art-historical styles like Baroque and Art Deco are. But these very facts about the cute – its vernacular origin, or lack of a clearly established archive; its radical diffusiveness, or way of soaking into culture as a whole – help account for the astonishing variety of artistic movements in which it has made an imprint: from Pop Art to craft-based and street art, to abstraction and even Conceptualism. Artists of all types are attracted to the cute, one could say, for the way in which it makes our social totality porous; links between seemingly divergent activities, from robot design to the domestication of animals, suddenly come into relief when revealed as touched by its logic.

The Cute's subject distinguishes it from – while also connecting it in new ways to – other surveys in the Documents of Contemporary Art series. Rather than taking up an institution, a mood, or a technique, *The Cute* explores the artistic ramifications of an *aesthetic category*: a perception of form, sutured by a specific affect or affects to a verbal evaluation. In contrast, however, to *Beauty* and *The Sublime*, whose subjects are aesthetic categories too – and, indeed, the elevated ones which prevail in academic histories and philosophies of art, tacitly organising our overall approach to art's concept in accordance with their images – this survey zooms in on a philosophically and morally unprestigious one. Cute is in fact an aesthetic 'of' or 'about' minorness – or what is generally perceived to be diminutive, subordinate, trivial, and above all, unthreatening.

But is this aestheticisation of minorness itself truly minor, given the cute's influence across radically diverse realms of social practice around the globe, from the automotive industry to poetry, packaged food to social media platforms, electoral politics to our perpetually shifting system of fine arts? How, and for what varying reasons, have artists ranging from Andy Warhol to Alake Shilling taken on the risk of using, as opposed to simply commenting on cuteness in their works? And what ultimately sets the cute apart from other, similarly 'minor' aesthetics or sensibilities – the sentimental, the pastoral, the naive, the ridiculous – with which it so often collaborates? The porousness that culture assumes in light of cuteness, as we notice it saturating everything from theories of biological evolution to the history of Mickey Mouse, makes this ordinary aesthetic a surprisingly useful tool for posing critical questions about society as whole. Artists in this survey accordingly mobilise the cute for insights into difference and belonging, into globalised relations of production and consumption, into adjacent aesthetics, and into art's delimited agency in capitalist society. What makes the cute such a powerful index of not only these questions, but also the historical present in which we encounter them? These issues are addressed across the entirety of *The Cute* as it reconstructs its concept by drawing on texts from multiple disciplines: biology and science, comparative literature, disability studies, queer theory, area studies, and of course, contemporary art.

But first: what is an 'aesthetic category', exactly, and what sets it apart from a style, a manner, or any of the other concepts more traditionally utilised in – and tacitly shaping – the study of art? And how might cuteness, as surveyed through the texts in this book, help concretise our understanding of this utterly familiar, yet curiously undertheorised thing? I want to emphasise that here we are dealing with a double-sided entity: a registration of form – and by 'form' I mean: socially pre-shaped perception – affectively laminated to a verbal judgment triggered in response to that form. An aesthetic category thus connects a structured way of seeing to an equally structured way of speaking. It names the bond between a sensuous 'look' and a discursive evaluation, between an appearance and a speech act. Both sides of that relation are saturated with affect: the element that sutures them together into a single, spontaneous experience.

Because the two sides of any aesthetic category – form and judgment, perception and discourse – are non-identical, they can be related through disconnection, asymmetry or conflict. 'Gimmick', for example, is a negative evaluation of a form we perceive as impoverished but as nonetheless making outrageously extravagant claims to value. It thus names an aesthetic experience in which judgment and form are at odds, or in which one directly indicts the other. Zaniness saturates contemporary capitalist life as a performative style, but one rarely hears 'zany' used as an evaluation. The axiological charge of the judgment seems to have waned over time, such that the term is now almost entirely descriptive. Given that the zany hinges on a stressful blurring of the border separating work from play, what does the diminished strength of its cultural impact as judgment tell us about our increasing resignation, in an age of flexible accumulation, to work's unremitting expansion into all other aspects of life? Conversely, 'interesting' is ubiquitous as an evaluation in both everyday and intellectual discourse, where its affective minimalism signals that one is registering a difference that has not yet been assigned a concept (but which could be, at some point). What the interesting 'looks like' as a style is, however, not as immediately obvious; while to the Conceptual Artists of the 1970s, its 'same but somehow or indeterminately different' ethos could be visualised with a series of binders filled with information, to a nineteenth-century writer like Henry James, the interesting looked like the novel, an infamously formless form featuring typical individuals in states of transition. In every case, however, the shifting relation between the formal and evaluative sides of an aesthetic category tells us something about its historical meaning.

If the zany is visually omnipresent but evaluatively recessed in contemporary capitalist culture, and the interesting is evaluatively strong but formally weak, the cute is striking for its symmetrical and increasing strength on both fronts. So on the one hand, cuteness refers to the 'look' of objects that come across to us as appealingly powerless – soft, malleable, diminutive – which is why its paradigmatic object is still the plush toy or *Kuscheltier*. (The German noun serves us better here, because in contrast to the comparatively cold-blooded 'stuffed animal', it contains an explicit reference to the act of snuggling.) On the other hand, 'cute' is also an aesthetic judgment. It is the thing we say to others, in a tellingly specific way often involving a cooing voice, a childish diction, and unconscious shrinking of one's body, in spontaneous response to our perception of an object's form as soft, malleable, diminutive, and so on. Directed as much if not more to an imaginary public of other subjects standing apart from the object itself, this affective response, 'Cuuuuuuute!!' – or as Roland Barthes prefers, 'Adorable!' – is also an evaluation: one that seems primarily positive but that is ultimately ambivalent. Calling something or someone 'cute' can be as much of a dismissal as a compliment.

Hence while all aesthetic categories conjoin our recognition of a relatively codified appearance to an equally conventional speech act, cuteness does so in a particularly revealing way: our judgment ends up mimicking the appearance it evaluates, collapsing the distance between object and subject in an instantiation of the 'immediacy' we seek in the aesthetic overall.[1] If, as I and others have argued, cuteness enables consumers to enjoy a certain fantasy of ourselves as having power over domestic commodities that, in reality, are much more in control of us, we find this dynamic allegorised in the surprising capacity of the subordinate object to soften and deform the language of its evaluator, re-shaping it in conformity to *its* malleable form.

This situation, in which the cute can exert a sort of 'revenge' by cutifying the language of the cutifier, points to what we might regard as the cute's primary paradox: the immense affective and cultural force exercised by its aestheticisation of powerlessness. In my earliest writings on this topic, I suggested that one of the reasons we see this paradox dramatised so frequently in modern and contemporary art – from the volatile flips of Takashi Murakami's 'Mr DOB' from vulnerable mouse to frightening monster, to, say, the daunting scale of Jeff Koons's *Puppy* – is because it highlights an ambiguity surrounding art's own power in contemporary capitalist life. Cuteness, one could argue, offers artists a place in which to inhabit and think through the complex question of whether art is or should be essentially unthreatening. But this everyday aesthetic also enables artists to investigate issues that take us well beyond self-reflexive inquiries into the agency of art: from Nayland Blake's exploration of the racialisation of rabbits in supremacist United States culture; to Mariko Mori's dramatisation of cuteness as a strategic gender performance and mode of affective labour in the digital economy; to Mika Rottenberg's repeated use of the cute to mark spots in which feminised practices of global consumption and production intersect.[2]

An experience of something as cute can easily tip over into disgust, as viscerally demonstrated by the unsettlingly babylike quality of the old men who shit on and torture one another in Tala Madani's paintings; this ambivalence runs through nearly all the texts in this survey. Hating on cuteness is frequently enjoyed. Indeed, from Wyndham Lewis's remarks on the baleful takeover of modernism by what he calls the 'Child-Cult' in the first decades of the twentieth century; to Carrie Rickey and Peter Schjeldahl on the aesthetically dubious resurgence of what they respectively call 'simplemindedness' and 'Cutism' in the 1980s–90s US artworld, some of the most prescient diagnosticians of the rise of cuteness in this survey are not exactly fans. And yet fans have been known to be equally forceful, and even militant, in cuteness' defense, as we see in the case of K-Pop's BTS Army.[3] The ur-text of 'militant cuteness' in twentieth-century art, however, is arguably Henry Darger's massive illustrated manuscript, *The Story of the Vivian Girls, in What Is Known as the Realms of the Unreal, of the Glandeco-Angelinian War Storm, Caused by the Child Slave Rebellion* (1910–1938/9). Peggy Ahwesh draws a connection between Paul Chan's repurposing of Darger's collective protagonist for his video *Happiness (Finally) After 35,000 Years of Civilization – After Henry Darger and Charles Fourier* (2000–2003), and her own use of a 'rescaled cartoon world' in *She-Puppet* (2001) (one of the earliest works of video-game-based animation), noting Chan's video is 'an intense and dire mash-up of the "cute" with the brutality of war and violence'.[4]

Having laid out these recurring motifs, let us turn to this book's organisation. Our survey begins with a general anatomy of the cute, *Theses on Cuteness*. Whether arch or academic, each text shows how cuteness' oscillation between power and powerlessness in the field of culture gets mirrored by the contradictory affects its experience conjoins: attraction and repulsion, tenderness and aggression, compassion and contempt. We see it recur as well in the well-nigh dialectical frequency with which the cute and anti-cute appear bound up in a single gadget or Gizmo, as Daniel Harris shows via the 1980s film *Gremlins* (a film readable also, Wendy Allison Lee suggests, as an allegory of US anti-Asian xenophobia); and in the *productivity* unleashed by a lethargic aesthetic primarily shaped by *consumption* (as Harris, Lori Merish, and I stress; though for a dissenting viewpoint, see Joshua Dale).[5] From here our survey pivots to a consideration of the cute's historical precedents and aesthetic adjacencies, *Para- and Proto-Cuteness*. For the cute converges with a number of other aesthetic concepts with their own distinctive genealogies: the simple, the grotesque, the pastoral, the sentimental.[6] These older if similarly 'minor' aesthetic traditions might be said to anticipate forms of cuteness before its historical emergence proper. Their lineages throw the cute into sharper relief, illuminating the edges at which it intersects while remaining distinct from the others. Such moments of external differentiation ultimately allow for more precise comparisons in the field of cuteness itself. How, for instance, does Ghoutam Ghosh's relationship to the 'naive', as revealed in his interview, inflect the way in which his paintings intermittently veer towards the cute? The naive seems to have nothing to do, however, with the cynical, sadistic variant of cuteness that informs Madani's paintings. Meanwhile, the fact that Mike Kelley's use of soft toys stems from his interest in craft practices, while Cosima von Bonin's clearly does not, helps explain how their works engage cuteness in such radically different ways.[7]

The next section of the survey considers cuteness as a technique of social differentiation – and one which has produced or reinscribed existing kinds of disenfranchisement and marginalisation. Artists conscious of this ideological aestheticisation of vulnerability nonetheless mobilise it to work on and transform the cute. They do so in ways that not only deepen or complicate its meanings (as Adrienne Edwards argues in her reading of Juliana Huxtable's 'kewt' aesthetic), but also reshape their artistic practices (as we see in Kevin Young's account of Kara Walker's turn to the pop-up book). Cuteness is something around which people tend to gather, and these scenes of public intimacy can enter into the content of art objects as well, as we see in Lauren Berlant and Lee Edelman's exchange on the 'adorable' and its function in works by Miranda July and Larry Johnson; or in Marilyn Ivy's reading of Yoshitomo Nara's relation to his fans as the key to understanding the basic forms and themes of his corpus.[8]

In my earlier writings on the cute, I stressed its status as an aesthetic 'about' (reproductive) consumption, heuristically and thus somewhat artificially isolating this activity from capitalist production and circulation. Yet our actions and fantasies as consumers are inextricably bound up with labour practices around the globe (which are in turn inflected by the categories of social difference examined in the preceding section).[9] 'The Machine and the Commodity' thus takes up a challenge posed by Lauren Berlant: 'How do we think about labour and consumer related subjectivities in the same moment, since…one cannot talk about scandals of the appetite – along with food, there's sex, smoking, shopping, and drinking as sites of moral disapprobation, social policy, and self-medication – without talking about the temporality of the workday [and] the debt cycle […]?'[10] Mika Rottenberg's corpus invites us to do the same; her work focuses on women working at global hubs of production and circulation, often explicitly at sites for the fabrication and sale of cute commodities, from the pink pearl-crusted bunnies in *NoNoseKnows* (2015) to the mountains of plastic decorations threatening to crush their tired female guardians in *Cosmic Generator (Tunnel Variant)* (2017). And so, in an utterly different way, do Dean Kenning's appealingly forlorn machines. As John Roberts puts it, the 'broken DIY machine wants you to be its friend […] – to get you to see through the technological sadism of the "new" – even when […] all you want to do is punish it for its sickly pleading presumptuousness and run a mile from its demand for love'.[11] Recognising cuteness as integrated into capitalist production was a key intervention on the part of the anthology *The Affects and Aesthetics of Cuteness*, and I have followed suit by focusing on artworks that explore 'cute' at the seam between leisure and labour. Whether or not we agree with Hal Foster's evaluation that most works of 'relational aesthetics' boil down to 'remedial work in socialization', it seems striking that when cuteness organises 'socially engaged' artworks, it does so in conjunction with the simulation of services involving affective or caring labour: from Mammalian Diving Reflex's *Haircuts by Children* (2006–19), discussed by Leigh Claire La Berge, to Adrian Howells's therapeutic offerings of intimacy (by appointment) in *Held* (2007).[12]

How can the cute help us periodise, or just make better sense of, 'the contemporary' itself? Serving as a bridge from the previous section, Jennifer Doyle's discussion of *Held* kicks off the final chapter of our survey, which focuses on how cultural producers use cute as a tool to process some aspect of our complicated, overwhelming 'now' and the various futures encoded in it: from Deborah Roberts' collages meditating on the 'violent adultification' of Black youth, to Charlemagne Palestine's feat of filling the gargantuan space at 356 S. Mission Road with 18,000 stuffed animals.[13] Though they evoke masses of living beings displaced by environmental disaster and, simultaneously, the look of environmental disaster itself, this battalion of cheap toys also elicits a fantasy of the collectively undertaken rescue of an earth damaged in part by their own toxic production.[14] A very different response to environmental crisis might be at work in Cosima von Bonin's unhealthy-looking 'seascapes' of floppy, humiliated sharks and disconsolate crabs, or in the little sweaters Annette Messager relentlessly knits for her vast grids of dead birds. Meanwhile, the washed-out cuteness of the stoneware figurines made by Diana Yesenia Alvarado and Narumi Nekpenekpen, whose curiously 'degraded' look Lily Scherlis describes as that of 'cuteness in decay', suggests that there is something tired or failing about the youth-obsessed aesthetic itself, which now appears on its last legs even as it continues to be ruthlessly 'worked.'[15] In a similar vein, as Bryan Markovitz notes, the 'decadent' version of cute we encounter in Alake Shilling's paintings of voluptuous, googly-eyed animals hints at a desire *to end* cuteness, or to imagine it as receding into the historical past, swallowed back into the older category of the grotesque.[16] In a striking departure from artists like Koons or Murakami, who represent cute at the height of its powers, interest in the wearing-out of this aesthetic paradoxically marks the cutting edge of work on the cute today.

Though the cute arguably has closer ties to some traditions than others (say, to Pop Art, or Outsider Art), it neither originates from nor belongs to any single artistic movement. Yet consider Peter Schjeldahl's startling, but not unconvincing thesis that 'Cutism' came to infiltrate the pores of the United States artworld through the gateway of Conceptualism, 'fill[ing] its austere self-referring forms [...] with cheery self-referring content of the artist's personal quirks and obsessions'. One wonders why this genealogy might be the case (if true): was it because the conceptualist critique of 'administration' realised it needed to take in place in an affective register diametrically opposed to severity? Or because art ends up exaggerating its charisma when confronted with the indifference of data?[17] Does Schjeldahl's hypothesis eerily anticipate the commodification of data today, which hinges on the unremitting cutification of ourselves on the internet?[18] Where would social media platforms themselves be without the cute? In any case, from Fluxus and neo-Dada to Situationism and even Minimalism and Earth Art, rich veins of cuteness streak through the 'hardest' post-war avant-gardes; indeed, one of the most surprising things about the cute is the sheer multiplicity of movements into which it threads, even within this provincial compass of a survey focused on the art of Global North.[19]

Cuteness' politics are, at best, ambiguous. Indeed, the ideology of an aesthetic that accentuates, eroticises, and sometimes performatively instantiates the powerlessness of others seems so obviously problematic that its critique has come to generate equally thought-provoking counter-critiques. These remind us to not overlook the agency of those who willfully act or have been made cute (Dale); that cuteness can be strategically chosen as well as externally imposed (Kinsella); that it can be a survival strategy (Gould); that it can be a lubricant for socialisation in general (Dale); or a way to foster alternative counterpublics (Berlant and Edelman).[20]

This said, it is telling that nearly all who embrace or defend cuteness in this reader are also wary of it. As critics have noted, cuteness is used in the workplace to make workers work harder, or squeeze more unpaid surplus labour from them.[21] Cuteness is often mixed with various kinds of racism and misogyny (as Kara Walker, Sean-Kierre Lyons, Yoshitomo Nara and others know well) – as is also, of course, right-wing or fascist anti-cuteness (Edmund Burke, Wyndham Lewis). Yet the ambiguity of the aesthetic's politics is often precisely why the artists in this survey have felt compelled to make use of it: as content (Nara, Darger, Nekpenekpen, Alvarado, Ahwesh), as form (Kelley, Chan, Palestine, von Bonin, Kenning), and as method (Howells, Robbins, Mammalian Diving Reflex). Feminist, queer and anti-racist uses of the cute *and* anti-cute – often in riskily close quarters – are deliberately foregrounded in this survey as an area of especially intensive exploration by artists today.

'To name a sensibility, to draw its contours and to recount its history, requires a deep sympathy modified by revulsion', notes Susan Sontag.[22] This is the approach taken by this survey, in close attunement with the artists included in it. It is the concatenation of affects that most defines the aesthetic experience and judgment of the cute itself.

1   On 'immediacy' as the most recent permutation of late capitalist logic – a drive towards 'direct presence' and 'self-identical thisness' in all areas of cultural production, from Immersive Van Gogh to NFTs – see Anna Kornbluh, 'Immediacy, or, The Style of Too Late Capitalism', unpublished manuscript, University of Illinois, Chicago.

2   For an in-depth study of cuteness as feminised affective labour on the internet, see Gabrielle Lukács, 'The Labor of Cute: Net Idols in the Digital Economy', in *Invisibility by Design: Women and Labor in Japan's Digital Economy* (Durham, NC and London: Duke University Press, 2020).

3   See Bonni Rambatan and Jacob Johanssen, 'The Online Militancy of the Cute', in *Event Horizon: Sexuality, Politics, Online Culture, and the Limits of Capitalism* (Winchester: Zero Books, 2021).

4   Peggy Awesh and Johanna Gosse, 'Cut to Cute: Fact, Form, and Feeling in Digital Animation' (2018); reprinted in this volume, 198–203.

5   Wendy Allison Lee, 'Cute. Dangerous. Asian American. 'Gremlins' @35', in *Public Books* (July 5 2019) (www.publicbooks.org/cute-dangerous-asian-american-gremlins-35/). For a theory of cuteness as an 'appeal to others' eliciting affiliative or prosocial behavior in general, rather than a commodity aesthetic linked to nurturing affects in particular, see Joshua Paul Dale, 'The Appeal of the Cute Object: Desire, Domestication, and Agency', in *The Affects and Aesthetics of Cuteness*, eds. Joshua Paul Dale, Joyce Goggin, Julia Leyda, Anthony P. McIntyre, and Diane Negra (London: Routledge, 2017) 35-54.

6   My approach here follows the same reasoning behind Rosalind Galt's synthesising/particularising approach to the concept of 'pretty'. See Rosalind Galt, 'Introduction: The Pretty as Troublesome Image', in *Pretty: Film and the Decorative Image* (New York: Columbia University Press, 2011) 8.

7   From nineteenth-century German painter Hermann Sondermann to British multi-media artist Heather Phillipson, the diverse range of works appearing in 'Too Cute! Sweet is about to get Sinister' (Birmingham Museum and Art Gallery, 26 January–12 May 2019), an exhibition culled from the Arts Council and Birmingham Museum's collections by artist Rachel Maclean, enables questions like this to come to the fore. For a video accompanying the exhibition created by Maclean, see www.rachelmaclean.com/too-cute/

8   Here I emulate a move I admire on the part of the editors of *The Affects and Aesthetics of Cuteness*, who also consider the cute's role in reinforcing social divisions alongside its role in generating communities.

9   Lauren Berlant, *Cruel Optimism* (Durham, NC: Duke University Press, 2017) 105.

10   Ibid.

11   John Roberts, 'Dean Kenning's Kinetics' (2020); reprinted in this volume, 157–61. Roberts' characterisation of Kenning's kinetic artworks dovetails in surprising ways with the industrial design of domestic robots. See Catherine Caudwell and Cherie Lacey, 'What do home robots want? The ambivalent power of cuteness in robotic relationships', *Convergence: The International Journal of Research into New Media Technologies*, vol. 26, no. 4 (2020) 956–968. See also the soft robots and kinetic sculptures created by artist and programmer Eevi Rutanen: www.eevirutanen.com/

12   Hal Foster, 'Chat Rooms', *Participation* (Documents in Contemporary Art), ed. Claire Bishop (London and Cambridge, MA: Whitechapel Gallery and MIT Press, 2004) 194.

13   Amarie Gipson, 'On Deborah Roberts', *Artforum* (21 September 2021). (www.artforum.com/print/reviews/202107/deborah-roberts-86369). 365 S. Mission Road is a Los Angeles warehouse originally transformed into a gallery by Laura Owens to accommodate her own outsized paintings of cute squiggles on grids.

14   Christopher Knight, 'Teddy Bears to the Rescue' (2018); reprinted in this volume, 207–8.

15   Lily Scherlis, personal communication with author (Word doc), 16 June, 2021.

16   Bryan Markovitz, personal communication with author (e-mail), 19 September, 2021.

17   I owe these thoughts to Anthony Iles. Personal communication with author, 28 September, 2021.

18   See Damon Young, 'Sarcastic Cuteness', in 'Ironies of Web 2.0', *Post45* (2 May 2019) (https://post45.org/2019/05/ironies-of-web-2-0/).

19   On cuteness in Italian Futurism, see Giancarlo Capri, 'A Cute Futurism', in *Futuriste: Women in Art and Literature* (New York: Casa Italiana Zerilli Marimò at New York University, 2009) 10–15. See also Giancarlo Carpi, 'Futurism: From Modernism to Cuteness', in Markku Valkonen and EMMA (Espoo Museum of Modern Art), *Uusi taide: Nopeus, vaara, uhma: Italian futurismi 1909–1944* [*A new art: speed, danger, defiance: Italian futurism 1909–1944*] (Espoo: EMMA, 2012).

20   See Dale, 'The Appeal of the Cute Object', op. cit.

21   Allison Page, 'This Baby Sloth Will Inspire You To Keep Going: Capital, Labor, and the Affective Power of Cute Animal Videos', in *The Aesthetics and Affects of Cuteness*, eds. Joshua Paul Dale, Joyce

Goggin, Julia Leyda, Anthony P. McIntyre, and Diane Negra (London and New York: Routledge, 2017) 75–94. See also Hiroshi Nittono, et al. 'The Power of Kawaii: Viewing Cute Images Promotes a Careful Behavior and Narrows Attentional Focus', *Plos One*, vol. 7, no. 9 (2012).

22   Susan Sontag, 'Notes on 'Camp', in *Against Interpretation and Other Essays* (New York: Octagon Books, 1978) 276.

THE CUTE COMMODITY, FOR ALL ITS PATHOS OF POWERLESSNESS, IS THUS CAPABLE OF MAKING SURPRISINGLY POWERFUL DEMANDS

THESES ON CUTENESS

Frances Richard
Fifteen Theses on the Cute//2001

I

Draw a circle, and ray out from it the *abject*, the *melancholic*, the *wicked*, the *childlike*. Now in the zones between add the *erotic*, the *ironic*, the *narcotic*, and the *kitsch*. Intersperse the *Romantic/Victorian*, the *Disney/consumerist*, and the *biologically deterministic*. At the centre of this many-spoked wheel lies a connective empty space. Label it CUTE.

II

What is cute? The technical definition encompasses revealing distinctions that tend to be elided in normal conversation, where cute is cute and everyone knows what this means. Cute by the book derives etymologically from 'acute,' and its establishing usage dates to circa 1731. From this root comes cute's first meaning, as clever or underhandedly shrewd, and its second, as impudent or smart-alecky – 'Don't get cute'. The standard connotation of dainty or delicate prettiness then leads to what might be termed mannerist cute – the cutesy, which (like the folksy) is defined by its excessive or self-conscious appeal to the unembarrassed core quality.[1]

III

Such interconnections echo a number of distinctions present in the larger motif. Fundamentally, cute serves to displace, or neutralise, or reconceptualise in a positive/non-threatening direction; this is possible only to a certain degree, at which point the pendulum swings back the other way. Because it is a device of masking and semblance, cute is inherently circular (see Thesis I). Note how the dictionary definition enacts this closed progression, which has to do at every stage with things not being wholly what they seem. Cleverness shields or distances; it plays potentially hurtful games. Impertinence simplifies this game, softening the con artist's plot into a joke. Prettiness and daintiness further soften a barbed joke into an appeal or flirtation; self-conscious or excessive appeal becomes suspect. Suspicious appeal shades toward a con.

IV

Cute marks a crucial absence. It guarantees, by definition, the non-appearance of malice, premeditation, irony, self-consciousness, accusation, or mercenary agenda. However, in its manufactured forms cute remains a major locus for – in some ways is synonymous with – the manipulative gesture, the prepackaged, consumable demonstration of (necessarily factitious) innocence, spontaneity, and need. Cute arises by manipulating the guarantee of non-manipulation. Professing its own demure and complete powerlessness, it gains power over and directs all interactions with it: parents wait upon the infant, not the other way around. Simultaneously referring to and negating its own vulnerability, cute functions as a self-fulfilling system, maintaining its image as 100% stolid and happy and obvious only by virtue of utter contingency.

V

Cute displaces and protects against violence by caricaturing the object of potential violation. Drop-kicking a stuffed animal or crumpling an animal-baby poster, for example, might generate a faint transgressive whiff; either could conceivably make a small child cry. But neither compares to the moment for which such acts are prophylactic: it is horrifying to feel the fragile bones and heartbeat-warmth of the actual kitten in one's hands, and to feel those hands flexing, as if of their own atavistic accord, to crush. Even more so when the live kitten functions as a surrogate for said small child.

VI

Put another way: William the cat is very cute each morning when he stalks, torments, and kills the cute stuffed robin and presents it to Rebecca and Ira in the bathroom, at their feet at the breakfast table, or in their bed. Actual dead robins, complete with mites and trailing blood, appearing in the same situations with the same frequency, would not be cute. Cute emerges as a ritualised and declawed sublimation of violence, a pantomime or parody neutralising mortal threat. This threat arises at that juncture where the destructive meets the generative: Rebecca and Ira cradle William furry-belly-up in their arms, laughing, asking, 'Have you met our son?'

VII

The sexy- or porn-cute obviously constitutes a whole genre *sui generis*, characterised by the Playboy bunny, the chick, the arm-candy, the hey-baby. Boy-cute geared toward both females and males tends to cutesify adult or macho animal imagery – *Tiger Beat*, beefcake – rather than indulging ostentatiously infantile girl-cute models. As a term for 'sexually desirable', cute marks a middle path: where 'hot' and 'innocent' might both be overwhelming (for different reasons), cute is available, plausible, manageable. One respondent queried about the meaning of cute insisted that males of her acquaintance identified sexually appealing women as cute only when they were also intelligent – a reversion, conscious or not, to the word's eighteenth-century origin in mental acumen, if not subterfuge. (See Thesis II.)

VIII

Cute might be thought of as a watered-down version of pretty; which is a watered-down version of beautiful; which is a watered-down version of sublime; which is a watered-down version of terrifying. In this regard, the cute is akin to the ridiculous, which is a watered-down version of the absurd, which is again a watered-down version of that which terrifies. By extension, this suggests that all representation, whatever its stylistic bent, is tinged with an experience of terror: the terror of the convincingly ersatz, the killing disjuncture of the otherised, the pseudo-real. (See Theses IV, VI.)

IX

> The trouble with a Kitten is that
> Eventually it becomes a Cat
> –Ogden Nash

In keeping with its status as representational rather than natural, cute suggests an inherently fleeting, forgettable, throwaway quality, but this is distinct from ephemerality, since by its very vapidity or inoffensiveness, cute remains indestructible. Cute stabilises infancy, or the frailty of old age, or the foolishly unconscious actions of a supposedly competent adult, by reframing them in an atemporal, non-biological, and consequence-free zone, not entirely unrelated to the fixed reality inside a picture.

X

What, then, of organic cute, the reflexive and visceral response stimulated by a playful baby or winsome gesture, animal or human? If beauty is symmetrical, proportionate, and shades toward perfection, while sublimity is awe-inspiring, jagged, and larger than life, then organic cute is disproportionate, asymmetrical, and smaller – lighter, more humorous, and less ironic – than life. The stabbing suddenness of organic cute, the irrepressible swoon it evokes, echoes back again to the acute not in its intelligence, but in its directness.

XI

Morphologically – that is, aesthetically – cute relies on big eyes, round heads, fat bellies. The limbs of the cute are stubby or non-existent, its mouth abstracted or disproportionately tiny, its nose button, its ears enormous, or alternatively, invisible. Cute tumbles, toddles, waddles, rolls; it is visibly dependent, apparently engineered by natural selection to stimulate a nurturing response. If this is true in evolutionary terms, it follows that the surplus cuteness manufactured by culture might denote the culture's attempt to trick itself into kindness. One respondent defined it thus: 'Cute makes you do things you wouldn't do otherwise.' (See Thesis V.)

XII

The evil (or drunken) clown; the devil-possessed doll; *Star Trek's* 'Trouble with Tribbles': like porn-cute, wicked-cute depends on camp. When cute goes bad, it deepens rather than transforms. Poisoned cute retains its outward appearance while proliferating cancerously toward a toxic/comic exaggeration of itself. Its colours tend to darken from pure pastel; its contours sharpen or skew to the grotesque. Cute melodies lilt or rollick and repeat – when sped to mania or slowed to dirge, their whimsy boomerangs on and guts itself. (See Thesis X.)

XIII

The linguistic analogue of cute is formed by a prolonged nonsense exhalation filtered through the mouth aligned as if to smile; when inflected improperly, these sounds become not porn-cute but directly porno-graphic: 'awww', 'oooohh', 'mmmm'. Since this lexicon is ostensibly derived from baby talk, perhaps it makes sense that it also gestures to the origin of babies. When such sounds coalesce into words, they often function as aliases for cute and rely on repetition and diminution, as if unconsciously articulating the concept's dual nature: 'boo-boo', 'snookums'. The infamous suffixes – '-ie' or '-y' and, to a lesser extent in English, '-ette' – reverse toward the abstract, pulling normal words back into their malleable infancy as preverbal sound. Of course, this also has the predictably paradoxical effect of making unremarkable words foolish, of cutesifying them. (See Thesis VII.)

XIV

Cute in German: *liebe* or *süss*. Cute in Spanish: *lindo*. Cute in French: *mignon*. In Japan (which vies with the United States as self-anointed world capital of cute – it might be relevant that the most extreme and deliberate form of cute, the cutesy, originated as a term circa 1944, while these two powers were at war – see Theses II, IX) cultural categorisation identifies not only cute people and cute objects, but cute handwriting – an extreme rounding of the kanji which renders them almost illegible (see again Thesis X). This style is variously referred to as 'round writing' (*marui ji*), 'comic writing' (*manga ji*), 'fake-child writing' (*burikko ji*) and 'kitten writing' (*koneko ji*) (See Thesis IX.) An American theorist of Japanese cute also reports cute food – sugary, bland, pale in colour, soft in texture – and, of course, many sartorial examples (see Thesis VII). Sayuri Koshino, a public-relations representative at Sanrio, the company responsible for the efflorescence of cute that is the Hello Kitty product line, explains:

> I believe we are all born with actual physical organs of cute, tiny and valentine shaped, pulsing away in our cerebella. But I also believe that many of us, having developed harsh and realistic life attitudes, have repressed our cute impulses.[2]

XV

Toward a thesaurus of cute: adorable, amiable, animated, appealing, artless, artificial, attractive, available, bland, boring, bowdlerised, callow, cartoon, charming, childish, childlike, cloying, comfy, comic, consumable, cuddly, dainty, darling, dear, delicate, desirable, diminutive, dippy, easy, effeminate, embarrassed, engaging, flirtatious, foolish, free, friendly, frilly, frivolous, frolicking, furry, fuzzy, gentle, genuine, girlish, guileless, happy, happy-go-lucky, helpless, honest, idiotic, immature, inexperienced, infantile, ingenuous, ingratiating, innocent, innocuous, inoffensive, itsy-bitsy, juvenile, lovable, naive, non-threatening, maudlin, miniature, mindless, mushy, natural, nostalgic, passive, pastel, pathetic, pert, petite, pink, popular, precocious, pretty, pure, quaint, quiet, round, rotund, saccharine, sappy, saucy, sexy, shallow, shy, silly, simpatico, simple, sincere, small, smarmy, smiley, soft, squashable, sugary, sweet, sympathetic, syrupy, tasteless, teeny, timeless, tiny, touching, unconscious, unironic, unsophisticated, unstructured, vapid, vulnerable, weak, winning, winsome, waiflike, wee.

1   See *Merriam-Webster's Collegiate Dictionary*, Tenth Edition.
2   Sharon Kinsella, 'Cuties in Japan', in *Women, Media, and Consumption in Japan*, eds. Lise Skov & Brian Moeran (Honolulu: University of Hawaii, 1995) 253.

Frances Richard, 'Fifteen Theses on the Cute', *Cabinet*, no. 4 (Autumn 2001) 94–5.

John Morreall
Cuteness//1991

What Cuteness Looks Like

[…] In using the word 'cute' I do not have in mind the older sense, 'clever, keen-witted, sharp, shrewd', but the newer sense in which babies, puppies, koala bears, certain adults, and certain cottages, villages, and cars are said to be cute. The category I have in mind is primarily a visual one, applying to things and actions, though a voice or melody may in some cases be cute. There are, I take it, no cute textures, tastes, or smells. […]

I will begin with the cuteness of babies, and then try to show how the term gets extended. The approach here is evolutionary: my guiding hypothesis is that in the evolution of our mammalian ancestors, the recognition and appreciation of the specialness of the young had survival value for the species. And so certain features evolved in the young which got them noticed and appreciated; these features constitute cuteness. The need to have adults find them appealing, and so take care of them, exists in all young mammals, but is by far the greatest in human babies, who are the most helpless creatures on earth. It is no accident, therefore, that as a species we appreciate the specialness of our offspring to a degree not found in other animals.

What are the features of babies that get them noticed and appreciated by adults? One is smallness, the baby's size relative to other humans. But cuteness is not mere smallness. Young crabs are much smaller in relation to adult crabs than our babies are to us, but young crabs are not cute, because they are merely miniatures of adult crabs. In the history of art, too – in colonial American painting, for example – infants have often been represented simply as miniature adults, and such portrayals are not cute. A baby is cute not just by being smaller than we are, but by showing some important differences from us in its appearance and behaviour.

Some of the distinctively babyish features, which get infants noticed and cared for, were investigated by the ethologist Konrad Lorenz. They include:

(1) a head large in relation to the body; (2) a large protruding forehead, with the eyes set relatively low in the head. (In adult humans the eyes are positioned about half-way down the head; in infants, they are about two-thirds of the way down the head); (3) round, protruding cheeks; (4) plump, rounded body shape; (5) short, thick extremities; (6) soft body surfaces which are pleasurable to touch; (7) behaviour indicating weakness and clumsiness.[1]

These characteristics are precisely, I suggest, what make a human baby cute. Cute features are just those which have the disposition to elicit from adults a response of wanting to hold, cuddle, and care for the baby. They are, to use the language of ethology, 'releasing stimuli' for tender feelings and affectionate behaviour; or in the language of popular psychology, they evoke 'bonding' between the parents and the child.

Our innate disposition to hold and touch the cute baby is revealed in the collocation 'cute and cuddly'. We also often say of the cute baby that it is 'sweet' and we playfully say to the baby things such as 'I'm going to eat you up!' A kind of natural synaesthesia is operating here based on the close relationship between nuzzling and kissing, on the one hand, and eating, on the other. Indeed a common way of showing affection for the baby is to take mock bites out of its legs, arms and belly.

The pleasurable feelings of tenderness we have for babies are often enhanced by other kinds of enjoyment, most notably by humorous amusement.[2] We can understand the connection between humour and cuteness in babies if we consider the list of cute features above, in light of the dominant theory of humour, the incongruity theory. [...] Babies can seem incongruous to adults because of their different body proportions, their inability to fend for themselves, their awkward and often undirected movements, and their lack of understanding of the world around them. Under the right circumstances these kinds of incongruity can be amusing, and that amusement contributes to our enjoyment of babies.

The Survival Value of Cuteness
Cultures around the world find babies cute. Indeed, bigots will often admit the cuteness of infants in the groups they despise, and even be inclined to hold those infants. Adults kiss and nuzzle babies in all cultures, even those in which adults do not kiss each other. This universal response to cuteness can be explained in evolutionary terms, by the survival value which nurturing responses to cuteness have for the young, and so for the species. The adult's desire to cuddle the baby, obviously, increases the likelihood that it will be protected and fed. And the adult's affection will satisfy the infant's biological need for tactile stimulation, a basic need in humans, indeed in all mammals. (Dogs, cats, and most other mammals need to be licked off by their mother soon after birth, for example; those which are not licked off usually die because their excretory systems do not begin to function normally.) Unfortunately, the human need for tactile stimulation was not recognised by biologists and physicians until well into this century. Foundling hospitals early in the 1900s provided little or no tactile stimulation for babies, and so, despite their adequate feeding and medical care, frequently had mortality rates of over 90%. There was even a name coined for

the 'disease' uncuddled babies 'died of' – '*marasmus*', Greek for 'wasting away'. When hospitals realised what was wrong and started showing the babies affection, many fewer died and all showed improvement in various ways.[3] Very recent research has shown that premature babies, who have until now been handled by the 'minimal touch rule', thrive on massage. They gain weight about 50% faster than untouched babies, their nervous systems mature more rapidly, and they are able to leave hospital an average of six days earlier.[4]

Cuteness has other benefits for babies besides getting them held and touched. Since they cannot do anything for themselves, require almost constant attention, and cause great inconvenience for their parents, all without a hint of gratitude, there has to be some compensation to the parents for what in an adult or older child would simply be selfish, rude behaviour. The pleasure that the baby's cuteness provides is part of this compensation. The baby wakes the parents at 3a.m., or throws the plate of food on the floor, or does any of the hundred potentially troubling things infants do; but its cute appearance, along with its powerlessness, innocence, and lack of awareness of what it is doing, appease the parents. The baby does not even have to smile in order to be seen as cute by the parents: adults' perceptions of babies' cuteness are relatively stable across various facial expressions – even crying.[5] Because babies' thoughtlessness and inability to fend for themselves are seen as attractive rather than as an imposition on adults, we are much more likely to be patient with them, and that is essential in our willingness to spend the time we must spend in teaching them such skills as language. Baby-talk is quite different from correct adult language, but not in the annoying way a poorly written business letter or a cliché-ridden speech is. Instead of feeling impatient with the young child for talking baby-talk, we find it delightful.

Besides this delight, there are other benefits to adults in finding babies cute. Perhaps the most important is the way it fills adult needs for affection. [...]

So cuteness has survival value because it prompts adults to care for the young, and it evokes adult behaviour which meets the tactile needs of both adults and young. A species in which the young were helpless, but in which there were no releasing stimuli such as cuteness to prompt adults to care for them, would be at a great disadvantage in the struggle for survival; indeed such a species probably never could have evolved. Simpler species such as the insects, which are born with much more ability to fend for themselves than mammals have, need little or no care at the beginning of life, and so get along without cuteness. For mammals, however, and especially for humans, cuteness seems indispensable.

Cuteness Beyond Babies
If we as a species have a built-in disposition to respond to cuteness in babies in certain ways, then it stands to reason that we will have a similar disposition to

respond to other things which have all or many of those characteristics which make babies cute. The infants of other animals are the most obvious case here, especially the infants of the species we care most about, our pets. […]

The second case I want to discuss of the extension of cuteness beyond babies is to human adolescents and adults. Teenage boys talk of teenage girls as cute, and vice versa to a lesser extent, as do men and women. I suggest that this use of 'cute' is based on the similarity between the romantic affection we have for each other and the affection we have for babies. There are many ways in which lovers see baby-like features in each other and treat each other in baby-like ways. They make up silly pet-names, for example, which are often diminutives and forms of baby-talk. […] Perusing a page of personal Valentine's Day messages in the newspaper recently, I turned up pet-names such as the following: Pee-Wee, Pookie, Tweetie, Little Monkey, Bunchlet, Scootchie, Scootchums, Honey Bunny Bear, Cuddles, Puddin' Pops, Pinkie, Little Shrimp, and Shiska-Bob-Bob. Notice how any of these could just as easily have been a nickname for a baby as for a lover. Notice, too, that some of them have a connotation of food, suggesting the connection between cuteness and eating or nuzzling. […]

When we extend the word 'cute' from humans and animals to inanimate objects such as cottages, villages and cars, we make a rather large jump. For obviously there is no urge to hug a cottage or village, nor, despite advertising hyperbole, to cuddle a car. None the less, there are elements which these cute things have in common with cute babies. For one thing, the cute cottage, village or car is small relative to things of its kind. We emphasise this aspect of cuteness with our redundant collocation 'cute little'. A large village could not be cute. A five-bedroom house could not be cute, though individual rooms within it could be. Beyond the small size of a cute cottage, village or car, there must be a certain innocence and non-threateningness like that of a baby. We must be able to feel something like the attraction we feel for the cute baby. A small village of tall, thin houses with many sharp angles to their steep roofs might be attractive in its own way, but it would not evoke the kind of affection we feel when we find something cute. Similarly, a small car that had sharp fins and an oversized engine would not be cute. Its aggressiveness would be the opposite of the charming gentleness of cuteness. A cute cottage or car also is usually well cared for, perhaps indicating that the appropriate nurturing is already being done – a dilapidated cottage or dirty rusted car would not be cute, just as a starving child is not cute.

In calling an inanimate object cute, in short, we are extending the schema of small/gentle/innocent/inviting that we first discerned in babies. The process here, I think, is the one Mark Johnson has written about in his account of metaphorical thinking.[6] I do not have a full account of how it works with everything we find cute, but I am confident that the elements I have been talking about play a role. A full account of how we extend the concept of cuteness, I think, would also add evidence to Johnson's view that our thinking is constitutionally metaphorical and anthropocentric.

Cuteness as an Aesthetic Category

I want to close with a few reflections on the fact which I mentioned at the beginning – that cuteness has not been an important category in art and aesthetics. Of the many reasons which might be given for this fact, I want to simply mention one and to discuss another. The first is a political reason: the traditions of Western fine art have been male dominated, and males have not valued the tender feelings involved in cuteness as an important aspect of art works. Madonnas notwithstanding, the nurturing of children has not been a major theme in Western art, and aesthetic features eliciting nurturing responses have not been considered important by male artists or male aestheticians.

Secondly, cuteness has not been important in the high traditions of Western art because it is an unsubtle property, and unsubtle properties have usually been treated as inferior aesthetic properties. If my analysis of cuteness is correct, it is a feature that we are genetically hard-wired to discern easily and react to automatically. Cuteness requires no taste or aesthetic education to discern. That is why, of course, it is so common in Kitsch. And from an evolutionary standpoint, it is obvious that cuteness would have to be like this in order to have survival value for the species. Subtle aesthetic features which are discerned only by the few and which are susceptible of several interpretations, do not, by definition, have a single effect on adults in general. But cuteness had to have such an effect. If hungry babies had needed aesthetes as parents in order to be fed, our race would have never gotten started.

Cuteness is not often mentioned in aesthetics and art criticism, but when it is, it is almost always thought of negatively. To judge a work of art 'cute' is usually not to take it seriously. The central objection to cuteness in the arts, I think, is a version of the objection to sentimentality. By sentimentality here I mean the reliance of an art work for its primary effect on evoking simple, shallow emotions in an obvious way. Melodramas of the nineteenth century and their film counterparts in the twentieth, for example, often had as their primary effect getting the audience to feel pity by presenting a one-dimensional innocent character being abused by a villain. What is objectionable here is not the evocation of pity – after all, tragedy does that – but the unsubtlety of the evocation and the shallowness of the emotion. When I find myself crying at just the intended moment in a sentimental film, I feel ashamed that I have let the director manipulate me in so obvious a way. […] I want to respond as a free person, not as a limbic system wired to a body. But the director found an easy 'pity-releaser', say a completely innocent person being mistreated by a completely evil one, presented it in an unambiguous way, and here I am crying right on cue. The director has simply pushed my pity-button. Unlike the pity evoked by great tragedy, the pity evoked by melodrama is emotion that is not coupled with any larger emotions, or with insight into the characters, or with any new perspective on the human condition. It is quick, easy, thoughtless emotion.

It was in part his negative reaction to sentimentality in the plastic arts that led Clive Bell to his wholesale rejection in art of emotions related to real life, and his insistence that true art will evoke only the 'aesthetic emotion'. This view has rightly been criticised as extreme, but if we see behind it the opposition to sentimentality, it becomes more understandable.

Cuteness, with its automatic evocation of tender feelings, is objectionable in the arts much as the pitiable is in melodrama. Certainly I am glad that I can feel affection for the cute, just as I am glad that I can feel pity for the suffering. And I realise that our race has benefited from having these capacities. I am even glad that I can react to cuteness in a baby in an unthinking, automatic way, and that I can react to innocent suffering in a similarly automatic way. But admitting all that, I still want more than simple automatic emotions from my experience of art works. I want emotions that are complex and even mixed with opposite emotions, emotions linked to a greater understanding of life, and emotions that within my experience of the artwork develop and deepen and perhaps even get resolved. The human race is lucky to have its automatic reactions, in short, but those reactions could never be the stuff of great art.

1   Konrad Lorenz, 'Die angebomen Formen moglicher Erfahrung', *Zeitschrift Tierpsychologic,* vol. 5 (1943) 235–409; and *Studies in Animal and Human Behavior,* vol. 2, trans. Robert Martin (Cambridge, MA: Harvard University Press, 1971) 154.

2   Adult amusement at babies and children was analysed as long ago as the eighteenth century by David Hartley in 'Of Wit and Humour', in *Observations on Man,* Part I, ch.4, reprinted in John Morreall (ed.), *The Philosophy of Laughter and Humor* (New York: State University of New York Press, 1987) 44.

3   [Footnote 5 in source] Ashley Montague, *Touching: The Human Significance of the Skin* (New York: Columbia University Press, 1971) 84–6.

4   [6] 'The Experience of Touch: Research Points to a Critical Role', *New York Times* (2 February 1988) sec. C.

5   [7] Katherine Hildebrandt, 'The Effect of Facial Expression Variations on Ratings of Infants' Physical Attractiveness', *Developmental Psychology,* vol. 16 (May 1983) 414–7.

6   [11] Mark Johnson, *The Body in the Mind: The Bodily Basis of Meaning, Imagination, and Reason* (Chicago: University of Chicago Press, 1987).

John Morreall, extracts from 'Cuteness', *British Journal of Aesthetics,* vol. 31, no. 1 (January 1991) 39–47.

Lori Merish
Cuteness and Commodity Aesthetics//1996

[...] [The] cute always in some sense designates a commodity in search of its mother, and is constructed to generate maternal desire; the consumer (or potential consumer) of the cute is expected [...] to pretend she or he is the cute's mother. Valuing cuteness entails the ritualised performance of maternal feeling, designating a model of feminine subjectivity constituted against those (ethnic, class or national) Others who lack the maternal/sentimental endowments (and aesthetic faculties) to fully appreciate the 'cute'. The Hallmark store, as much as the art museum and the opera, is a site for the interpellation of gendered/class/ racial subjects, a site in which those identifications are inscribed on citizens' very bodies.

[...] [Appreciating] the cute – loving the 'adorable' as culturally defined – entails a structure of identification, wanting to be like the cute – or, more exactly, wanting the cute to be just like the self. Appreciating cuteness expresses the double logic of identification, its fundamental inseparability from desire: it bespeaks a 'presumption of identification' that is, in the words of Doris Sommer, 'appropriation in the guise of an embrace'.[1] Assimilating commodity desire into a structure of familial, expressly maternal emotion, the cute generates an aesthetic response mediated through familial resemblance. Maternal desire becomes the vehicle through which being and having are synthesised: the cute is identified as part of the 'family,' indeed part of the self; the pleasure of the cute involves 'recognising' it as such. [...]

But the chief social power of cuteness is exercised as a drama of socialisation. Drawing affective force from the Victorian sentimentalisation of childhood, cuteness enacts the fundamental ambivalence of the child in a liberal-capitalist order: as at once consenting 'subject' and property 'object'.[2] Evoking an ideal of maternal or benevolent ownership, cuteness stages a problematic of identification that centres on the child's body. This problematic involved anxieties about the cultural 'ownership' of the child, and the racial identifications of children, that were acutely felt in the late nineteenth and early twentieth centuries, a period of massive immigration into the United States along with renewed nativist concern with racial 'purity' and the transmission of Euro-American culture.[3] Focusing on the child – the privileged locus for the transmission of culture and the ('uncivilised') Other in that culture's midst – cuteness represents lines of interpersonal, intergenerational identification, promoting affective bonds of social affiliation and cohesion.

Specifically, cuteness engenders an affectional dynamic through which the Other is domesticated and (re)contextualised within the human 'family'. Cuteness aestheticises the most primary social distinctions, regulating the (shifting) boundaries between Selves and Others, cultural 'insiders' and cultural 'outsiders,' 'humans' and 'freaks'. [...]

Freaks And (Child) Prodigies: Historicising Cuteness

[...] As a strategy for managing the radical Otherness of the child, cuteness is [...] intimately bound up with the history of the 'freak'. There are obvious parallels between child and freak: both are liminal figures, residing on the boundaries that separate the 'fully human' from the 'less-than-human'.[4] That 'cute' child and 'freak' are reciprocally defined is supremely evident in the film *E.T.*, which constructs an identification between child and freak (only the children can communicate with E.T.) in order to position the freakish extraterrestrial as a (cute) monster to be adopted. The monstrosity of the 'alien' E.T. does not diminish but rather intensifies his cuteness – in part because his desire for 'home' (as well as his docility) renders him sentimentally recuperable, available to assimilation within normative domestic and affectional structures.

As the example of E.T. suggests, the categories of 'cute' and 'freak' have historically been mutually articulated. Indeed, the cute child can be situated in a historical lineage that extends from Hellenistic times through the Middle Ages and Renaissance when dwarfs and midgets were kept as accoutrements of court life, entertainers and pets. In the eighteenth century such figures were put on display in public taverns and at carnivals and circuses; by the 1840s, these exhibitions were consolidated in the commercialised spectacles known as 'freak shows'.[5] Tellingly, a popular term for 'freak show' was 'kid show'.[6] Midgets – a term reserved, in general usage, for perfectly shaped and proportioned 'little people' – were especially popular in these shows, as well as in popular theatre and, later, vaudeville.[7] In nineteenth-century popular culture, there was a productive exchange between the cute child's performance and the midget's commercial display: part of the pleasure of watching precocious child and 'little person' perform derived from how they unsettled, in a contained but dramatic fashion, the conventional boundary between child and adult. This interplay between the categories of cute child and 'little person' was registered by drama critic Laurence Hutton. Commenting in 1890 on the 'Infant Phenomena' of the American stage, Hutton observed that entertaining and precocious children occupy 'the neutral ground between the amateurs and the monstrosities, without belonging to either class'.[8] The history of freakish spectacles of 'little people' is embedded within the performance of the cute child. [...]

'Cuteness' As Feminine Spectacle: The Tom Thumb Wedding

The structure of maternal sentiment activated by the cute child performer also organised the exhibition of midgets. Leslie Fiedler invokes the process whereby 'little people' were divested of their ancient aura of the sacred and magical during the nineteenth century and domesticated, converted into objects of compassion and pity: There was 'something sacred and otherworldly about dwarfs and midgets' in ·ancient civilisations such as Egypt, where gods like Ptah and Bes were 'portrayed in the form of dwarfs. [...] Even after they had become buffoons and court pets in the Middle Ages and Renaissance there still clung to them an aura of the magical.' According to Fiedler, the Victorian era 'complete[d] the process of demythification by converting them into public exhibits, subjects for medical study, and occasions for pity-like orphans, abused animals, or the deserving poor.' Although they, like all 'freaks', were known as 'curiosities', the curiosity engendered by midgets was tempered by sympathy. As Neil Harris has noted, unlike other freakish spectacles in [P.T.] Barnum's museum, the audience's sympathies were (partially) with the exhibited 'little people': 'Crowds identified with [them], rather than against [them].'[9] Like the cute child's body, the bodies of little people have been the site of a particular kind of erotic investiture, engendering in their viewers the dynamic play between similitude and difference, identification and appropriative desire. [...]

Cuteness as Racialised Style: Shirley Temple and the Construction of Cute (white) Girlhood

Shirley's position as cute child prodigy was anticipated by 'little people' such as Tom Thumb and Lavinia Warren, who inspired in their audiences a mixture of fascination and proprietary desire. But the freakish Otherness at the heart of the cute is particularly registered in Shirley's intimate connection with racial Others. Shirley's ties to racial Otherness are featured in several films, particularly those about the Old South, *The Littlest Rebel* and *The Little Colonel.* Indeed, embedded within her song-and-tap-dance numbers are historical traces of Jim Crow performances and resonances of a Sambo-like obsequiousness in her always-ready smile and effort to please. This racial doubling of Shirley's body is rendered explicit in those scenes in which she is paired with Bill Robinson ('Bojangles') as dance partner. References to antebellum 'Jim Crow' and the history of slavery complicate the structure of feeling (of maternal cherishing) the cute works to construct, exposing the forms of power and coercion at its core.

Cuteness as a comic theatrical style available to children was intimately bound up with the history of race. The comic child in nineteenth-century America was a racialised construction, a fact evident when one considers the cultural icon, *Uncle Tom's Cabin* – phenomenally popular as novel, play, and, later, film. Harriet Beecher Stowe presents the minstrel sprite Topsy as a comic figure and foil for the pious, spiritualised, and deeply serious Little Eva (a role Shirley Temple would adapt in *Dimples*). Mass culture in the late nineteenth century featured an iconography of blackness, derived from plantation humor, that depicted African Americans as comical, inept and childlike. Some of the first commodity trademarks – such as the Gold Dust Twins and the Pears Soap children – recycled racial stereotypes, featuring black kids with cute features (e.g., large round heads and eyes, chubby limbs). These African American comic figures, however, usually bore explicit traces of the grotesque or the threatening: in particular, they were often depicted with exaggerated grins or teeth. By the 1930s, blonde, blue-eyed Shirley Temple would purge the cute of its unsettling racial resonances, performing an absorption and domestication of comic styles associated with 'blackness' and the black child performer. Shirley's cherubic, dimpled smile mimes, even while it tames, the exaggerated, painted grin of minstrelsy. Even that epitome of cuteness, Shirley's famous 'O my goodness!' expression – her face momentarily frozen with wide saucer eyes and pursed lips extruding in an affectionate kiss – should be seen as a racialised style. […]

Cuteness And Cultural Others

Emphasising that what is 'often referred to as a "freak of nature"' is actually a '"freak of culture"', Susan Stewart observes, 'We find the freak inextricably tied to the cultural other, the Little Black Man, the Turkish horse, the Siamese twins […] the Irish giants.' Accounts of pygmies, Stewart notes, can be found in Homer, Hesiod, Herodotus and Ovid, and thus date back to the West's earliest encounters with other traditions. Nineteenth century examples of racialised freaks include Admiral Dot, the 'North Carolina Twins' Millie and Christine, and Zip the Pin Headed Man – all of whom, like Tom Thumb and Lavinia Warren, were employed by Barnum.[10]

In Shirley Temple films, the essential freakishness of the cute child is expressed by her ties to racial Otherness as fully as by her status as prodigious 'little person'. Signifying and animating the forms of familial sentiment through which the child is socialised and incorporated within culture, cuteness domesticates Otherness in a double move through which that Otherness is at once affirmed and denied. But the very banality of cuteness – its (mass) production and display in a whole range of commercial contexts – suggests the fragility and tenuousness of the cute's hold on us; it bespeaks the need to compulsively rehearse the most basic social forms to ensure their idealisation and transmission. Haunted by its own freakishness, the cute ineluctably points to other possibilities of embodiment, other forms of subjectivity and desire. […]

1   [Footnote 5 in source] Doris Sommer, 'Resistant Texts and Incompetent Readers,' *Poetics Today*, vol. 15, no. 4 (Winter 1994) 543. For an extended analysis of the complex psychic processes of identification and the highly unstable 'identification/desire' opposition in psychoanalytic theory, see Diana Fuss, *Identification Papers* (New York: Routledge, 1995).

2   [8] In the late nineteenth century, the popular conception of the child as the 'natural property' of the parent appears in narratives of white child slavery (in which children appear as 'capital' through which adults satisfy their 'horrible cravings'), and in accounts of child abuse published by the newly formed national network of child protection and anticruelty societies. 'White Child Slavery', *Arma*, no. 1 (April 1890) 589–603. For a sociological summary of the reconstruction of the child from an 'object of use' to an 'object of sentiment' between 1870 and 1930, see Viviana A. Zelizer, *Pricing the Priceless Child* (New York: Basic Books, 1985).

3   [9] For an extended analysis of the 'negative associations of childhood' with racial Others and an 'atavistic savagery' in nineteenth century literature and anthropology, focusing on the British national context, see Cora Kaplan, 'A Heterogeneous Thing: Female Childhood and the Rise of Racial Thinking in Victorian Britain', in Diana Fuss (ed.), *Human, All too Human* (New York: Routledge, 1995) 168–202.

4   [12] Susan Stewart identifies the constitutive liminality of the freak: 'the physiological freak represents the problems of the boundary between self and other (Siamese twins), between male and female (the hermaphrodite), between the body and the world outside the body (the *monstre par excès*), and between the animal and the human (feral and wild men)'. Susan Stewart, *On Longing*, (Baltimore: John Hopkins University Press, 1987) 109.

5   [13] Robert Bogdan, *Freak Show: Presenting Human Oddities for Amusement and Profit* (Chicago: University of Chicago Press, 1988).

6   [14] Leslie Fiedler, *Freaks: Myths and Images of the Secret Self* (New York: Anchor, 1978) 31.

7   [15] On the politics of these terms, see Joan Ablon, *Little People in America: The Social Dimensions of Dwarfism* (New York: Praeger, 1984).

8   [16] Laurence Hutton, *Curiosities of the American Stage* (New York: Harper and Bros., 1891) 253.

9   [27] Fielder, op. cit., 48; Neil Harris, *Humbug: The Art of P.T. Barnum* (Boston: Little, Brown, 1973) 49.

10   [44] Stewart, *On Longing*, 109–10.

Lori Merish, extracts from 'Cuteness and Commodity Aesthetics: Tom Thumb and Shirley Temple', in *Freakery: Cultural Spectacles of the Extraordinary Body*, ed. Rosemarie Garland-Thomson (New York: New York University Press, 1996) 185–203.

Daniel Harris
Cuteness//2001

[…] Everywhere we turn we see cuteness, from cherubic figures batting their peepers on Charmin toilet paper to teddy bears frozen mid-embrace, the stubs of their pawless arms groping for hugs. In the eyes of most people, whose conditioned responses to this most rigid of styles prevent them from recognising its artificiality, things like calendars with droopy-eyed puppies pleading for attention or greeting cards with kitty cats in raincoats are the very embodiment of innocence and as such represent an absence of the designed and manipulated qualities of what is in fact a heavily mannered aesthetic. For them, the foreshortened limbs and sad, saucer eyes of a doll like [Galoob's] So Shy Sherri are part of a unique and readily identifiable iconography whose distortions trigger, with Pavlovian predictability, maternal feelings for a mythical condition of endearing naiveté. The chilling paradox of the fetishes over which we croon so irrepressibly is that their cuteness suggests guilelessness, simplicity, and a refreshing lack of affectation, the very antithesis of what we would expect if we were to judge these toys on the basis of their extreme stylisation alone.

Cuteness is not an aesthetic in the ordinary sense of the word and must by no means be mistaken for the physically appealing, the attractive. In fact, it is closely linked to the grotesque, the malformed. So Shy Sherri, for instance, is an anatomical disaster. Her legs are painfully swollen, her fingers useless pink stumps that seem to have been lopped off at the knuckles, and her rosy cheeks so bloated that her face is actually wider than it is long. Medieval or renaissance images of the Christ child, those obese monstrosities whose muscularity always strikes the modern viewer as bafflingly inaccurate, make an interesting comparison. In an era like our own, which prides itself on its ability to achieve effects of uncanny realism, the disfigured putti of the 'Baby Face' series of dolls mark a decline rather than an advance in the representation of children, an eerie throwback to the slant-eyed sphinxes in Sienese icons: alien, carnivorous-looking creatures who are, in many ways, as pictorially inexact as So Shy Sherri.

Far from being an accident of bad craftsmanship, the element of the grotesque in cuteness is perfectly deliberate and must be viewed as the explicit intention of objects that elicit from us the complex emotions we feel when we encounter the fat faces and squat, ruddy bodies of creatures like the Trolls, with their pot bellies, pug noses, and teased-up mops of brightly coloured hair. The grotesque is cute because the grotesque is pitiable, and pity is the primary emotion of this seductive and manipulative aesthetic that arouses our sympathies by creating anatomical pariahs, like the Cabbage Patch Dolls or even E.T., whose odd proportions and lack of symmetry diverge wildly from the relative balance and uniformity of ordinary bodies. The aesthetic of cuteness creates a class of outcasts and mutations, a ready-made race of lovable inferiors whom both children and adults collect, patronise and enslave in the protective concubinage of vast harems of homely dolls and snugglesome misfits. Something becomes cute not necessarily because of a quality it has but because of a quality it lacks, a certain neediness and inability to stand alone, as if it were an indigent starveling, lonely and rejected because of a hideousness we find more touching than unsightly.

The koalas, pandas and lambs of the stuffed animal series 'Lost 'n Founds' directly allude to this state of homeless destitution. With their 'adorable "so-sad" eyes' that shed real tears, these shameless examples of the waif or pauper syndrome seem to be begging to be rescued from their defenceless state, so tellingly emphasised by paws as cumbersome as boxing gloves – absurd appendages that lie uselessly in their laps, totally free of any of the prehensile functions hands usually serve. Because it generates enticing images like these of ugliness and dejection, cuteness has become essential to the marketplace, in that advertisers have learned that consumers will 'adopt' products that create, often in their packaging alone, an aura of motherlessness, ostracism, and melancholy, the silent desperation of the lost puppy dog clamoring to be befriended – namely, to be bought.

Cuteness, in short, is not something we find in our children but something we *do* to them. Because it aestheticises unhappiness, helplessness and deformity, it almost always involves an act of sadism on the part of its creator, who makes an unconscious attempt to maim, hobble and embarrass the thing he seeks to idolise, as in the case of 'Little Mutt', a teddy bear with a game leg that a British manufacturer has even fitted with an orthopedic boot. The process of conveying cuteness to the viewer disempowers its objects, forcing them into ridiculous situations and making them appear more ignorant and vulnerable than they really are. Adorable things are often most adorable in the middle of a pratfall or a blunder: Winnie the Pooh, with his snout stuck in the hive; the 101 dalmatians of Disney's classic, collapsing in double splits and sprawling across the ice; Love-a-Lot Bear, in the movie *The Care Bears*, who stares disconsolately out at us with a paint bucket overturned on his head; or, the grimmest example of the cruelty of cuteness, the real fainting goat, which has acquired of late a perverse chic as a pet (bred with myatonia, a genetic heart defect, it coyly folds up and faints every time you scream at it). Although the gaze we turn on the cute thing seems maternal and solicitous, it is in actuality transformative and will stop at nothing to appease its hunger for expressing pity and big-heartedness, even at the cost of mutilating the object of its affections. The French-manufactured 'Vet Set' takes the neediness of cuteness to macabre extremes: the kit is equipped with a wounded stuffed puppy whose imploring eyes seem to wince as it patiently awaits the physician, who can alleviate its suffering with a wide array of bandages, tourniquets, syringes, and even a stethoscope to monitor the irregular, fluttering thump of a mechanical heart that actually beats.

If cuteness is the aesthetic of deformity and dejection, it is also the aesthetic of sleep. Although adorable things can be bright eyed and bushy tailed, the pose we find cutest of all is not that of a rambunctious infant screaming at the top of his lungs but that of the docile sleepyhead, his chin nestled drunkenly in the crook of someone's neck, wearing the PJs in the FAO Schwarz catalogue that consist of a full-length leopard suit made of spotted fur or a 'sweet confection of lace' with fuzzy marabou touches of pristine white down sewn like a tutu around the waist. The world of cute things is transfixed by the spell of the Sandman, full of napping lotus eaters whose chief attraction lies in their dormant and languorous postures, their defenseless immobility.

Turning its targets into statues and plush dolls, cuteness is ultimately dehumanising, paralysing its victims into comatose or semi-conscious things. In fact, the 'thingness' of cute things is fixed firmly in our minds by means of the exaggerated textures and hues so characteristic of stuffed animals, with their satins and their luscious coats of fur, or dolls with their luxuriant profusion of hair, often of absurd length and body (as with the Cutie Kids of the 'Cutie Club' series, a set of dolls whose psychedelic coiffures cascade down their sides in corkscrew curls longer than their own bodies). 'Anxiously awaiting power snuggles', FAO Schwarz's huge grizzly bear is a slouching, seemingly invertebrate mammoth rippling with 'serious spreads of soft spots' that are 'just asking to be hauled and mauled', while their elephant, as large as a St. Bernard, is described as 'big, plump, and deliciously soft with soulful brown eyes that encourage big-time hugging and smooching'. Vacant and malleable, animals like these inhabit a world of soothing tactile immediacy in which there are no sharp corners or abrasive materials but in which everything has been conveniently soft-sculpturised to yield to our importunate squeezes and hugs. If such soulless insentience is any indication, cuteness is the most scrutable and externalised of aesthetics in that it creates a world of stationary objects and tempting exteriors that deliver themselves up to us, putting themselves at our disposal and allowing themselves to be apprehended entirely through the senses. In light of the intense physicality of our response to their helpless torpor, our compulsive gropings even constitute something one might call cute sex or, in point of fact, given that one of the partners lies there groggy and catatonic, a kind of necrophilia, a neutered coupling consummated in our smothering embrace of a serenely motionless object incapable of reciprocating. Far from being content with the helplessness of our young as we find them in their natural state, we take all kinds of artificial measures to dramatise this vulnerability even further by defacing them, embarrassing them, devitalising them, depriving them of their selfhood, and converting them, with the help of all of the visual and sartorial tricks at our disposal, into disempowered objects, furry love balls quivering in soft fabrics as they lapse into withdrawal for their daily fix of TLC. [...]

The strange consequence of the need to increase huggability is that all stuffed animals, from marsupials to pachyderms, are covered in fur, regardless of the fact that the real-life counterparts of Beatrice the Boa and Willy the Walrus have scales that are wet and slimy or hides that are bristly and tough. Behind the pleasure we take in the bodies of such cartoon heroes as Kermit and Snoopy is the fear of another sort of body altogether, the distasteful subtext of our plush toys: the excreting bodies of real live babies which, far from being clean and dry, are squalling factories of drool and snot. Our unenviable role as the hygienic custodians of children, whose dirty bottoms we must regularly wipe, noses we must blow, and soiled underwear we must launder, has led to a recurrent parental fantasy, that of the diaperless baby, the excretionless teddy bear, a low-maintenance infant whom we can kiss and fondle free of anxiety that it will throw up on our shoulder as we rock it to sleep or pee in our laps as we dandle it on our knees.

Exaggerating the vast discrepancies of power between the sturdy adult and the enfeebled and susceptible child, the narcissism of cuteness is evident in the way that the aesthetic ascribes human attributes to non-human things. Anthropomorphism is to a large extent *the* rhetorical strategy of children's books, which often generate their narratives from a kind of animal transvestism in which dogs, cats, bears and pigs have the clothing and demeanour of human beings. Calendars, another rich source of cuteness, also employ animal transvestism as a major theme: mice as prima ballerinas in toe shoes and tutus, dogs in party hats and sunglasses, or swallow-tailed hamsters in tuxes and cummerbunds rearing up on their hind legs to give each other what appears to be an affectionate peck on the cheek. Even an artist as respected as William Wegman subtly refashions, in the appropriative style of postmodernism, the low-brow aesthetic of cuteness by decking out his lugubrious mastiff, an irresistibly funereal pooch cheerlessly resigned to his fate, in everything from Christian Dior to Calvin Klein jeans. Examples like these reveal that the cute worldview is one of massive human chauvinism, which rewrites the universe according to an iconographic agenda dominated by the pathetic fallacy. Multiplying our image a thousand-fold and reverberating like an echo chamber with the familiar sounds of our own voices, the cute vision of the natural world is a world without nature, one that annihilates 'otherness', ruthlessly suppresses the non-human, and allows nothing, including our own children, to be separate and distinct from us.

The imitative nature of cuteness can also be seen in the relation of the aesthetic to precocity. One of the things we find cutest in the behaviour of our children is their persistence in mimicking us, not only in such time-honoured traditions as dress-up (the anthropomorphic version of which is played out obsessively in children's literature) but in that most basic form of child's play, mothering, whether it be of a doll or of a family pet. The spectacle of toddlers rocking their babies, changing the diapers of the many incontinent toys on the market, placating anxious dolls, or thrashing disobedient teddy bears elicits some of our most gloating and unrestrained responses to cuteness. Nothing delights us more than the strange sight of a one-year-old in a stroller meeting a barely ambulatory two-year-old, who, rather than seeking to establish spontaneous *esprit de corps* with his peer, breaks rank and gibbers baby talk at the bewildered object of his curiously perfunctory affections. As co-conspirators in this game of make-believe maturity, we reward children who at once feign helplessness and assume adult authority in mothering others, reinforcing simultaneously both infantilism and precocity. The child is thus taught not only to be cute in himself but to recognise and enjoy cuteness in others, to play the dual roles of actor and audience, cootchy-cooing as much as he is cootchy-cooed. In this way, our culture actively inculcates the aesthetic doctrines of cuteness by giving our children what amounts to a thorough education in the subject, involving extensive and rigorous training in role-playing. By encouraging our children to imitate the way we ourselves fawn over their own preciousness, we give them the opportunity to know cuteness from both sides of the equation, not only from the standpoint of the object receiving the attention but from the standpoint of those giving it as well, from their appreciative audience cum-artistic directors, whom they impersonate for brief and touching intervals in their own highly informative charades of child-rearing. We teach our children the nature and value of cuteness almost from the dawn of consciousness and initiate them into the esoteric rituals of its art, passing on to them the tribal legacy of its iconographic traditions, its strange, self-mutilating ceremonies, as alien in their way, at least to a culture unindoctrinated in cuteness, as the scarification customs of Africa or New Guinea. Because imitation allows children to observe their own behaviour with the analytic detachment with which they in turn are observed by their admirers, cuteness is unique among aesthetics because it lays the foundations for its own survival by building into itself a form of proselytising. […]

Daniel Harris, extracts from 'Cuteness', in *Cute, Quaint, Hungry and Romantic: The Aesthetics of Consumerism* (New York: Basic Books, 2001) 1–9, 10–15.

Sianne Ngai
The Cuteness of the Avant-Garde//2012

[...] In spite of the prominent example of the Kantian sublime, there has been surprisingly little attention to how a class of judgements underwritten by mixed or even contradictory feelings might put interesting new pressures on the theory of aesthetic judgement in general, including the longstanding assumption that aesthetic judgements must always be based on a single and unequivocal feeling: 'disinterestedness' or 'conviction'. Surely there are other feelings and/or combinations of feelings on which the appraisals of value or quality we feel compelled to share with others in public might be based?

[...] Yet rare aesthetic experiences underwritten by unequivocal feelings continue to be the dominant ones appealed to as models in contemporary theories of art. Theorists of the postmodern avant-garde, in particular, have been repeatedly drawn to Kant's account of the sublime: an aesthetic of sheer force or power explicitly not based on art [...]. Yet it is cuteness, a 'soft' aesthetic emerging from the sphere of mass culture as opposed to high art and explicitly about the appeal of powerlessness as opposed to power, that seems best suited for the analysis of art as it develops in dialectical relation to commodity culture over the twentieth century. Indeed, if the slackening of tension between autonomous art and the commodity form is the one development that has arguably had the greatest impact on the development of twentieth-century art overall (and on changes in avant-garde theory and practice in particular), one might read the 'relaxing' effect of cuteness as an allegory of the development leading to its own eventual cultural hegemony. With all this in mind, let us [...] embark on the analysis of this diminutive aesthetic: one that epitomises the minorness of not just 'minor aesthetic categories' but arguably all art in an age of high-tech simulacra and media spectacles.

Cute Willies

[...] While the cute has thus played an ongoing role in the commodification of social difference, Marx implies that there may be something 'indecently "cute"' about the commodity itself. The second chapter of the first volume of *Capital*, 'The Process of Exchange', opens with a comparison of the subject's relation to commodities to that of a man's relation to his children or wards: since commodities 'cannot go to market and perform exchanges in their own right', Marx invites his readers to imagine themselves as their 'guardians'. [...] [Marx further] likens the commodity, now from the point of view of the other commodities with which it is always already in congress, to [...] Maritomes from *Don Quixote*, sexually interchangeable with other women to the oblivious hero, who thus ends up becoming her lover in spite of her infamous lack of charm. The mocking tone in which Marx makes these comparisons – one that immediately distances the speaker from his act of anthropomorphising comparison even as that act is being performed – suggests that Marx may be presenting the commodity in what he pointedly wants the reader to recognise as an almost cutely or preciously anthropomorphising, 'story-time' way.

[....] Yet for all his distancing sarcasm, Marx seems compelled to repeat commodity fetishism's personification of the commodity, Barbara Johnson argues, in his very effort to demystify it as false belief. This use of a personification whose 'cuteness' Marx clearly wants to highlight and immediately express his disdain for, even as he cannot help but also make use of it, comes to a head when Marx asks his reader to imagine commodities speaking like child actors herded up on stage: 'If commodities could speak, they would say this: our use-value may interest men, but is no part of us as objects. What does belong to us as objects [...] is our value. Our own intercourse as commodities proves it. We relate to each other merely as exchange-values.' Forcing his reader to mentally act out a scene in which commodities themselves are compelled to act out or recite lines, Marx's account dramatises how human producers of commodities come to empathise with the commodity or perceive it from what they imagine to be its own perspective on itself: as an object defined entirely by its 'social' relation to other objects in exchange. [...]

Noting how Marx makes commodities speak precisely in order to make them confess the illusion of animation they promote, Johnson suggests that 'this scene of prosopopoeia is [...] a sign that the very thing [Marx] is arguing for is too strong for him'. One could infer from this that it is difficult to critique the fetishism of commodities [...] without somehow entering into its logic. We could also read the moment as an effort on Marx's part to underscore the objectivity of the fantasy that the .... theory of fetishism enables him to describe, giving us a better picture both of the illusion qua illusion and of how intimately the subject of capital comes to inhabit it. In other words, fetishism's fantasy of animation may be totally kitschy…yet like the cute object, as Johnson notes, it seems to be 'irresistible'. Indeed, Marx stresses that the fantasy is compulsory: it 'attaches itself to the products of labor as soon as they are produced as commodities and is therefore inseparable from the production of commodities'.

Cuteness might be regarded as an intensification of commodity fetishism's [...] phantasmatic logic but also as a way of revising it by adding yet another layer of fantasy. For as an aesthetic in which the object is imagined not just as an animated being but as one inviting the aesthetic subject to handle it physically, the cute speaks to a desire to recover what Marx calls the 'coarsely sensuous objectivity of commodities as physical objects' that becomes immediately extinguished in exchange. Cuteness is thus a kind of consumer fetishism redoubled; it tries to seize hold of and manipulate, as its 'raw material', the unavoidable fantasy of fetishism, itself already an effort to find an imaginary solution to the irresolvable 'contradiction between phenomenon and fungibility' in the commodity form (as Adorno puts it in *Minima Moralia*). Although cuteness retains fetishism's overarching illusion (that of the object's animate qualities), it actually wants to deny what, in Marx, these animated commodities go on to say: 'Our use-value may interest men, but is no part of us as objects [...] We relate to each other merely as exchange values.' It is precisely the qualitative, phenomenological experience of 'use' – occulted by the commodity form much in the same way as labour power occults the qualitative, phenomenological experience of labour – that cuteness attempts phantasmatically to recover at the level of consumption. For as pure 'value', the commodity is no longer legible as the product of any concrete form of labour but becomes reduced to what Marx calls 'human labor in the abstract'; it thus becomes, in a way eerily mirrored by the blobbishness of the prototypically cute object, a 'merely congealed quantit[y] of homogeneous labor'.

[...] Let us now delve further into these feelings by considering, as a ready-at-hand example, the frog-shaped sponge or baby's bath toy [...]. With its enormous face (it is in fact nothing but face) and exaggerated gaze (but interestingly no mouth), the bath toy underscores the centrality of anthropomorphism to cuteness. Yet what is striking is how crudely simplified the sponge's features are, as if cuteness were a commercial as opposed to high-modernist primitivism. Realist verisimilitude and formal precision tend to work against or even nullify cuteness, which becomes most pronounced in objects with simple round contours and little or no ornamentation or detail. By this logic, the epitome of the cute would be an undifferentiated blob of soft doughy matter. Since cuteness is an aestheticisation of powerlessness ('what we love because it submits to us'), and since soft contours suggest pliancy or responsiveness to the will of others, the less formally articulated the commodity, the cuter. The bath sponge makes this especially clear because its purpose is to be pressed against a baby's body and squished in a way guaranteed to repeatedly crush and deform its already somewhat formless face. The non-aesthetic properties associated with cuteness – smallness, compactness, formal simplicity, softness or pliancy – thus call up a range of minor negative affects: helplessness, pitifulness, and even despondency. Cuteness might also be said to epitomise the process of affective 'objectification' by which all aesthetic judgements are formed. In cuteness it is crucial that the object has some sort of imposed-on mien – that is, that it bears the look of an object unusually responsive to and thus easily shaped or deformed by the subject's feeling or attitude toward it. Although a glamorous object must not have this mien or aspect – in fact, the meta-aspect of looking as if its glamour were being imposed on it would instantly shatter its aura of cool self-sufficiency and thus its glamour – the subject's latent awareness, as she coos at her cute object, that she may in fact be imposing that cuteness upon it is likely to augment rather than detract from her aesthetic experience of it as cute. If aestheticisation is always, at the bottom line, objectification (of our subjective feelings and the evaluations underpinned by them), the latter in turn seems epitomised by cutification: the more objectified the object, or the more visibly shaped by the affective demands and/or projections of the subject, the cuter. […]

The qualitative and quantitative sides of the commodity cannot be pried apart; in the narrative of *Capital*, as Fredric Jameson notes, their fundamental opposition, set in motion with the act of exchange, seems to give rise to all the other contradictions of capital. By returning us to a simpler, sensuous world of domestic use and consumption, populated exclusively by children and their intimate guardians, cuteness is the pastoral fantasy that, somehow, the commodity's qualitative side as use-value, or as a product of concrete, phenomenological labour, can be extracted and therefore 'rescued'. Yet this romantic fantasy requires force, a willfulness of imagination arguably reflected in the physical distortions of cute form. 'We may twist and turn a single commodity as we wish', Marx writes in his storytelling voice; 'it remains impossible to grasp it as a thing possessing value.' The desire to fondle and squeeze the object that cuteness similarly elicits – even to the point of crushing or damaging that object – might thus be read as an effort to 'grasp' the commodity as a product of concrete human labour. It is as if, in a society fully governed by the rule of exchange, phantasmatically recovering the commodity's occulted use-value, or what Marx calls its 'plain' and 'homely' form, requires so much counterfactual force on the part of the imagination that 'use' can be made visible only in the melodramatic mode of 'abuse'. Precisely because the qualities of the commodity seem to disappear right in front of us, our need to 'twist and turn' its physical body intensifies, as if to foreground how a certain degree of mental violence becomes necessary for regaining intimacy with its phenomenal form. […]

As noted earlier, our desire for the cute commodity mirrors the desire it appears to have for us, a mimesis repeated in the compulsion to imitate the 'soft' properties of the object in our speech. Conflating desire with identification, or 'wanting to have' with 'wanting to be or be like', as [Lori] Merish notes, the experience of cuteness thus produces what Mary Anne Doane describes as a 'strange constriction of the gap between consumer and commodity', a shrinking of distance that, like the affect of empathy which indexes it, is strongly aligned with the feminine. […]

'False Simplicity'

Given […] what Kanako Shiokawa describes as *kawaii*'s unprecedented surge in popularity during the rapid expansion of Japan's culture industry in the 1960s, it is unsurprising that a self-conscious foregrounding of the violence underpinning the aesthetic runs throughout the work of Yoshitomo Nara and Takashi Murakami, Japanese artists who grew up in the 1960s and began exhibiting in the early 1990s, whose bodies of work allow us to grasp cuteness in one of its most probingly or theoretically worked-out forms. […] Evoking the expression 'You're so cute I could just eat you up', Nara's use of food-related objects for his interrogation of *kawaii* becomes extended and exaggerated in *Fountain of Life* (2001), a sculpture in which seven of what appear to be disembodied dolls' heads are stacked on top of one another in an oversized teacup with accompanying saucer, with tears/water flowing out of their closed eyes. Underscoring the aggressive desire to master and overpower the cute object that the cute object itself appears to elicit, the tie between cuteness and eating that Nara's work makes explicit finds its consumer culture counterpart in the characters generated by San-X, [a] more contemporary incarnation of Sanrio, the company that invented the iconic Hello Kitty. One of San-X's most currently popular figures is Kogepan, who is a slightly burned and dejected-looking bread bun. Described on San-X's website as 'a bread [that) has gone sourpuss for being burned […] that can't help making negative words like "You'll dump me anyway"', Kogepan is occasionally depicted not only with a bite taken out of the top of its head, but even baking miniature versions of itself. Kogepan's obvious state of abjection and simultaneous potential for acts of cruelty to less than fully baked Kogepans suggest that the ultimate index of an object's cuteness may be its edibility. Underscoring this link, an untitled drawing by Nara (2001), in which one of his stylistically simplified children pops out of a package with the label 'JAP in the BOX', also highlights cuteness' role in the merchandising and packaging of racial difference.

[…] Although one can buy Nara dolls […] postcards, ashtrays, T-shirts, and, of course, dinner plates, it is Murakami who has pushed these bounds furthest, not only by creating both cheap and expensive wares based on his gallery paintings and sculptures (including, in the spring of 2003, a series of Louis Vuitton handbags) but also by inventing a character, Mr. DOB, a red and blue mouse-like figure originally drawn with an exaggeratedly large head and tiny mouth which Murakami copyrighted in the early 1990s. Created in what Murakami describes as an effort 'to investigate the secret of the market survivability […] of characters such as Mickey Mouse, Sonic the Hedgehog…Hello Kitty and their knock-offs produced in Hong Kong', Mr. DOB's origin as an experiment in species 'survivability' echoes Stephen Jay Gould's famous argument about how the 'progressive juvenilisation' of Mickey Mouse over the twentieth century – his gradual transformation from spiky rodent into a rounder, softer, more wide-eyed character – testifies to the power of biological cuteness as an evolutionary strategy.

DOB is often shown smiling, as he is in the painting *DOB with Flowers* (1998), situated in a 'landscape' composed of anthropomorphised flowers as happy as he is. Although things are changed slightly in the installation *DOB in the Strange Forest* (1999), which places DOB in [an] implicitly menacing environment and depicts him as confused or distressed rather than contented, the menacing objects … arguably remain as cute as both DOB and the smiling flowers that surround him in the earlier painting.

In *And Then, and Then and Then and Then and Then* (1996–1997), however, an acrylic painting roughly 9 by 11 feet in size, DOB's cuteness seems questionable or under stress, in part because of the huge proportions of his image and the fact that he now has bared teeth. Suggesting a pun on *kawaii*'s sonorous proximity to *kowai*, which means 'scary', the surprisingly menacing look DOB assumes in this image is pushed further in subsequent piece like *GuruGuru* (1998), a vinyl chloride helium balloon 106 inches – nearly 9 feet – in diameter, and *The Castle of Tin Tin* (1998), an acrylic painting nearly 11 by 11 feet. In both, DOB has become virtually all eyes, teeth, and blisters, although the signature 'D' and 'B' on the character's ears still remain legible.

These works blurring the line between *kawaii* and *kowai* are only two of hundreds of permutations, and increasingly distorted, deformational permutations, to which Murakami has subjected the original DOB ever since his debut as a painting in 1993. Hence while cuteness exaggerates vulnerability, as [Daniel] Harris emphasises by noting that objects are cutest when maimed or hobbled, Murakami's stylistic mutilation of DOB calls attention to the violence always implicit in our relation to the cute object while simultaneously making it more menacing to the observer. The more DOB appears to be the object or victim of aggression, the more he appears to be an agent of aggression. Murakami's DOB project thus suggests that it is possible for cute objects to be helpless and aggressive at the same time. Given the powerful affective demands that the cute object makes on us, one could argue that this paradoxical doubleness is embedded in the concept of the cute from the start, as even commercial generators of cuteness such as San-X seem to realise. Kogepan's cuddliness does not seem incompatible with or compromised in any way by his potential to use and abuse the more diminutive Kogepans, whom he seems to treat either as food or as pets.

How are we to read the unusual readiness with which cute reverses into its opposite? Is it a sign of the aesthetic's internal instability, or how the experience of cuteness often seems to lead immediately to feelings of manipulation and betrayal? And how are we to read the vehemence of the reversal? Is the explosion of DOB's body a testament to the intensity of cuteness' deferred utopian dream? Or does it say something more about our own phantasmatic investment in the narrative of a cute object's 'revenge'? […]

Mute Poetics

We have seen how cuteness cutifies the language of the aesthetic response it compels, a verbal mimesis underscoring the judging subject's empathetic desire to reduce the distance between herself and the object. This cutification of the language of aesthetic judgement can be witnessed in the origins of the word 'cute' itself. Since 'cute' derives from the older 'acute' in a process linguists call *aphaeresis* (the process by which words lose initial unstressed syllables to generate shorter and 'cuter' versions of themselves; 'alone' becomes 'lone', 'until' becomes 'til'), its etymology strikingly replicates the logic of the aesthetic it has come to name. But there is a key difference between 'cute' and these other examples. While cuteness is an aesthetic of the soft or amorphous that therefore becomes heightened when objects are depicted as sleepy, 'acute' means 'coming to a sharp edge or point' and suggests mental alertness, keenness, and quickness. Cute thus exemplifies a situation in which making a word smaller – or, if you like, cuter – results in an uncanny reversal, changing its meaning into its exact opposite.

Like the flip-flop of power relations dramatised in the DOB series, this reversal mirrors the deverbalising effect that prototypically cute objects – babies, puppies, and so on – have on those who judge them as such. Resulting in a squeal or a cluck, a murmur or a coo, the cute object seems to have the power to infantilise the language of its infantiliser. Note, for example, how Gertrude Stein's admiring and critical reviewers alike seem compelled to approximate her language and, moreover, to savour or take pleasure in these acts of imitation even when the intent is clearly ridicule: 'Babble, baa, baa, Bull'; 'Her art is the sophisticated development of the child's "Tiddledy diddlety-fiddlety-doo".' In much the same way in which Huxley seems to relish neologisms like 'orgy-porgy' and 'bumblepuppy' even while mobilising them to attack the easy delights of his brave new world, we find a member of the American literati no less refined than H.L. Mencken pushed into saying words like 'tosh' when negatively commenting on Stein's 'bebble'. Even Wyndham Lewis seems compelled to mimic (and to enjoy mimicking) the lisping speech of the female consumer he despises ('Oh! Pease, pease'). This process of verbal cutification once again redounds on the very word 'cute', which is easily reduced to even more diminutive versions of itself: the noun 'cutie', the adjective 'cutesy', and the adjective 'cutesy-poo', all of which receive separate entries in the OED.

Cuteness is thus the name of an encounter with difference – a perceived difference in the power of the subject and object, in particular – that does something to everyday communicative speech: weakening or even dissolving syntax and reducing lexicon to onomatopoeia. More specifically, it names an encounter with difference that alters the speech of the subject attempting to manage that difference by imposing cuteness on the object. In this manner, cuteness incites a fantasy of the cute object's capacity for retaliation that we already have seen Murakami explore. The same fantasy may shed new light on why *Tender Buttons* features so many 'little things' – a cup and saucer, a petticoat, a cushion, a shawl, a purse – described as 'hurt' but also as 'enthusiastically hurting' other objects of their own genre or kind, not unlike the way Kogepan relates to his pets. [...]

Twentieth-century poetry's complicated relation to the commodity aesthetic of cuteness thus helps enrich our understanding of the latter by drawing out certain leitmotifs. First, cuteness is not just a style of object but also a style of language, one characterised by non-discursive 'twittering' or 'babbling' and by a mode of address that in its intensity and intimacy bears a striking similarity to lyric. Second, our experience of the cute involves an intimate address that often fails to establish the other as truly other, as if due to the excessive pressure of the subject's desire for intimacy or to the force of the aesthetic's mimetic compulsion. Failure like this might seem endemic to an aesthetic of powerlessness. Yet it is the very aestheticisation of powerlessness in the experience of cute that seems to give rise to a fantasy about the cute object's power, one epitomised by the boomeranging of the aggressive affect projected onto the object back outward and toward the subject. All these cute leitmotifs [...] underscore the aesthetic's defining dialectic of power and powerlessness. In accordance with the animating logic of fetishism, cuteness seems to always include a fantasy of the agency of its hyperobjectified objects, even in their most congealed or inert form. After all, as Merish and others note, the cute object seems to insist on getting something from us (care, affection, intimacy) that we in turn feel compelled to give. On the one hand, this underscores the way in which all aesthetic judgements, however cloaked as constative statements, are really performative utterances and, more specifically, demands. On the other, it is this compulsion to answer the demand of an object we regard as weaker or subordinate that, as Natalie Angier notes, produces the sense of being strong-armed or manipulated by cuteness, a secondary feeling that can paradoxically undermine the aesthetic power of the original feeling. The subject confronting the cute object thus experiences a sense of both mastery and surrender, explicit relations to force that the cute leitmotif of violence helps cast in sharper relief. [...]

Sianne Ngai, extracts from 'The Cuteness of the Avant-Garde', in *Our Aesthetic Categories: Zany, Cute, Interesting* (Cambridge, MA: Harvard University Press, 2012) 53, 57–9, 60–62, 63–5, 67, 73, 78–88, 98 [footnotes omitted].

Peter Schjeldahl
On Cutism: Allen Ruppersberg//1992

In the late 1970s a spate of winsome conceptual art moved me to propose a new movement: Cutism. That was mean – meaner, for the joke's sake, than I meant, because I didn't want to condemn, exactly. I did want to mark work that filled austere self-referring forms of conceptual art with cheery self-referring content of the artist's personal quirks and obsessions, as if art were a playpen for frisky narcissists. Somewhat a frisky narcissist myself, I had cause to go easy. What bothered me was just a little too much cosiness in presumptions of mutual approval between artists and audiences.

It was a matter of degree. Some artists, such as Chris Burden and William Wegman, were spectacularly narcissistic in their work, but with enough attendant rigour, melancholy, doggedness (Wegman in more than one way), or pugnacity hardly to be Cutist. Maybe no artist could be purely Cutist. Cutism was simply the extreme of a collective drift toward theatricalised self-absorption. It was easy to insult. Critic Carrie Rickey wrote of 'Naive Nouveau,' Craig Owens of 'Puerilism'.

I now drop the past tense. Never having quite gone away, Cutism is back, tincturing work by perhaps most of the up-and-coming young American artists of an emerging 1990s spirit. It precipitates regularly in the liveliest downtown galleries, including Feature, 303, American Fine Arts, Cugliani, Hearn, Gorney and Andrea Rosen. Much of it is a variant – whose doyen is Mike Kelley – that I think of as Rancid Cutism, fascinated with the emotion of treacly stuff (stuffed toys are the early-90s material) nudging over into revulsion. (Rancid Cutism eclipses the Cryogenic Cutism of, for instance, Jeff Koons, who vests treacly stuff with icy glamour. Expensive looks are insufferable to the new taste.) The strongest, so far unnamable trend, seen in the likes of Jim Shaw, Karen Kilimnick and Jack Pierson, is toward shaggy autobiographical engagement with sexy and dire effects of American extended adolescence. All of it is Cutist to the extent that it needs complicit viewers and makes their complicity a work's main pivot of pleasure. Such art croons antic or husky undertones to seduce viewers into sharing its maker's smitten or, sometimes, appalled self-contemplation.

Economic recession helps explain the timing of Neo-Cutism. As during the draggy 1970s, a down art market foreshortens the horizon for competition among artists. With fame and fortune largely out of the question, available career rewards shrivel toward in-group popularity. It might be the serious kind of popularity indicated by the phrase 'an artist's artist'. But Cutism is quicker. If in doubt, be fun. In times of fear and frustration, fun may be no joke. When taking demoralisation head-on, art in a Cutist vein realises the serious value of giving morale new footings. Such was the effect of a marvelous recent group show at American Fine Arts, imported from Los Angeles by curator Ralph Rugoff, with the Zen-Cutist title *Just Pathetic*. (The artists included David Hammons, Cady Noland and Raymond Pettibon – three powerfully poetic souls I will call, because I cannot help myself, Trans-Cutists.) The imperative to ingratiate may be only good manners when people are depressed. And dedicated self-display, if the self in question is sufficiently interesting, can provide an exemplary public service when people are struggling for rudimentary senses of identity.

What launched me on this ramble is a show of five installational works, four from the 70s and early 80s and one brand new, by Allen Ruppersberg. Ruppersberg, born in 1944, is a Classic Cutist, perhaps, as well as something of an artist's artist – a veteran, perennially both esteemed and obscure, of an early 70s generation that is coming in for timely renewed attention. Like Wegman and Alexis Smith, seen in current retrospectives at the Whitney Museum, Ruppersberg got his bearings in Southern California. He displays the distinctive combination of stringent conceptual strategies and voluptuous self-involvement (part Marcel Duchamp, part Joseph Cornell) that used to make Los Angeles feel like the art culture of the future and now increasingly makes it feel like the art culture of the present. Unlike Wegman and Smith, and unlike Cutist eminence grise John Baldessari, Ruppersberg has never been at pains to formularise an eye-grabbing, crowd-pleasing style. Though given to flavourful nostalgias for decayed popular culture, arcane Americana, and beloved books […] he makes art that is strangely ascetic. […]

Ruppersberg's new installation surrounds, with five silkscreen-printed, old cheap movie screens, a blank screen on which a 25-minute sequence of slides is projected to syrupy musical accompaniment (the score of *The Princess Bride*). The prints are from stills of antique educational films – 1,300 reels of which were lately rescued from a school basement by Ruppersberg, a connoisseur of cultural dreck right up there with Jim Shaw. The images include the title frame of something called *How to Remember* and an oddly lugubrious shot of a hand drawing a cartoon little bear. […]

Today many people's main first-hand aesthetic experience is of second-hand content, with a nagging sense of being always too late for, and everywhere peripheral to, a world palpably real. Some folks are more comfortable than others with this state of things. The more sanguine may deserve to be insulted. (Why should the rest of us be the only ones with hurt feelings?) Ruppersberg seems neither sanguine nor not sanguine, just uncannily resigned – mildly depressed and mildly piqued at being caught in a position of obvious weakness. His other 70s 'drawing project' at Burgin includes himself, photographed stuperously supine on a couch, beneath drawings from a loopy old children's Bible-story book illustrating a cautionary tale of greed and ambition. The work is, in a word, cute, but with a cuteness about as light-hearted as the planet Saturn. Ruppersberg owns one particular existential response to the urgency of life: take it lying down.

Peter Schjeldahl, extracts from 'Allen Ruppersberg: Personal Art', in *Columns & Catalogues* (Berkeley and Great Barrington, MA: The Figures, 1992) 59–62.

Not managing
to name the specialty
of his desire for
the loved being,
the amorous subject
falls back on this
rather stupid word:

adorable!

Roland Barthes, "Adorable!"', in *A Lover's Discourse*, 1978

PARA- AND PROTO-CUTENESS

Stephen Jay Gould
A Biological Homage to Mickey Mouse//2008

Age often turns fire into placidity. Lytton Strachey, in his incisive portrait of Florence Nightingale, writes of her declining years:

> Destiny, having waited very patiently, played a queer trick on Miss Nightingale. The benevolence and public spirit of that long life had only been equaled by its acerbity. Her virtue had dwelt in hardness […] And now the sarcastic years brought the proud woman her punishment. She was not to die as she had lived. The sting was to be taken out of her; she was to be made soft; she was to be reduced to compliance and complacency.

I was therefore not surprised – although the analogy may strike some people as sacrilegious – to discover that the creature who gave his name as a synonym for insipidity had a gutsier youth. Mickey Mouse turned a respectable fifty last year. To mark the occasion, many theatres replayed his debut performance in *Steamboat Willie* (1928). The original Mickey was a rambunctious, even slightly sadistic fellow. In a remarkable sequence, exploiting the exciting new development of sound, Mickey and Minnie pummel, squeeze, and twist the animals on board to produce a rousing chorus of 'Turkey in the Straw'. They honk a duck with a tight embrace, crank a goat's tail, tweak a pig's nipples, bang a cow's teeth as a stand-in xylophone, and play bagpipe on her udder.

Christopher Finch, in his semi-official pictorial history of Disney's work, comments: 'The Mickey Mouse who hit the movie houses in the late twenties was not quite the well-behaved character most of us are familiar with today. He was mischievous, to say the least, and even displayed a streak of cruelty.' But Mickey soon cleaned up his act, leaving to gossip and speculation only his unresolved relationship with Minnie and the status of Morty and Ferdie. Finch continues: 'Mickey […] had become virtually a national symbol, and as such he was expected to behave properly at all times. If he occasionally stepped out of line, any number of letters would arrive at the Studio from citizens and organizations who felt that the nation's moral well-being was in their hands […] Eventually he would be pressured into the role of straight man.'

As Mickey's personality softened, his appearance changed. Many Disney fans are aware of this transformation through time, but few (I suspect) have recognised the coordinating theme behind all the alterations – in fact, I am not sure that the Disney artists themselves explicitly realised what they were doing, since the changes appeared in such a halting and piecemeal fashion. In short, the blander and inoffensive Mickey became progressively more juvenile in appearance. (Since Mickey's chronological age never altered – like most cartoon characters he stands impervious to the ravages of time – this change in appearance at a constant age is a true evolutionary transformation. Progressive juvenilisation as an evolutionary phenomenon is called neoteny. More on this later.)

The characteristic changes of form during human growth have inspired a substantial biological literature. Since the head-end of an embryo differentiates first and grows more rapidly *in utero* than the foot-end (an anterior-posterior gradient, in technical language), a newborn child possesses a relatively large head attached to a medium-sized body with diminutive legs and feet. This gradient is reversed through growth as legs and feet overtake the front end. Heads continue to grow but so much more slowly than the rest of the body that relative head size decreases.

In addition, a suite of changes pervades the head itself during human growth. The brain grows very slowly after age three, and the bulbous cranium of a young child gives way to the more slanted, lower-browed configuration of adulthood. The eyes scarcely grow at all and relative eye size declines precipitously. But the jaw gets bigger and bigger. Children, compared with adults, have larger heads and eyes, smaller jaws, a more prominent, bulging cranium, and smaller, pudgier legs and feet. Adult heads are altogether more apish, I'm sorry to say.

Mickey, however, has travelled the ontogenetic pathway in reverse during his fifty years among us. He has assumed an ever more childlike appearance as the ratty character of *Steamboat Willie* became the cute and inoffensive host to a magic kingdom. By 1940, the former tweaker of pig's nipples gets a kick in the ass for insubordination (as the Sorcerer's Apprentice in *Fantasia*). By 1953, his last cartoon, he has gone fishing and cannot even subdue a squirting clam.

The Disney artists transformed Mickey in clever silence, often using suggestive devices that mimic nature's own changes by different routes.

To give him the shorter and pudgier legs of youth, they lowered his pants line and covered his spindly legs with a baggy outfit. (His arms and legs also thickened substantially – and acquired joints for a floppier appearance.) His head grew relatively larger and its features more youthful. The length of Mickey's snout has not altered, but decreasing protrusion is more subtly suggested by a pronounced thickening.

Mickey's eye has grown in two modes: first, by a major, discontinuous evolutionary shift as the entire eye of ancestral Mickey became the pupil of his descendants, and second, by gradual increase thereafter.

Mickey's improvement in cranial bulging followed an interesting path since his evolution had always been constrained by the unaltered convention of representing his head as a circle with appended ears and an oblong snout. The circle's form could not be altered to provide a bulging cranium directly. Instead, Mickey's ears moved back, increasing the distance between nose and ears, and giving him a rounded, rather than a sloping, forehead.

To give these observations the cachet of quantitative science, I applied my best pair of dial calipers to three stages of the official phylogeny – the thin-nosed, ears-forward figure of the early 1930s (stage 1), the latter-day Jack of *Mickey and the Beanstalk* (1947, stage 2), and the modern mouse (stage 3). I measured three signs of Mickey's creeping juvenility: increasing eye size (maximum height) as a percentage of head length (base of the nose to top of rear ear); increasing head length as a percentage of body length; and increasing cranial vault size measured by rearward displacement of the front ear (base of the nose to the top of front ear as a percentage of base of the nose to top of rear ear).

All three percentages increased steadily – eye size from 27 to 42% of head length; head from 42.7 to 48.1% of body length; and nose to front ear from 71.7 to a whopping 95.6% of nose to rear ear. For comparison, I measured Mickey's young 'nephew' Morty Mouse. In each case, Mickey has clearly been evolving toward youthful stages of his stock, although he still has a way to go for head length.

You may, indeed, now ask what an at least marginally respectable scientist has been doing with a mouse like that. In part, fiddling around and having fun, of course. (I still prefer *Pinocchio* to *Citizen Kane*.)

But I do have a serious point – two, in fact – to make. We must first ask why Disney chose to change his most famous character so gradually and persistently in the same direction?

National symbols are not altered capriciously and market researchers (for the doll industry in particular) have spent a good deal of time and practical effort learning what features appeal to people as cute and friendly. Biologists also have spent a great deal of time studying a similar subject in a wide range of animals.

In one of his most famous articles, Konrad Lorenz argues that humans use the characteristic differences in form between babies and adults as important behavioral cues.

He believes that features of juvenility trigger 'innate releasing mechanisms' for affection and nurturing in adult humans. When we see a living creature with babyish features, we feel an automatic surge of disarming tenderness. The adaptive value of this response can scarcely be questioned, for we must nurture our babies. Lorenz, by the way, lists among his releasers the very features of babyhood that Disney affixed progressively to Mickey: 'a relatively large head, predominance of the brain capsule, large and low-lying eyes, bulging cheek region, short and thick extremities, a springy elastic consistency, and clumsy movements'.

(I propose to leave aside for this article the contentious issue of whether or not our affectionate response to babyish features is truly innate and inherited directly from ancestral primates – as Lorenz argues – or whether it is simply learned from our immediate experience with babies and grafted upon an evolutionary predisposition for attaching ties of affection to certain learned signals. My argument works equally well in either case for I only claim that babyish features tend to elicit strong feelings of affection in adult humans, whether the biological basis be direct programming or the capacity to learn and fix upon signals. I also treat as collateral to my point the major thesis of Lorenz's article – that we respond not to the totality or *Gestalt*, but to a set of specific features acting as releasers. This argument is important to Lorenz because he wants to argue for evolutionary identity in modes of behaviour between other vertebrates and humans, and we know that many birds, for example, often respond to abstract features rather than *Gestalten*. Lorenz's article, published in 1950, bears the title '*Ganzheit und Teil in der tierischen und menschlichen Gemeinschaft*' – 'Entirety and part in animal and human society'. Disney's piecemeal change of Mickey's appearance does make sense in this context – he operated in sequential fashion upon Lorenz's primary releasers).

Lorenz emphasises the power that juvenile features hold over us, and the abstract quality of their influence, by pointing out that we judge other animals by the same criteria – although the judgment may be utterly inappropriate in an evolutionary context. We are, in short, fooled by an evolved response to our own babies, and we transfer our reaction to the same set of features in other animals.

Many animals, for reasons having nothing to do with the inspiration of affection in humans, possess some features also shared by human babies but not by human adults – large eyes and bulging forehead with retreating chin, in particular. We are drawn to them, we cultivate them as pets, we stop and admire them in the wild – while we reject their small-eyed, long-snouted relatives who might make more affectionate companions or objects of admiration. Lorenz points out that the German names of many animals with features mimicking human babies end in the diminutive suffix *chen*, even though the animals are often larger than close relatives without such features – *Rotkehlchen* (robin), *Eichhörnchen* (squirrel), and *Kaninchen* (rabbit), for example.

In a fascinating section, Lorenz then enlarges upon our capacity for biologically inappropriate response to other animals, or even to inanimate objects that mimic human features. 'The most amazing objects can acquire remarkable, highly specific emotional values by "experiential attachment" of human properties […] Steeply rising, somewhat overhanging cliff faces or dark storm-clouds piling up have the same, immediate display value as a human being who is standing at full height and leaning slightly forwards' – that is, threatening.

We cannot help regarding a camel as aloof and unfriendly because it mimics, quite unwittingly and for other reasons, the 'gesture of haughty rejection' common to so many human cultures. In this gesture, we raise our heads, placing our nose above our eyes. We then half-close our eyes and blow out through our nose – the 'harumph' of the stereotyped upper-class Englishman or his well-trained servant. 'All this', Lorenz argues quite cogently, 'symbolizes resistance against all sensory modalities emanating from the disdained counterpart.' But the poor camel cannot help carrying its nose above its elongate eyes, with mouth drawn down. As Lorenz reminds us, if you wish to know whether a camel will eat out of your hand or spit, look at its ears, not the rest of its face.

In his important book *Expression of the Emotions in Man and Animals*, published in 1872, Charles Darwin traced the evolutionary basis of many common gestures to originally adaptive actions in animals later internalised as symbols in humans. Thus, he argued for evolutionary continuity of emotion, not only of form. We snarl and raise our upper lip in fierce anger – to expose our non-existent fighting canine tooth. Our gesture of disgust repeats the facial action associated with the highly adaptive act of vomiting in necessary circumstances. Darwin concluded, much to the distress of many Victorian contemporaries: 'With mankind some expressions, such as the bristling of the hair under the influence of extreme terror, or the uncovering of the teeth under that of furious rage, can hardly be understood, except on the belief that man once existed in a much lower and animal-like condition.'

In any case, the abstract features of human childhood elicit powerful emotional responses in us, even when they occur in other animals. I submit that Mickey Mouse's evolutionary road down the course of his own growth in reverse reflects the unconscious discovery of this biological principle by Disney and his artists. In fact, the emotional status of most Disney characters rests on the same set of distinctions. To this extent, the magic kingdom trades on a biological illusion – our ability to abstract and our propensity to transfer inappropriately to other animals the fitting responses we make to changing form in the growth of our own bodies.

Donald Duck also adopts more juvenile features throughout time. His elongated beak recedes and his eyes enlarge; he converges on Huey, Louie and Dewey as surely as Mickey approaches Morty. But Donald, having inherited the mantle of Mickey's original misbehaviour, remains more adult in form with his projecting beak and more sloping forehead.

Mouse villains or sharpies, contrasted with Mickey, are always more adult in appearance, although they often share Mickey's chronological age. In 1936, for example, Disney made a short entitled *Mickey's Rival*. Mortimer, a dandy in a yellow sports car, intrudes upon Mickey and Minnie's quiet country picnic. The thoroughly disreputable Mortimer has a head only 29% of body length, to Mickey's 45, and a snout 80% of head length, compared with Mickey's 49. (Nonetheless, and was it ever different, Minnie transfers her affection until an obliging bull from a neighboring field dispatches Mickey's rival.) Consider also the exaggerated adult features of other Disney characters – the swaggering bully Peg-leg Pete or the simple, if lovable, dolt Goofy.

As a second, serious biological comment on Mickey's odyssey in form, I note that his path to eternal youth repeats, in epitome, our own evolutionary story. For humans are neotenic. We have evolved by retaining to adulthood the originally juvenile features of our ancestors. Our australopithecine forbears, like Mickey in *Steamboat Willie*, had projected jaws and low vaulted craniums.

Our embryonic skulls scarcely differ from those of chimpanzees. And we follow the same path of changing form through growth: relative decrease of the cranial vault since brains grow so much more slowly than bodies after birth, and continuous relative increase of the jaw. But while chimps accentuate these changes, producing an adult strikingly different in form from a baby, we proceed much more slowly down the same path and never get nearly so far. Thus, as adults, we retain juvenile features. To be sure, we change enough to produce a notable difference between baby and adult, but our alteration is far smaller than that experienced by chimps and other primates.

A marked slowdown of developmental rates has triggered our neoteny. Primates are slow developers among mammals, but we have accentuated the trend to a degree matched by no other mammal. We have very long periods of gestation, markedly extended childhoods, and the longest life span of any mammal. The morphological features of eternal youth have served us well. Our enlarged brain is, at least in part, a result of extending rapid prenatal growth rates to later ages. (In all mammals, the brain grows rapidly in utero but often very little after birth. We have extended this fetal phase into postnatal life.) But the changes in timing themselves have been just as important.

We are pre-eminently learning animals, and our extended childhood permits the transference of culture by education. Many animals display flexibility and play in childhood but follow rigidly programmed patterns as adults. Lorenz writes, in the same article cited above: 'The characteristic which is so vital for the human peculiarity of the true man – that of always remaining in a state of development – is quite certainly a gift which we owe to the neotenous nature of mankind.'

In short, we, like Mickey, never grow up although we, alas, do grow old. Best wishes to you, Mickey, for your next half-century. May we stay as young as you, but grow a bit wiser.

Stephen Jay Gould, 'A Biological Homage To Mickey Mouse', *Ecotone*, vol. 4, issue 7 (Winter 2008) 333–40.

William Ian Miller
Anatomy of Disgust//1998

[...] Both contempt and disgust are emotions that assert a superior ranking as against their objects. But the experience of superiority based on the one is quite different from that based on the other. We can enjoy our feelings of contempt, mingled as they often are with pride and self-congratulation. Contrast disgust which makes us pay with unpleasant sensation for the superiority it asserts. Whereas disgust finds its object repulsive, contempt can find its object amusing. Contempt, moreover, often informs benevolent and polite treatment of the inferior. Disgust does not. Pity and contempt go hand in hand, whereas disgust overwhelms pity.

Consider in a related vein how differently the two emotions intersect with love. Not only are love and contempt not antithetical but certain loves seem to be necessarily intermingled with contempt. What is the judgment that some persons or animals are cute but a judgment of their endearing subordinance and unthreateningness? We love our pets and our children and we find them cute and adorable. Even love between equals is less a matter of admitting constant equality than of taking turns at being up or being down, so that even 'true' adult love can admit judgments of cuteness and adorableness, as long as they don't run in one direction only. Where there are rankings there is contempt doing the work of maintaining them. I do not mean my claim of the unavoidable mingling of contempt and some genuine kinds of love to be all that contentious, yet it is just the kind of claim that will elicit resistance. But contempt has a light side as well as a dark one; and though we might not wish to admit it, there is good reason to suspect that contempt can be as complex and varied as love itself. Why not admit that helplessness and need may be elicitors of love as much as strength and autonomy? Perhaps one of the most adaptive traits of humanity is that we find some kinds of helplessness endearing, or feel that it raises a duty in us to help and succor. How else do parents bond to their infants no matter how colicky or obnoxious they may be, whether related by blood or adoption? Contempt is more than just a sneer of hostility. The notion of looking down is consistent with softer and gentler sentiments: pity, graciousness, and love. [...]

William Ian Miller, extract from *Anatomy of Disgust* (Cambridge, MA: Harvard University Press, 1998) 32.

Roland Barthes
'Adorable!', Compassion, and Tenderness//1978

'Adorable!'

adorable | adorable

Not managing to name the specialty of his desire for the loved being, the amorous subject falls back on this rather stupid word: *adorable!*

Diderot

1.   'One lovely September day, I went out to do some errands. Paris was *adorable* that morning...', etc. A host of perceptions suddenly come together to form a dazzling impression (to dazzle is ultimately to prevent sight, to prevent speech): the weather, the season, the light, the boulevard, the Parisians out walking, shopping, all held within what *already* has its vocation as memory: a scene, in short, the hieroglyph of kindliness (as [Jean-Baptiste] Greuze might have painted it), the good humour of desire. All Paris is within my grasp, without my wanting to grasp it: neither languor nor lust. I forget all the reality in Paris which exceeds its charm: history, labour, money, merchandise – all the harshness of big cities; here I see only the object of an aesthetically *restrained* desire. From the top of Pere Lachaise, Rastignac hurled his challenge to the city: *Between the two of us now*; I say to Paris: *Adorable!*

After an impression of the night before, I wake up softened by a happy thought: 'X was adorable last night.' This is the memory of … what? Of what the Greeks called *charis*: 'the sparkle of the eyes, the body's luminous beauty, the radiance of the desirable being'; and I may even add, just as in the ancient *charis*, the notion – the hope – that the loved object will bestow itself upon my desire.

2.   By a singular logic, the amorous subject perceives the other as a Whole (in the fashion of Paris on an autumn

DIDEROT   like Lessing, elaborates a theory of the *pregnant moment.*

afternoon), and, at the same time, this Whole seems to him to involve a remainder, which he cannot express. It is the other *as a whole* who produces in him an aesthetic vision: he praises the other for being perfect, he glorifies himself for having chosen this perfect other; he imagines that the other wants to be loved, as he himself would want to be loved, not for one or another of his qualities, but for *everything*, and this *everything* he bestows upon the other in the form of a blank word, for the Whole cannot be inventoried without being diminished: in *Adorable!* there is no residual quality, but only the *everything* of affect. Yet, at the same time that *adorable* says everything, it also says what is lacking in everything; it seeks to designate that site of the other to which my desire clings *in a special way*, but this site cannot be designated; about it I shall never know anything; my language will always fumble, stammer in order to attempt to express it, but I can never produce anything but a blank word, an empty vocable, which is the zero degree of all the sites where my very special desire for this particular other (and for no other) will form.

3.   I encounter millions of bodies in my life; of these millions, I may desire some hundreds; but of these hundreds, I love only one. The other with whom I am in love designates for me the specialty of my desire.

This choice, so rigorous that it retains only the Unique, constitutes, it is said, the difference between the analytical transference and the amorous transference; one is universal, the other specific. It has taken many accidents, many surprising coincidences (and perhaps many efforts), for me to find the Image which, out of a thousand, suits my desire. Herein a great enigma, to which I shall never possess the key: Why is it that I desire So-and-so? Why is it that I desire So-and-so lastingly, longingly? Is it the whole of So-and-so I desire (a silhouette, a shape, a mood? And, in that case, what is it in this loved body which has the vocation of a fetish for me? What perhaps incredibly tenuous portion – what accident? The way a nail is cut, a tooth broken slightly aslant, a lock of hair, a way of spreading the fingers while talking, while smoking? About all these folds of the body, I want to say that they are adorable. Adorable means: this is my desire, insofar as it is unique: 'That's it! That's it exactly (which I love)!' Yet the more I experience the specialty of my desire, the less I can give it a name; to the precision of the target corresponds a wavering of the name; what is characteristic of desire, proper to desire, can produce only an impropriety of the utterance. Of this failure of language, there remains only one trace: the word 'adorable' (the right translation of 'adorable' would be the Latin *ipse*: it is the self, himself, herself, in person).

4.   Adorable is the futile vestige of a fatigue – the fatigue of language itself. From word to word, I struggle to put 'into other words' the ipseity of my Image, to express improperly the propriety of my desire: a journey at whose end my final philosophy can only be to recognise – and to practice – tautology. *The adorable is what is adorable.* Or again: I adore you because you are adorable, I love you because I love you. What thereby closes off the lover's language is the very thing which has instituted it: fascination. For to describe fascination can never, in the last analysis, exceed this utterance: 'I am fascinated'. Having attained the end of language, where it can merely repeat its last word like a scratched record, I intoxicate myself upon its affirmation: is not tautology that preposterous state in which are to be found, all values being confounded, the glorious end of the logical operation, the obscenity of stupidity, and the explosion of the Nietzschean yes?

Nietzsche

**'I have an
Other-ache'**
compassion | compassion
The subject experiences a sentiment of violent compassion with regard to the loved object each

LACAN 'It is not every day that you encounter what is so constituted as to give you precisely the image of your desire.'
PROUST Scene of the specialty of desire: Jupien and Charlus meet in the courtyard of the Hôtel de Guermantes (at the beginning of *Cities of the Plain*).

Nietzsche

Michelet

time he sees, feels, or knows the loved object is unhappy or in danger, for whatever reason external to the amorous relation itself.

1. 'Supposing that we experienced the other as he experiences himself – which Schopenhauer calls compassion and which might more accurately be called a union within suffering, a unity of suffering – we should hate the other when he himself, like Pascal, finds himself hateful.' If the other suffers from hallucinations, if he fears going mad, I should myself hallucinate, myself go mad. Now, whatever the power of love, this does not occur: I am moved, anguished, for it is horrible to see those one loves suffering, but at the same time I remain dry, watertight. My identification is imperfect: I am a Mother (the other causes me concern), but an insufficient Mother; I bestir myself too much, in proportion to the profound reserve in which, actually, I remain. For at the same time that I 'sincerely' identify myself with the other's misery, what I read in this misery is that it occurs without me, and that by being miserable by himself, the other abandons me: if he suffers without my being the cause of his suffering, it is because I don't count for him: his suffering annuls me insofar as it constitutes him outside of myself.

2. Whereupon, a reversal: since the other suffers without me, why suffer in his place? His misery bears him far away from me, I can only exhaust myself running after him, without ever hoping to be able to catch up, to coincide with him. So let us become a little detached, let us undertake the apprenticeship of a certain distance. Let the repressed word appear which rises to the lips of every subject, once he survives another's death: Let us live!

3. So I shall suffer with the other, but without pressure, without losing myself. Such behaviour, at once very affective and very controlled, very amorous and very civilised, can be

NIETZSCHE: *The Dawn.*
MICHELET: Saying, 'I have a France-ache.'

given a name: *delicacy*: in a sense it is the 'healthy' (artistic) form of compassion. (Ate is the goddess of madness, but Plato speaks of Ate's delicacy: her foot is winged, it touches lightly.)

Tenderness

tendresse / tenderness
Bliss, but also a disturbing evaluation of the loved object's tender gestures, insofar as the subject realises that he is not their privileged recipient.

1.   There is not only need for tenderness, there is also need to be tender for the other: we shut ourselves up in a mutual kindness, we mother each other reciprocally; we return to the root of all relations, where need and desire join. The tender gesture says: ask me anything that can put your body to sleep, but also do not forget that I desire you – a little, lightly, without trying to seize anything right away.

Sexual pleasure is not metonymic: once taken, it is cut off: it was the Feast, always terminated and instituted only by a temporary, supervised lifting of the prohibition. Tenderness, on the contrary, is nothing but an infinite, insatiable metonymy; the gesture, the episode of tenderness (the delicious harmony of an evening) can only be interrupted with laceration: everything seems called into question once again: return of rhythm – *vritti* – disappearance of *nirvana*.

2.   If I receive the tender gesture within the field of demand, I am fulfilled: is this gesture not a kind of miraculous crystallisation of presence? But if I receive it (and this can be simultaneous) within the field of desire, I am disturbed: tenderness, by rights, is not exclusive, hence I must admit that what I receive, others receive as well (sometimes I am even afforded the spectacle of this).

MUSIL: 'Her brother's body pressed so tenderly, so sweetly against her, that she felt she was resting within him even as he in her; nothing in her stirred now, even her splendid desire' (*The Man Without Qualities*, II).
ZEN: *Vritti*, for the Buddhist, is the series of waves, the cyclic process. *Vritti* is painful, and only nirvana can put an end to it.

> Where you are tender, you speak your plural.
> ('L was stupefied to see A give the waitress in the Bavarian
> restaurant, while ordering his schnitzel, the same tender
> look, the same angelic expression that moved him so when
> these expressions were addressed to him.')

Roland Barthes, '"Adorable!"', 'Compassion', and 'Tenderness', in *A Lover's Discourse*, trans. Richard Howard (New York: Hill and Wang, 1978) 18–21, 57–8, 224–5.

Elizabeth Honor Wilder
On Cosiness, or Making a Scene//2019

[…] Cosiness derives its primary effects from the ways bodies find pleasure in differentiation, in heightened awareness of the distinction between individual objects and the environment. Despite its ultimate pleasures, this process of differentiation frequently works through a contrastive incorporation of discomfort into, or in proximity to, the scene of cosiness. In *Barnaby Rudge* (2003), for instance, Dickens describes the ruse a man practices on himself to induce a cosy feeling:

> Mr Willet walked slowly up to the window, flattened his fat nose against the cold glass, and shading his eyes that his sight might not be affected by the ruddy glow of the fire, looked abroad. Then he walked slowly back to his old seat in the chimney-corner, and, composing himself in it with a slight shiver, such as a man might give way to and so acquire an additional relish for the warm blaze, said, looking round upon his guests: 'It'll clear at eleven o'clock'.

Cosiness here works through the contrast between the warm, bright interior of a tavern and the cold dark of the night outside it (enabled by the transparency of the windowpane, which allows those inside just enough intimacy with nighttime chill to foster an active appreciation of their shelter). Semi-permeable partitions like screens and windows help to stage the oppositions (dark/ bright, exterior/interior, cold/warm, outsider/intimate) that are central to the operations of cosiness by giving controlled entry to those elements of difference or discomfort needed for a strong impression of contrast. But even this amount of difference isn't enough for Mr. Willett's needs; he has to force a shiver by the fire as a way to 'acquire an additional relish for the warm blaze'. Crucially, Willett wills, or 'compos[es]', his shivering as a way to top off a sense of wellbeing, underlining the extent to which the experience of cosiness is a condition of conscious (and in this case, intentional) enjoyment. Cosiness is not about moving from a cold outside to a warm inside so much as it is about an awareness of coldness and warmness happening at the same time. In this sense, we might think about cosy contrast as a form of *simultaneity*.

The effect of simultaneity can be produced discursively by the movement from one scene to another, one chapter to another, or graphically by the juxtaposition of word and picture. A page from the serial version of [Dickens'] *The Old Curiosity Shop* (2011) combines a chapter break with juxtaposition to create a contrast [...]. Chapter sixty-seven of the novel ends with the gruesome details of Quilp's death, followed by a vignette of his corpse foundering in the Estuary marshes. The next chapter begins after this with a paradigmatically cosy scene: 'Lighted rooms, bright fires, cheerful faces, the music of glad voices, words of love and welcome, warm hearts, and tears of happiness – what a change this is!' As Malcolm Andrews notes in his reading of this page: 'The page as a whole, the composite of text and illustration, spectacularly epitomises the design of the novel as articulated in chapter 53: 'Everything in our lives, whether of good or evil, affects us most by contrast'.[1] The contrast here, however, is not contained within the cosy scene itself but within both the logic of the novel's narrative structure and formatting, which are amplified by the narrator's interest in the simultaneity of these two events happening at once; only readers – not the characters themselves – can perceive the effect.

It makes sense, then, that cosiness fails in the presence of too much continuity or uniformity between self and world; as Ishmael has it in *Moby Dick* (2020), to be in a warm bed in a warm room is not the height of comfort but rather one of the 'luxurious discomforts of the rich'. It is worth pausing on this thought because it suggests that what most threatens to disrupt a cosy experience is not fear, pain, or strangeness, but rather excessive, uncalibrated, or poorly scaled conditions of comfort. Cosy scenes are apt to feel dingy or stuffy in the absence of sufficient contrast ....

Contrast does not differentiate symmetrically in cosy scenes. Instead, interiors are individuated and particularised in proportion to the obscurity or formlessness of the exterior view. The darker or mistier it is outside, the more clearly the details of the inside are drawn into visibility. Barthes reflects on this phenomenon as it plays out in Jules Verne's novel, *The Mysterious Island*, in which 'the enjoyment of being enclosed [in a submarine] reaches its paroxysm when, from the bosom of this unbroken inwardness, it is possible to watch, through a large window-pane, the outside vagueness of the waters, and thus define, in a single act, the inside by means of its opposite'.[2] [...]

The Cosy Mood

The word *comfortable* stands at some remove from comfortable things. It is a neutral word, which is not to say that it does not have generally positive associations, but that it is able to designate them without being overly implicated in the objects or scenes it describes. In contrast, the word 'cosy' partakes of the linguistic and affective register of cosiness: cosy is a cosy word. To use the word 'cosy' is to be cosy. 'Snug' likewise sends up a signal-flare for cosiness; it is not a word that describes comfort so much as evokes it. Other words are cosy without belonging to the semantic field of comfort. Take, for instance, 'topsy-turvy,' a favourite word in Dickens. 'Topsy-turvy' is typical of the vocabulary of cosiness in its cute diminutive ending, tone of hearty cheer, and companionable compound form. Compound words give a sentence a rhythmical, sing-song quality, and when they're hyphenated can suggest a clubby complicity between the halves. […]

As these examples suggest, a sense of cosiness can emerge not only from the signification of a word, or the feeling it imparts, but also from the relationship it suggests between speaker and auditor. William Empson called this relationship mood, which he defines as 'a mixed class giving the hints of the speaker about his own relations to the person addressed, or the person described, or persons normally in the situation described'.[3] Empson provides examples of several types of moods, but he focuses on one in particular: the cosy mood.[4] Words communicated in this mood carry the sense that the speaker is appealing to a common understanding with the auditor, the sense that 'we agree about this, we who know, don't we?'. Empson's primary example of the cosy mood is the British use of the word 'quite', a word whose emotive meaning departs from its semantic meaning in a range of situations. To illustrate, Empson quotes a couplet from Pope: 'But something much more our concern/And quite a scandal not to learn'. 'The feeling here is 'how cosy', Empson remarks. This cosy feeling – the implied sense of complicity or shared understanding between speaker and auditor – brings the communicative relationship to the fore in the dynamics of the meaning of this word. […]

Theatricality

'Every literary description is a view,' Barthes writes. 'It could be said that the speaker, before describing, stands at the window, not so much to see, but to establish what he sees by its very frame: the window frame creates the scene.'[5] The window frame is especially integral to consolidating scenes of cosiness *as scenes*: Frankenstein's creature monitors the De Lacey family in their cottage through a chink in a boarded-up window; Fagin and Monks stand at a window to watch Oliver Twist dozing over his studies; Cathy and Heathcliff balance on a flower-pot to look into the Lintons' drawing-room window; a starving Jane Eyre gazes at the women of the Rivers household 'near the hearth, sitting still amidst the rosy peace and warmth suffusing it', a 'scene [that] was as silent as if all the figures had been shadows and the fire-lit apartment a picture'.[6] Yet each of these episodes underwrites the attractions of domesticity with a pervasive awareness of the way such attractions incorporate precarity, threat and exclusion: Frankenstein's creature and Jane Eyre are both outcasts who have been turned away at many doors by the time they look longingly through the keyhole of domestic paradise; Fagin and Monks kidnap Oliver; Cathy and Heathcliff are appalled by the Linton siblings' spoiled behavior in their lavish home. Given this, we can agree that Victorian novelists engaged the paradox of domestic ideology that Karen Chase and Michael Levenson call the 'spectacle of intimacy'. 'One of the abiding activities of midcentury life,' they argue, 'was the production of family tableaus, the ceaseless manufacture in text and image of scenes of home life, the publication of a privacy. But to see the 'public opinion of privacy' as only an invasion is to miss one of the leading features of the age: the extent to which domestic life itself was impelled toward acts of exposure and display'.[7] Cosiness, as the primary aesthetic attached to positively-valued 'family tableaus', participates in these 'acts of exposure'. It's important to note, however, that novelistic evocations of cosiness (whether these take the form of a spectacle seen by an outside observer or are experienced by a character from within) perform this act of suspicious reading on themselves. It is not the case that cosy scenes are securely installed as hermetically sealed zones. After all, part of what makes a scene cosy is recognising it *as a scene*. The theatricality of cosiness – its dependence on display, and on the differential operations of distance or discomfort required by display – are, as this chapter has been at pains to demonstrate, central to the reflexivity that constitutes so much of the pleasure this mode offers. […]

Crucially, however, the theatre provides not only an origin for novelistic conceptions of the scene, but also during this period serves as one of the prominent *destinations* for these scenes, as popular novels were rapidly adapted into tableaus and plays for performance. The illustrations that accompanied much serial fiction at the time played a central role in this process of adaptation, primarily by acting as storyboards for novels that could then be turned into a series of *tableau vivants*. [In *Realizations: Narrative, Pictorial, and Theatrical Arts in Nineteenth-Century England* (1984)] Meisel describes how illustrations bridged the distance between novel and play by offering a pre-selected menu of key scenes and postures that playwrights could easily 'realise' with actors on stage. He cites as a main example Edward Stirling's discovery, while working on the comic opera, *Pickwick Papers: or, The Age We Live In* (1837), that 'the most economical and acceptable method of dramatising such fiction' was 'by concentrating on the pictures, not just for the narrative line, but as the basis of the dramaturgical unit and as the prime vehicle of effect'. Illustrations – often, especially in the case of Dickens, with strict instructions from the author – served an interpretive function of determining and accentuating the scenes the reader would take to be most important. The fact that these same illustrations, which already emphasised selected scenes from the text by repeating them in picture form, also often became the basis for stage adaptations of the novel points to the ways illustrations helped determine what counted as a scene in a novel and the ongoing debt this concept owed to drama.

It is worth picking up on Meisel's cue to dwell on the importance of illustrations to the cosy scene, for Hablot K. Browne's etchings amplify the theatricality of cosiness in *David Copperfield* (2004) by emphasising the visual and dramatic aspects of 'scene' as a narrative unit. Because of its medial position in the two-way traffic between novel and drama, illustrations for serialised novels effectively give readers an iconography of the scene. The most frequent subject of illustration in *David Copperfield* – apart from David himself – is the houseboat, which appears not only in the title page vignette of Little Em'ly playing outside it, but is also pictured during David's first visit to the 'seaside cottage'; as a backdrop for the departing carriage at the end of this visit; and once again, in the scene Meisel references, of Steerforth and David greeting the Peggotty family. What is striking about these etchings is how they play up the homology between the curvature of the houseboat and the oval framing of picture itself.

The repeated insistence on the structural similarities between the boathouse and Browne's own method of representing novel scenes as spherical vignettes that dissolve or fade at the borders suggests that in this novel cosiness migrates beyond the representation of snug spaces to attach to the formal unit of the scene itself. Channeling a kind of tunnel vision, as though reading a novel might be akin to navigating an underground warren, the illustrations for David Copperfield craft a peephole from which a wide range of scenes – including ones that take place outdoors or in distinctly non-cosy spaces – appear in a cosy perspective. [...]

Phiz's illustrations make the shape of a scene literal, but the idea of the scene as a spherical form has a much longer history, one that clarifies how the circle joins together the theatrical and the cosy. Barthes, for example, in offering examples of some 'subversions of the rectangle' – the rectangular frame of aesthetic theory – recalls the roundedness of classical theatre: 'Theatre of antiquity: circular (Greek), semicircular (Latin) orchestra. Stage = to begin with, a tent for actors. They would come out and perform in front of it: *the proscenium*: conflict between the rectangle and the circus'.[8] More figuratively, Henry James imagines the dramatic form of his novel *The Awkward Age* (1987), in distinctly round and cosy terms as 'the neat figure of a circle consisting of a number of small rounds disposed at equal distance around a central object'. He goes on to explain his method for the novel: 'The central object was my situation, my subject in itself, to which the thing would owe its title, and the small rounds represented so many distinct lamps, as I liked to call them, the function of each which would be to light with all due intensity one of its aspects'. It is not just the intimacy of the circle, the connotation of closeness and maternal comfort, then, that makes a round scene cosy but its theatrical vividness and immediacy. As Barthes notes, if a lamp functions 'as an object-center, a crystallizer of proxemics', in part it is because a lamp 'isolates the writing desk, the armchair, produces a lit being and a dark nothingness'.9 The scene, like a lamp, brightly illuminated and illuminating, stands out against a dark or indistinct backdrop.

For this reason, scenes are, perhaps, what are best remembered about a novel. [...]

1   'Illustrations', in *A Companion to Charles Dickens*. ed. David Paroissien (Malden, MA and Oxford: Blackwell, 2008) 118.

2   Roland Barthes, *Mythologies* (New York: Hill and Wang, 1972) 67.

3   [Ed. note] William Empson, *The Structure of Complex Words* (Cambridge, MA: Harvard University Press, 1989) 17. All subsequent quotations are from this title unless noted otherwise.

4   [Footnote 5 in source] In a letter to I.A. Richards, Empson reflects on this choice of name: 'You can keep your Tone; and your Gesture; I want a monosyallable. My "£" is now called a "Mood", which gives a suggestion of grammar (as in Subjunctive M) which goes all right. The only pain is to lose the assonance of "cosy tone".' Empson's regret about the name change is especially interesting for us in light of what I have said about the importance of phonetic and orthographic aspects of linguistic cosiness. 'Cosy tone' would have been a cosier term because of the rhyme, but Empson is at pains to distinguish his 'mood' from his mentor's concept of 'tone.')

5   [7] Roland Barthes, *S/Z* (New York: Hill and Wang, 1974) 54.

6   [8] Charlotte Brontë, *Jane Eyre* (1847) (London: Penguin, 2006) 382–3.

7   [9] Karen Chase and Michael Levenson, *The Spectacle of Intimacy: A Public Life for the Victorian Family* (Princeton: Princeton University Press, 2000) 7.

8   [10] Roland Barthes, *The Preparation of the Novel* (2011) 115.

9   [11] Ibid., 112.

Elizabeth Honor Wilder, extracts from 'Coziness', in *Domestic Formalism* (Stanford University dissertation, 2019) 20–3, 36–9, 45–6, 52–3.

Carrie Rickey
Naive Nouveau and Its Malcontents//1980

I.

There's a fine line between simplicity and simplemindedness, and drawing it is a tough assignment. Apropos movies, the distinction is easy: Robert Bresson's *Lancelot du Lac* is simple, while *The American Gigilo,* by Bresson's American epigone Paul Schrader is simpleminded, because it embodies the pared-down form of Bressonian simplicity while lacking the pungency and concentration of Bresson's content. In pop music, The Ramones – whose musical vocabulary consists of about three chords – are simple; they use economic form to stress the wicked humour of their lyrics. The Flying Lizards, on the other hand, however amusing, are simpleminded: they impose a tired ironic attitude on old pop material – the content is cynicism. (As Oscar Wilde said, the cynic knows the price of everything and the value of nothing.) Georges Simenon is a writer whose simplicity is staggering. He crams a world of information into a six-word sentence. But the prose of Penelope Gilliatt's simple sentences, unlike Simenon's, relates little information and, consequently, often seems Simpleminded. Simplicity is a condensed account of a complicated concept. Simplemindedness a condensation of something vacuous.

I prize simplicity, believing that to be simple quite a difficult task. Yet it's impossible to ignore the significant number of artists taking up the corollary aesthetic of simple-mindedness. In the visual arts, this aesthetic seems particularly modern, paralleling, as it does, the development (one might call it regression) in the music of punk, new wave and no wave persuasions. The parallel is significant, for although modern art and music have a lot in common, most recently their shared territory has been minimalism – a reduction of means (as opposed to a simplification) that has resulted in a reduction of audience as well. That vanguard efforts in art (specifics later) aspire to popular culture, no less youth culture, marks the difference in attitude among artists, recalling the ambitions of certain abstract expressionists to make pictures having the personal, improvisational qualities of Black jazz.

A characterological profile of the artist extolling the aesthetic of the simple-minded would take into account youth, interest in domains outside the history of art (namely music and pop culture), and – most crucial – the emphasis on *attitude.* (I feel like a buzzard, circling the general territory, before setting my sights on specifics; they will come.) While partisans of simplicity treasure the *issues* simplicity enables them better to expose, adherents of simplemindedness reckon a posture toward an issue is more important than the issue itself. An issue is something one formulates an attitude toward. Issue orientation is primarily interested in content. Attitude-orientation is preoccupied with form and protocol. Attitude is the essence of the simpleminded aesthetic, a sensibility I call Naïf Nouveau.

Other traits of the Naïf Nouveau: the sense the artist knows more than he or she is telling, the making of paintings or sculpture (or music or fashion) that's childlike in presentation but sophisticated in execution. Disingenuousness reigns. The reason? I suspect it's because freed from the burden of art history and art seriousness, the artist can unpretentiously go about his or her business and make art – instead of Making Art. This work is about deschooling oneself of modernism and starting from scratch. But starting from scratch can only be a token gesture. Think of Nudist colonists who want to be in their original uncivilised natural states. Or think of Marie Antoinette and her ladies-in-waiting who glorified the bucolic life of milkmaids as sideshows to the most cynical. urbane court in the history of France. Likewise, Naïf Nouveau artists affect simple-mindedness in simplicity's clothing at a stunningly complex moment in culture.

Despite a preference for simplicity over simple-mindedness, for issues over attitudes, the work of Naïf Nouveau artists provokes equal measures of attraction and repulsion in me. On the attraction side, I like the idea of lightweight art after so much heavy-handed modernism; I like NN's lack of pretension; I like the obviation of modernist art 'problems' like the resolution of figure and ground (NN's view of the canvas is a vast ground, anything depicted becomes figure).

Irony (meaning *meaning*) is the aspect of Naïf Nouveau that divides me. Is the intent of these images to undermine the act depicted? To undermine the act of depicting it? Or is simplicity of depiction its only intent? Irony, of course, is in the eye of the beholder. But I'm of two eyes on this. One is repelled by the anti-intellectual character of Naïf Nouveau. By emulating the naturalness of authentic primitives, Naïf Nouveau's pretend that ignorance is bliss and suggest they know better. It's their way of being intellectual about anti-intellectualism. The other eye is attracted to Naïf Nouveau's fascination with cliché and the banal. Sometimes its downright analytical about the obvious in the same way Pop Art was. That its irony is the issue troubling me most in Naïf Nouveau reminds me of my ambivalent relations with that most elusive of phenomena, Camp. One of Susan Sontag's delicious descriptions of Camp distinguishes the unselfconscious from the conscious variety: 'The pure examples of Camp are unintentional; they are dead serious. The Art Nouveau craftsman who makes a lamp with a snake coiled around it is not kidding, nor is he trying to be charming. He is saying, in all earnestness, 'Voila! The Orient!' Naïf Nouveau's lack of sincerity – its stylishly educated choice to abandon education and feign naivety – makes it difficult to determine its intentionality. Self-conscious affectation of the genuine Naïf's pre-conscious behaviour is what the Naïf Nouveau attitude is about. The Naïf Nouveau artist who makes a simple image on canvas or piece of paper is maybe kidding, maybe disingenuous. He or she is saying, a double-edge to his/her tone, 'Voila! Art! Voila! Expression'. Figuring out whether or not this affectation is responsible for good art is the tricky issue.

II.

It's time to be specific, to name names. When I say Naïf Nouveau, I'm not talking about an organised movement or school (should I say preschool?). Although Richard Marshall designated some of these artists as New Imagists in his show at the Whitney in 1978, 'New Image Painting', and Douglas Crimp included others in his exhibition 'Pictures' at Artist's Space in 1977, I'm talking about a slightly more inclusive sensibility of the Simple whose attributes can be seen in the work of Nicholas Africano, Jared Bark, Troy Brauntuch, Eric Fischl, Michael Hurson, Neil Jenney, Christopher Knowles, Lois Lane, Thomas Lanigan-Schmidt, Thomas Lawson, Sherrie Levine, Robert Longo, David Salle and Jeff Way. There's no manifesto of Naïf Nouveau, and I can feel most of these artists cringing at being designated as such. There is, however, a house organ of NN, *Real Life Magazine*, edited by Lawson and addressing issues that seem to be on the minds (and definitely in the works) of its practitioners: pop culture, play activity (much in the intellectualised spirit of [Johan] Huizinga's *Homo Ludens*), music and movies. A smattering of the techniques they employ: Jenney makes fingerpaintings (at least they seem to be made that way), Bark builds matchstick houses, Levine draws silhouettes of famous profiles (American presidents and the like), Knowles makes stream-of-conscious doodles with magic marker on paper. Although methods and materials vary, the Peter Pan aspect of 'I won't grow up, I don't wanna go to school' pervades the work. […]

Carrie Rickey, extract from 'Naive Nouveau And Its Malcontents', *Flash Art* (Summer 1980) 36–9.

Friedrich Schiller
On Naive and Sentimental Poetry//1796

There are moments in our lives when we extend a kind of love and tender respect toward nature in plants, minerals, animals and landscapes, as well as to human nature in children, in the customs of country folk and the primitive world. We do this, not because it makes us feel good and not even because it satisfies our intellect or taste (in both cases the reverse can often occur), but merely *because it is nature*. Every more refined human being not utterly devoid of feeling experiences this when he wanders about in the open, when he resides in the country or lingers at the monuments of ancient times, in short, whenever in the midst of man-made contexts and situations he is taken aback by the sight of nature in its simplicity. It is this interest, often elevated to a need, that lies at the bottom of our many fondnesses for flowers and animals, for simple gardens, for walks, for the land and its inhabitants, for many an artefact of remote antiquity, and the like (provided that no predilection or any other serendipitous interest comes into play here). This sort of interest in nature takes place, however, only under two conditions. It is absolutely necessary, first, that the object instilling this interest in us be *natural* or at least be considered by us to be natural, and, second, that it be *naive* (in the widest sense of the term), that is to say, nature must contrast with art and put it to shame. The moment the latter condition is joined to the former, and not before, nature becomes something naive.

Regarded in this way, nature is for us nothing but the uncoerced existence, the subsistence of things on their own, being there according to their own immutable laws.

This image is absolutely necessary if we are to take an interest in the sorts of phenomena mentioned above. If somehow by means of the most perfect sort of deception one could give an artificial flower the look of being natural, if one could press the imitation of the naive in culture to a point where the illusion was complete, then the discovery that it is an imitation would utterly destroy the feeling I have been talking about.[1] On the basis of these considerations it becomes clear that this manner of enjoying nature is not aesthetic, but moral, for it is communicated by an idea and not immediately produced by observation. It is also in no way directed at the beauty of the forms of things. What else is it about a humble flower, a brook, a mossy rock, the chirping of birds, the humming of bees, and the like, that by itself pleases us so much? What else could even give them a claim to our love? It is not these objects, it is an idea portrayed by them that we cherish in them. We treasure the silent creativity of life in them, the fact that they act serenely on their own, being there according to their own laws; we cherish that inner necessity, that eternal oneness with themselves.

They *are* what we *were*; they *are* what we *should become* once more. We were nature like them, and our culture should lead us along the path of reason and freedom back to nature. Thus they depict at once our lost childhood, something that remains ever dearest to us, and for this reason they fill us with a certain melancholy. Because at the same time they portray our supreme perfection in an ideal sense, they transport us into a state of sublime emotion.

Yet their perfection is not something they have deserved, since it is not the result of a decision on their part. Hence they afford us the utterly distinctive pleasure of being models for us without putting us to shame. They surround us with a constant theophany, though one that is more exhilarating than blinding. What constitutes their character is exactly what ours lacks to be perfect. What distinguishes us from them is exactly what they lack to be divinelike. We are free and what they are is necessary; we alter, they remain one. Yet only if both are combined with one another – only if the will freely adheres to the law of necessity and reason maintains its rule in the face of every change in the imagination, only then does the divine or the ideal emerge. Hence in *them* we forever see what eludes us, something we must struggle for and can hope to approach in an endless progress, even though we never attain it. *In ourselves* we see an advantage that they lack, something that they either could never participate in at all, as in the case of beings devoid of reason, or can participate in only inasmuch as they proceed down the same path that *we* did, as in the case of children. Accordingly they afford us the sweetest sort of delight in the idea of our humanity, although they necessarily humble us as far as any *specific state* of our humanity is concerned.

Since this interest in nature is founded upon an idea, it is able to reveal itself only to minds receptive to ideas, that is to say, moral minds. Most people by far only affect that interest, and the universality of this sentimental taste in our times, expressing itself (especially since the appearance of certain writings) in maudlin journeys, gardens, strolls, and other penchants of this sort, is in no way a proof of the universality of this way of feeling. Still, nature will always have something of this effect even on the most callous individual. For the *potential* for morality, common to all people, is all that is needed to produce this effect and we all, without distinction, are driven to the contemplation of *this idea*, despite the tremendous distance between our *deeds* and nature's simplicity and truth. This sensitivity to nature expresses itself in the most universal manner and in a particularly powerful fashion when it is occasioned by those objects, for example, children and primitive peoples, that are more closely connected to us, placing in sharper relief for us a retrospective of ourselves and what is *unnatural* in us. People err if they believe that it is merely the image of helplessness that at certain moments makes us dwell on children with so much tenderness. That may perhaps be the case for those who would never feel anything but their own superiority in the face of weakness. However, the feeling I am talking about (that takes place only in quite distinctive moral moods and is not to be confused with the feeling stirred in us by the joyful activity of children) humbles more than it promotes self-love. Indeed, if along the way any advantage comes up for consideration, it is at least not on our side. We are moved with such emotion, not because we look down on the child from the heights of our power and perfection, but rather because we *look up* from our own *limitedness*, inseparable as it is from the *determination* we acquired at some point in time, to the boundless *determinability* in the child and to its pure innocence, and our feelings at such a moment are too visibly mixed with a certain melancholy for this source to be mistaken. In the child are exhibited the *potential* and the *calling*, in us their *fulfillment*, and the latter always remains infinitely behind that potential and that calling. The child is thus for us a realisation of the ideal, not, of course, the fulfilled ideal, but the projected one. So it is in no way the representation of its neediness and limitations that moves us; completely to the contrary, it is the representation of its pure and free power, its integrity, its infiniteness, that does so. Consequently, for a person of moral substance and sensitivity a child will be a holy object, an object, namely, that by virtue of the magnificence of an idea overwhelms anything magnificent in experience. Whatever this object may lose in the judgment of the understanding [*Verstand*], it gains in rich measure in the judgment of reason [*Vernunft*].

Out of precisely this contradiction between the judgement of reason and that of the understanding there emerges the quite unique phenomenon of those mixed feelings awakened in us by the *naive* manner of thinking. It combines *childlike* with *childish* simpleness [*Einfalt*], Through childish simpleness a weakness is exposed to the understanding, producing that smile by which we let our (*theoretical*) superiority be known. However, as soon as we have reason to believe that this childish simpleness is at the same time childlike, and that as a consequence it is not a lack of understanding or ability but rather a loftier (*practical*) strength, a heart full of innocence and truth that leads it, on the basis of an inner grandeur, to forsake the assistance art can provide, then that triumph of the understanding is superseded, and that belittling of the child's simplemindedness turns into wonder at its simplicity [*Einfachheit*]. We feel ourselves compelled to respect the object that we smiled about earlier and, since we cast a glance back at ourselves at the same time, we also cannot avoid feeling the need to complain that we are not like that. In this way there emerges the quite unique phenomenon of a feeling in which cheerful patronising, respect, and melancholy flow together.[2] For naiveté it is necessary that nature be victorious over art whether this happens against the person's knowledge and will or with full consciousness of it. In the former case it is the amusing naiveté of *surprise*, in the latter case the moving naïveté of *character*.

In the case of the naiveté of surprise, the person must be *morally* capable of denying nature. In the case of the naiveté of character, the person is not permitted to be morally capable of doing so, though we may not think the person *physically* incapable, if he is to strike us as naive. Thus the actions and prattle of children provide us with an unadulterated impression of naiveté, only as long as we are not reminded of their incapacity for art and in general only take notice of the contrast between their naturalness and the artificiality in us.

Naiveté is a *childlikeness, where it is no longer expected*, and precisely for that reason it cannot be attributed to actual childhood in the strictest sense.

However, in both cases, that of the naiveté of surprise as well as that of the naiveté of character, nature must be right and art wrong. […]

How is it that we are so infinitely surpassed by the ancients in everything that is natural, and yet at precisely this point we are able to revere nature to a higher degree, to cling to it more intimately, and to embrace even the inanimate world with the tenderest of feelings? This is so because nature has disappeared from our humanity, and we re-encounter it in its genuineness only outside of humanity in the inanimate world. Not our greater *naturalness* [*Naturmäßigkeit*], but the very opposite, the *unnaturalness* [*Naturwidrigkeit*] of our relationships, conditions, and mores forces us to fashion a satisfaction in the physical world that is not to be hoped for in the moral world. This is the satisfaction of that awakening urge for truth and simplicity that lies, like the moral predisposition from which it flows, in all human hearts as something indestructible and ineradicable. It is for this reason that the feeling with which we cling to nature is so intimately related to the feeling we have when we protest the passing of childhood and childish innocence. Our childhood is the only unmutilated nature that we still encounter in the cultivated part of humanity. Thus it is no wonder, if each footstep of nature outside us leads us back to our childhood.

In the case of the ancient Greeks it was very much different.[3] For them the culture had not degenerated to such a degree that nature was left behind in the process. The entire edifice of their social life was erected on feelings, not on some clumsy work of art. Their theology itself was the inspiration of a nai ve feeling, born of a joyful imagination and not of brooding reason as is the belief of the churches of modem nations. Hence, since the Greek had not lost the nature in humanity, he also could not be surprised by nature outside humanity, and for that reason could have no pressing need for objects in which he rediscovered nature. One with himself and content in the feeling of his humanity, the Greek had to stand quietly by this humanity as his ultimate and to concern himself with bringing everything else closer to it. We, on the other hand, neither one with ourselves nor happy in our experiences of humanity, have no more pressing interest than to take flight from it and to remove from sight so miscarried a form.

The feeling spoken of here is thus not something that the ancients had. It is rather the same as the sort of feeling we *have for the ancients*. They felt naturally, while we feel the natural. Undoubtedly, what filled Homer's soul, as he had his divine swineherd entertain Ulysses, was a completely different feeling from what moved the soul of the young Werther when he read this song following an evening in some irritating company. Our feeling for nature is like the sick person's feeling for health.

Just as nature eventually begins to disappear from human life as an *experience* and as the (acting and feeling) *subject*, we see it ascend in the world of poets as an *idea* and *object*. [...]

By virtue of the very notion of a poet, poets are everywhere the *guardians* of nature. Where they can no longer completely be this, and where they have already experienced within themselves the destructive influence of arbitrary and artificial forms or have had to contend with them, they will appear as nature's *witnesses* and *avengers*. They will either *be* nature or *seek* the lost nature. Two completely different manners of poetry spring from this fact, exhausting and demarcating the entire realm of poesy [*Poesie*]. Depending on the character of the age in which they flourish or on the impact that contingent circumstances have on their general formation and their passing states of mind, all poets who really are such will be either *naive* or *sentimental*. [...]

The poet, I say, either *is* nature or he will *seek* it. The former makes for the naive poet, the latter for the sentimental poet. [...]

1   'On Naive and Sentimental Poetry' first appeared as a complete text in the second part of *Kleinere prosaische Schriften* (Leipzig: Crusius, 1800) 43–76. The text was originally published in three successive issues of *Die Horen*. The first part *Über das Naive* appeared on 24 November,1795 (*Die Horen*, 4, no. 11, 3–216); the second part *Die sentimentalischen Dichter* toward the end of December (*Die Horen*, 4, no. 12); and the final part *Beschluß der Abhandlung über naive und sentimentalische Dichter nebst einigen Bemerkungen einer charakteristischen Unterschied unter den Menschen betreffend* on 22 January, 1796 (*Die Horen*, 5, no. 1). Kant, to my knowledge the first person to begin reflecting on this phenomenon, recalls that if we were to find the song of the nightingale perfectly imitated by a human and if, completely moved by it, we were to give ourselves up to this impression, all our pleasure would disappear with the destruction of this illusion. See the chapter 'On The Intellectual Interest in the Beautiful' in the *Critique of Aesthetic Judgment*. Anyone who has learned to wonder at the author only as a great thinker will be delighted to find here a trace of his heart and on the basis of this discovery to convince himself of the high philosophical calling of this man (a calling absolutely requiring the combination of both properties).

2   In his 'Remarks on the Analytic of the Sublime' (*Critique of Judgment*, 228 [of the second, 1793 edition]) Kant also distinguishes these three sorts of ingredients in the feeling of the naive, but he gives a different explanation of them. 'Something from both (the animal feeling of pleasure and the spiritual feeling of respect) are found together in naiveté that is the outbreak of the uprightness originally natural to humanity over against the art of dissembling that has become second nature. People laugh at the simplicity that does not yet understand how to pretend and still they also delight in the simplicity of nature that thwarts art in this respect. People would expect the commonplace custom of the artificial expression, carefully composed for show, and lo and behold it is the uncorrupted, innocent nature that they did not at all expect to find and that is revealed by someone who did not have the slightest intention of doing so. This sudden transformation of that beautiful, but

false show (that usually means so very much in our judgment) into nothing, the exposure, as it were, of the rogue in us for what it is – this puts the mind in motion in two opposite directions that give a therapeutic jolt to the body. The fact, however, that something infinitely better than all the customs that people have taken on, that is to say, the fact that the purity of the manner of thinking (or at least the potential for that purity) has not been utterly extinguished in human nature, mixes seriousness and esteem into this play of the power of judgment. Yet, because the phenomenon lasts only a short time and the veil of the art of dissembling is quickly drawn again, there is also in it a mixture of pity, a tender emotion, that can be playfully combined quite well with such a good-hearted laughter and in fact usually is. At the same time this pity usually compensates for the embarrassment on the part of the individual who provides the material for the embarrassment by not yet being wise in the ways of men.' I confess that this manner of explanation does not completely satisfy me and especially for this reason, that it maintains something about the naive in general that is at most true of one species of it, namely, the naiveté of surprise, of which I will speak later. Of course, it makes us *laugh* if someone in his naiveté *exposes himself,* and in many cases this laughter flows from a foregoing expectation that fails to materialise. But even the naiveté of the noblest sort, naiveté of character, always arouses a *smile* that is hardly based on some expectation that has come to nothing. Instead it is only to be explained generally by the contrast between some specific behaviour and the forms of conduct that are assumed and expected. I also doubt whether the pity intermingling in our feelings when confronted with naiveté of the latter sort is meant for the naive person and not rather for ourselves or rather for humanity at large, on whose demise we are reminded on such an occasion. It is all too obvious that, in the ordinary course of the world, uprightness is threatened less by physical evil than by a moral grief that necessarily has some more noble object. This object can be indeed none other than the loss of truth and simplicity in humanity.

3   But also only in the case of the Greeks. For in order to extend life to the inanimate and to pursue the image of humanity with this zeal it is necessary to have precisely the sort of animated movement and rich fullness of human life that surrounded the Greeks. The human world of *Ossian*, for example, was shabby and uniform, while the inanimate world around him was magnificent, colossal, mighty, and thus forced itself on him, asserting its rights over human beings. Accordingly; in the songs of this poet the inanimate nature far more (than the human beings) emerges as an object of feeling. Meanwhile, even Ossian himself complains about a decline of humanity. As inconsiderable as culture's scope and depravities were among his people, the experience of it was still sufficiently vivid and intrusive to make the singer, full of high-minded feelings as he was, turn back in fear to the inanimate and pour out over his songs that elegiac sound that makes them so touching and endearing to us.

Friedrich Schiller, extracts from 'On Naive and Sentimental Poetry' (1796), in *Essays*, ed. Walter Hinderer & Daniel O. Dahlstrom (New York, Continuum: 2005) 179–84, 194–6, 200.

Goutam Ghosh

On the 'Naive': In Conversation with Jason Havneraas and Kristian Skylstad//2015

[…]

Jason Havneraas and Kristian Skylstad What role does naivety play in your work?

Goutam Ghosh Naivety is a political word, but for me it can be seen as the maximum limit of a work through which I can collapse it, and then re-collect myself from there. To be naive is to allow yourself to go onward, so the work is no longer about right and wrong. If there were no naivety and I drew a straight line then that would be correct and if I drew a curved line that would be wrong.

Havneraas and Skylstad You kind of just summed up the content of *The Savage Detectives* by Roberto Bolaño…

Ghosh I say this because governments want you to behave in a certain way, any society gives you a certain amount of freedom, but that is always restricted and you may feel you have limited space to grow. Most of the time if you follow those rules and regulations you will spend your whole life drawing straight lines. Naivety within your private space is a very good idea; my curved line on my paper or canvas is not harming anybody. That allows you to express yourself and live exactly the way you want to; your entire system is cleared and that is very refreshing. I can empty myself of all the influences I get from different sources and that is why this act of naivety is so important and political.

Havneraas and Skylstad But can you decide to be naive? Isn't that something you just are?

Ghosh Well, I have to allow myself to be what I am; if I am naive it becomes a question of ethics that is easily misunderstood; but is naivety being stupid? I don't think so.

Havneraas and Skylstad When writing about Eichmann, Hannah Arendt proves that evil is another form of stupidity; can we say the same when it comes to aesthetics? Do you think you can use naivety to be political? That is very hard for me to understand; are you making your work more naive than you necessarily are as a person?

Ghosh If we see naivety as chaos, we have to remember that chaos also has its own rules and activations. I guess people think being naive is irresponsible, but there are many poles that cannot be clearly defined and there is a societal urge not to be naive. If I buy a plane ticket I have to go in a straight line to the airport or I will miss my flight, so naivety will not work in that situation. But in my work, whenever I try not to be naive I always end up in a mess, so it is better to try and understand the relationship between the straight and curved lines and make harmony between them. In some of my work you can see that I have used a graph structure that I see as being geopolitical; I then mess around within it and it creates an amount of harmony, which means it can be both naive and take an active role in society. I don't want to disappear completely into the forest; I want to keep the friction between the two sides.

Havneraas and Skylstad How does one of your works begin: with a naive impulse or a complex idea?

Ghosh It is a collective impulse that leads me towards the work; and you may say collective in terms of a combination of information, consciousness, morality, expression and so on. We all have the ability to interpret the starting point in our own way and it is not fixed. I cannot put my finger on where a particular impulse started, I think it was designed during the big bang and was finally realised in the naiveties you see now, and it was meant to be. […]

Goutam Ghosh, extract from 'The Magus: an Interview with Jason Havneraas and Kristian Skylstad', *Kunstkrittik: Nordic Art Review* (February 2015) (https://kunstkritikk.com/the-magus/).

Juliane Rebentisch
A Note on Camp Ridiculousness//2020

[...] While the ridiculous is a notoriously undertheorised phenomenon, it interestingly makes quite a prominent appearance in Adorno's *Aesthetic Theory*.[1] The stage for the ridiculous is set here, significantly, by a comparison between art and sex. According to Adorno, art proves its loyalty to the somatic happiness of sexuality precisely by abstaining from the pretension that it is capable of fulfilling this promise of happiness. Aesthetic sublimation is what distinguishes art from the culture industry, which betrays this happiness by purporting to satisfy it: 'Works of art', Adorno and Horkheimer state in the culture industry chapter of the *Dialectic of Enlightenment*, 'are ascetic and unashamed; the culture industry is pornographic and prudish'.[2] The degree to which crucial passages in Adorno's *Aesthetic Theory* revolve around sexuality and its true aesthetic sublimation or false fulfillment by the culture industry is indeed remarkable. One could say that *Minima Moralia* is about marriage whereas *Aesthetic Theory* is about sex.[3] The happiness of fulfillment that art is to retain in its brokenness has its model not least in the bodily happiness of sex. The ridiculous now appears precisely at the intersection of the respective alliance of sex and art, since each seems ridiculous to whoever is not driven by it. Like art, sex – or, as one should probably specify, non-reproductive sex – when viewed from the perspective of instrumental reason and self-preservation, appears as ridiculous.[4] Although both seem ridiculous from the perspective of a rationality oriented towards a logic of means and ends, Adorno insists that the alliance between art and sexuality can only come about across an unbridgeable gap; bridging this gap, he fears, would mean betraying both art's promise of happiness as well as the bodily joy of sexuality. Adorno presents a similar line of argument when he claims an alliance between art and 'base' pleasures such as circus, clowns, and children's play. Once again, he points out that the culture industry betrays both sides. The point of contact between the two poles in opposition to the 'middling domain'[5] of the culture industry is only possible if art rejects any direct association with either childish pleasures or sexuality. As art is to avoid leering at the happiness of sexuality, it too must stay clear from any direct participation in childish pleasure, the happiness of fooling around for example. 'If [art] remains on the level of the childish and is taken for such, it merges with the calculated fun of the culture industry.'[6]

It seems clear that Adorno would have deprecated the films of Jack Smith as a somewhat degenerated form of culture industry, for they delve into what Adorno considers a double no-go within art: they show sexuality and take pleasure in the childish. Ridiculousness does indeed appear on the side of content in Smith – as an essential feature of his creatures, in fact. For their sexuality is not only ridiculous from the perspective of instrumental reason, from which all non-reproductive sexuality might appear as ridiculous, but ridiculousness, the fooling around, is the mode in which, as Susan Sontag has observed, sexuality itself is being articulated.[7] One could say that ridiculousness modulates sexuality in such a way that it is not directed towards orgiastic fulfilment, transforming it instead into an arena for inhabiting the ridiculous itself, turning it into a praxis, the anarchic state of being silly. To stress this element within the aesthetic of the ridiculous means directing attention away from the pejorative meaning of the ridiculous – as that which is laughable from the position of the norm – and towards the pleasurable dimension its connotations with foolishness, fatuity, stupidity, idiocy and childishness take on once put into the verb form: to fool around, to act the fool, to play up, to kid around, and to go stupid are all examples of this.

Different from irony, these forms of being silly tend not to keep much of a distance. They are not even primarily about a subject's relation towards an object, but rather about a transformation in the subjectivity of the silly subject itself. It is not the superior stance towards something laughable that is characteristic of such states, but the dumbing down of the silly person themselves. Often triggered by something minor, the silly subject programmatically goes low, and enjoys it. The silly state, Gert Mattenklott writes, is accompanied by a 'loosening of the subject's demands on itself'; 'all dignity breaks down'.[8] In the extreme, this results in the reduction of the subject to its creatureliness in convulsive laughter. One says that one pisses oneself or dies laughing. 'In the paroxysms of silliness, the meaningful is shaken off or out of the body, sometimes to the degree of bodily exhaustion. This amounts not only to a destruction of what the bourgeoisie might consider meaningful, but, even more radical, the annihilation of the order of representation as such. There are only signifiers, no signified, only words or gestures, no sense.'[9] The laughter of the silly seems to be self-sufficient; it therefore has no critical sting and is thus an affront to any given form only to the degree in which it resists being captured by any order at all.[10] 'This is why silliness is a titillation in which all sense vanishes, a specific experience of nothingness.'[11]

But this somewhat revolutionary description of the phenomenon has a different side as well. For the state of silliness is not generalisable; it might be infectious to insiders, but it doesn't necessarily communicate to outsiders. It is for this reason that states of silliness are often not very pleasant for those who witness them from the outside. To the silly themselves, however, the witnessing of consciousness, the perspective from both outside and above, as it were, adds to the joy. Their distance towards soberness is part of what fuels the silly state. One takes pleasure both in one's own dumbing-down and in the annihilation of the meaningful. This is why the silly is free of any irony. Whereas irony always finds a way to communicate its distance to the low remark, and in such a way that the sovereignty of consciousness is not only maintained but in fact strengthened, silliness dethrones this sovereignty. This explains why, as Mattenklott observes, 'shame usually returns after the silly ecstasies and places a lid on the swirl',[12] even if this lid will never sit too tight – a tiny gesture, the blink of an eye might suffice to reopen the gap.

The extreme state of convulsive laughter is just one aspect of silliness, however. Another, less extreme variety is that of fooling about. Dieter Wellershoff characterises this as an anarchistic subculture of humour that unfolds its attraction below both the high standards of seriousness and established forms of the comical – which, differently from irony, may know reversals and crossings of reason, but not their principle maceration and deformation. In contrast to established forms of the comical, fooling about uses regression to aim at 'progressing chaotisation of rationality, thereby escaping the control of internalised norms of reason or taste. Fooling about is a voluntary loss of form and standard',[13] whereby the 'not fully socialized, infantile human being' is turned into an adult ideal of social resistance.[14] Consequently, the laughter fooling around might effect in its audience (if any) has its source not in this or that message, this or that object, stemming instead from a 'bewildered and enchanted perception of a bottomless freedom, for which there seem to be no standards or sanctions'.[15]

This is in fact a very apt description of the world of the Smithian creatures, which seem to be embedded in a fearless and playful atmosphere in which their programmatically improvised doings can then develop. For fooling about, or acting the fool, is always improvised. It knows no fixed form or institutional setting; spontaneity is needed in order to begin the process of ridiculous deformation.[16] This distinguishes the ridiculous from all 'higher' nonsense that can be recognised as intentional or skillful.[17] Smith's filmic means confirm this. He seems to be amongst his creatures most of the time, his hand-held camera often reacting spontaneously in the swirl of events. The deformation of conventions in the fooling around of the creatures is met here with a deformation of the conventions of its recording – an anarchist freedom of filmic form itself.

It is in this deformation that Smithian ridiculousness and his materialism are shown to be clearly part of the same project, for in both registers he joyfully and sensually draws the idealism of spirit down into the mud of its creaturely base. Jack Smith's camp aesthetic does not only combine the ridiculousness of his sexually childish (or childishly sexual) creatures with an emphasis on the perishability of their world; rather, both aspects are articulated through one another, mutually intensifying each other. If, within the Smithian world, damaged goods find their expressive quality because they are discarded from commodity circulation, his creatures find theirs not least because they escape circles of exploitation. For fooling around, after all, not only withdraws from the reach of instrumental reason, it is also decidedly nonproductive. Like their exposed vulnerability and perishability, their ridiculous activities are part of an aesthetic program that shifts the terrain of the beautiful – away from idealist beauty, product of sublimation, and triumph of the normative, and towards a beauty that holds its ground not against but by means of its creaturely dimension.

1   [Footnote 5 in source] 'Ridiculous' is the translation of '*albern*' in the English translation of *Aesthetic Theory* provided by Robert Hullot-Kentor. However, while Adorno does indeed often use the term '*albern*' (silly) in the sense of '*lächerlich*' (ridiculous), '*das Alberne*' in Adorno also plays into the meaning of childlike liberated play, the base pleasures of fooling around, which also constitute an essential element of the aesthetic of the ridiculous but belong more to the semantic horizon of silliness.

2   [6] See Theodor W. Adorno and Max Horkheimer, 'The Culture Industry: Enlightenment as Mass Deception', trans. John Cumming, in *Dialectic of Enlightenment* (London and New York: Continuum, 1976) 141–2.

3   [7] See *Christine Weder, Intime Beziehungen. Ästhetik und Theorie der Sexualität um 1968* (Göttingen: Wallstein, 2016) 293. The comparisons between art and sexuality in Adorno's *Aesthetic Theory* are based on a narrative of repression, as Weder summarises. In particular, Adorno criticises genital primacy and the suppression of the partial drives, a suppression he calls one of the 'pioneering atrocities of the Third Reich'. [Cf. Theodor W. Adorno, 'Sexualtabus und Recht heute', in *Eingriffe. Neun kritische Modelle* (Frankfurt/M.: Suhrkamp, 1963) 533–54, quotation on 537, trans. JR.] Consequently, Adorno also takes sides against the American idea of 'healthy sex' and the assumptions about nature that this carries with it. In view of the omnipresent fetishisation of sexuality in commodity society, Adorno believes that the only viable and not necessarily unattractive alternative might probably be sexual fetishism – and certainly not an ideological return to a supposedly original, unalienated sexuality. The decisive point in our context, however, is Adorno's thesis that the sexual taboo was not abolished in the post-war period but continues to exist in a repressive desublimation organised by the culture industry.

4   [8] Theodor W. Adorno, *Aesthetic Theory*, trans. Robert Hullot-Kentor (London and New York: Continuum, 2002) 119.

5   [9] Ibid., 106.

6   [10] Ibid., 119.

7   [11] In her defence of *Flaming Creatures* against the accusation of its being pornographic, Sontag

writes: 'The depiction of nakedness and various sexual embraces (with the notable omission of straight screwing) is both too full of pathos and too ingenuous to be prurient. Rather than being sentimental or lustful, Smith's images of sex are alternately childlike and witty.' Susan Sontag, 'Jack Smith's *Flaming Creatures*' (1964), in *Against Interpretation and Other Essays* (New York: Picador, 1966) 227.

8   [12] Gert Mattenklott, 'Albernheit', in *Ästhetische Opposition. Essays zu Literatur, Kunst und Kultur*, ed. Dirck Linck (Hamburg: Philo Fine Arts, 2010) 176 [trans. JR].

9   [13] Ibid., 175 [trans. JR].

10   [14] See ibid., 174 [trans. JR].

11   [15] See ibid., 175 [trans. JR].

12   [16] Ibid. [trans. JR].

13   [17] Dieter Wellershoff, 'Infantilismus als Revolte oder das ausgeschlagene Erbe Zur Theorie des Blödelns', in *Das Komische*, ed. Wolfgang Preisendanz and Rainer Warning (Munich: Fink, 1976) 335–357, quotation on 338 [trans. JR].

14   [18] See ibid. [trans. JR].

15   [19] Ibid., 340 [trans. JR].

16   [20] Ibid. [trans. JR].

17   [21] See Michael Glasmeier, Lisa Steib, *Albernheit* (Hamburg: Textem Verlag, 2011) 31.

Juliane Rebentisch, extract from 'A Note on Camp Ridiculousness', in *Camp Materialism* (Cologne: Galerie Buchholz, 2020) 21–6.

Wyndham Lewis
A Brief Account of the Child-Cult//1927

[...] I suppose that there is no one who has not noticed, passim and without attentiveness, perhaps, in a hundred different forms, the prevalence of what now amounts to a cult of childhood, and of *the Child.* This irresponsible, Peterpannish, psychology, is the key to the Utopia of the 'revolutionary' Rich; the people, namely, who have taken over, have degraded, and are enjoying the fruits of revolutionary scientific innovation – far from its creative ardours, cynically scornful of its idealisms, but creating out of its ferments, which they have pillaged, a breathless Millennium.

This subject has been so thoroughly analysed by me elsewhere that I do not propose to go into it again here. All that it is necessary to say is that it is essential, if you wish to understand at all a great deal of contemporary art and thought, even the developments of positive science, not only to gather up all the dispersed manifestations of this strange fashion; but – having done so – to trace this impulse to its source in the terrible and generally hidden disturbances that have broken the back of our will in the Western countries, and have already forced us into the greatest catastrophes. Whether these great disturbances are for the ultimate good of mankind or not, no one can claim that they are pleasant, or that they do not paralyse and weaken the system they attack. Many complaints break out in consequence in the midst of our thinking; and the instinctive recoil of the stricken system makes it assume strange shapes.

What you have to ask yourself is why, exactly, a grown person should wish to be a Child? – for to use the forms of infantile or immature life, to make an art of its technical imperfections, and to exploit its natural ignorance, is, in some sense, to wish to be a child.

That, to start with, it is connected with the cult of *the primitive* and the *savage,* is obvious. The same impulse that takes the romantic painter, Gauguin, to the South Sea paradise, takes a similarly romantic person of today to the Utopia of childhood, in the sense indicated above. Only the latter has the Heaven of Childhood inside himself (it is a *time-paradise);* whereas Gauguin had to go a long way to reach Samoa. That is the advantage that *time-travel* has over *space-travel.*

That was really Proust's Utopia, too. And the great appeal of that author is partly because he shows a method for capturing and retaming that spirit – the *recherche du temps perdu* and partly because he so feverishly expresses the will to that particular dream. As we read him, the 'I' of his books is that small, naïf, Charlie Chaplin-like, luxuriously-indulged, sharp-witted, passionately snobbish, figure, a model for many variations bred thickly everywhere. But that is not the whole story; and rather than give an imperfect notion of what a little investigation will reveal, I will, having started the enquiry, leave it at this point, or refer the reader to that part of my recent book dealing with this subject.

How *the demented* also joins hands with the child, and the tricks, often very amusing, of the asylum patient, are exploited at the same time as the happy inaccuracies of the infant; how contemporary inverted-sex fashions are affiliated to the Child-cult; and in fact all the different factors in this intricate sensibility, being evolved notably by such writers as Miss Stein, will be found there. Not to seize the secret of these liaisons is to totally misunderstand the nature of what is occurring around you today. […]

Wyndham Lewis, extract from 'The Revolutionary Simpleton', *Enemy*, no. 1 (January 1927); reprinted in *The Enemy*, ed. David Peters Corbett (Santa Rosa, CA: Black Sparrow Press, 1994) 75–6.

THE MORPHING
BLACK BODY
IS A FAMILIAR
TROPE NOT JUST
FOR RACISTS
BUT ALSO FOR
BLACK ARTISTS.

Kevin Young, 'Triangular Trade', 2007

Adrienne Edwards
Relishing the Minor: Juliana Huxtable's Kewt Aesthetic//2015

Am I altering your aura, your ideas, your dreams…?
– Audre Lorde[1]

Juliana Huxtable has mastered the affects of boredom and disinterest in her performances. Her stage is an insulated and insular arena in which she often paces back and forth or languorously reclines, reading her texts in a luminous, modulated, and slightly dissonant sex-kitten-cum-valley-girl voice while twirling her knee-length hair twists. She isolates her audience, though there is something striking about her stage presence. Her physical capacity to hold space and, thus, one's attention, contrasts with a seemingly lackadaisical, retro performance style – in a manner reminiscent of the spoken-word style popular both in the 1990s among artists like Saul Williams, and in the mid twentieth century among the Beatniks in downtown New York City – that is decidedly in the register of 'minor' aesthetics.[2] The minor things in which Huxtable revels defy easy interpretation, and are always far more complex than what one immediately experiences. While it could be interpreted as kitsch or, more specifically, camp, 'kewt' – a colloquial replacement for the word 'cute' among queer people of colour – better encapsulates Huxtable's affect. Indeed, she repeatedly drops the word in casual conversation, wielding it like a singular, definitive verbal gavel, conveying that the thing being judged falls somewhere in the range of clever, desirable and intriguing. The constituting force of kewt aesthetics is the wresting and shifting of power through minor acts that express themselves in surprising ways, which we can unexpectedly locate in the historical and cultural formations of the fetish and the ornament; like kewt and cute, they overlap and differ in ways that make their boundaries increasingly apparent.

[…] In *There Are Certain Facts that Cannot Be Disputed*, and possibly throughout Huxtable's work, kewt is expressed in a multitude of self-knowing ways. It is reflected in the manner in which Huxtable comports herself in relation to her viewers, literally the making-object of herself. In so doing, she offers up the intersection of race, gender and queerness for the gaze of others, which points to the longstanding, problematic history of representation of such subjects – which has been redressed in vastly different ways by artists such as Adrian Piper, Carrie Mae Weems, Mickalene Thomas, Wangechi Mutu, Lorna Simpson and Tracey Rose, to name only a few. This sly self-object-making move, or kewt-being, forces viewers to engage with their own feelings about Huxtable's playful significations of, for instance, femininity, which is to say all the socially constructed, embodied symbols that have operated to render them minor. In Huxtable's public demonstration of becoming-minor, the viewer becomes cannily aware that more is quite literally at play; Huxtable simultaneously flips this position while enacting it. She is reacting to a specific set of conditions realised in the very execution of the performance and in the broader world in which it takes part. Further, Huxtable's approach to her 'archive' – all the myriad source materials for her texts and performances – renders these references kewt. The narratives that we categorise as historical fact are not merely questioned but approached as minor, negligible and trivial. Huxtable makes history submit.

Here it is useful to comment on the proliferation of a strikingly broad range of people who have seemingly drawn Huxtable as a figure *in* art, as opposed to the artwork itself. A cursory review of her press clippings reveals an overwhelming number of references to her as a model or muse, as opposed to what she is: an artist. In this context, we can better understand her artistic choices in performance, particularly the affective registers of alienation in her slightly bored, distant voice, and her use of the papers she reads from as a kind of shield from direct encounter – despite the fact that she is *there*, ostensibly performing for the viewer and thereby available for our sensual (visual, aural, etc.) consumption. Huxtable's live presence, a thoroughly mediated encounter, is mimetic of online interfaces – literally the ways in which the screen filters our digital experiences, mitigates cyberspace encounters, and is the primary (self-) reflective surface for the banal and the spectacular alike – through which she first began to create and disseminate her art. She beckons, while simultaneously estranging. One can only get but so close, and any sense of proximity is already, always, a fantasy, a total projection of one's own imagination. This is to say that the performance itself is a highly fantastical, sensually enveloping wonderland. Nevertheless, vital to understanding Huxtable's performance is the fact that the alienated viewer is just as responsible for creating this world through projections of a desire that animates the encounter as Huxtable is for creating the conditions for its emergence. The performance is a vector wherein the viewer, sensually compressed – both fulfilled and denied by Huxtable's coolness – responds to such exertions of soft power[3] with an overwhelming desire not to merely watch but to rapturously consume, wanting to have, wanting to be like, wanting to be with.[4]

[…] That 'force' (a coming to a sharp edge or point) is fundamentally related to 'cute' (the most 'objectified of things') makes clear that the inherent relation of power to cuteness 'is thus the name of an encounter with difference – a perceived difference…that does something to everyday communicative speech'.[5] Juridical and judicial advances for LGBTQI people in the US have been a long time coming. Though as it relates to the trans community, there now lurks a kind of cultural fascination we can approximate to the fetish. Here we can truly contemplate the stride from cute to kewt in the fetish's contingent encounter with the cute and its historical relation to discourses on beauty, which is haunted by Immanuel Kant. We can also mark the shift whereas the fetish (especially as it relates to popular culture), with its foundational constitution in power and eccentricities, is equally ghosted by G.W.F. Hegel's total inability to value cultures of Africa.

Much as camp and kitsch negate the typical moral and aesthetic judgments assigned to beauty by philosophers of the *nature* of art, Huxtable's kewt art is an uncontainable expression unconcerned with symmetry, proportion, taste, or any other preordained delineation of what has been deemed beautiful in the historical arc of Western aesthetics. If anything, her work reveals the ways in which the project of aesthetic assessment is challenged, if not found entirely inadequate, when pressed through the vector of her imagination. Perhaps this is most substantially conveyed in the distinction between so-called high and low culture, and Huxtable's disavowal of formalisms in art for the power of quotidian speech and pop culture references – but not the kinds one might expect. For the everyday lexicon of queer communities of colour is extra-being, maximal, fifth-dimensional. The overall sensibility is more hieroglyphic, or rather, the hieroglyph as thought image, animating the ways in which minor aesthetics like kewt amplify psychic structures, distorting image, language and style to such an extent as to emphasise and create emotional responses to feelings, ideas and moods in the work.

Because the degree of our femininity has always been questioned (at best), black women tend to be spared stereotypical representations as girly girls or swooning women. As Audre Lorde reminds us, 'as we learn to bear the intimacy of scrutiny and to flourish within it, as we learn to use the products of that scrutiny for power within our living, those fears which rule our lives and form our silences begin to lose their control over us'.[6] She continues, 'for each of us as women, there is a dark place within, where hidden and growing our true spirit rises, "beautiful/and tough as chestnut/stanchions against (y)our nightmare of weakness and of importance"'.[7] The fact that Huxtable traffics in such motifs lends her work a transgressive sensibility; she plays with these tropes and, in so doing, casts a far darker shadow upon them. In this instance, kewt asserts itself with a confidence, as an 'artistic hegemony', trans-forming 'transgressive subjects into beloved objects…it exaggerates social difference'.[8] Betwixt the affection and aversion to these tropes the tension is heightened not just by the discomfort that comes with recognition of the stereotyped female, but also through the media, for 'all art in an age of high tech simulacra and media (performance) spectacles' incites double the response.[9] For this reason, more than speech acts, Huxtable's performance, as we experience it, does not merely hold space and time; it is its own suspended space and anachronistic time. [...]

While I have been interchangeably using kewt and cute up to this point, remarking [...] the instances in which they are mutually constituted in Huxtable's art, it is also necessary to elucidate the characteristics that extend beyond their commonalities in order to somehow grasp this 'place in the world' on which Huxtable remarks. If cute is in a minor aesthetic register, one can think of kewt as a kind of micro- or minor-minor aesthetic. Which is not to say 'less than' – in this sense it approximates what German Marxist theorist Ernst Bloch, in writing on art and utopia, described as 'an intensification of small things'.[10] Huxtable's small is to be understood not in terms of scale but in the context of a set of relations to power, as perceived and experienced from the vantage point of what Lorde called 'the shadows'. In this sense, the minor addresses a black and queer artist, a scene situated in nightlife, a promiscuous culling from popular, digital, and underworld cultures that is intensified through the assembly of a range of forces put to work to express a way of being of the world. Namely, the minor-scene is a community that fortifies such a reality, mining and (re) assemblage-ing images and language from overlooked corridors of history, employing fantasy (online and live) to highlight the absurd aspects of everyday life and to reveal some possibilities for one's escape.

This minor-scene intersects, with cute/kewt along one axis and the fetish/ornament on the other. There is an extensive art-historical discourse on the ornament that is impossible to fully outline here, but I do want to point to the set of circumstances involving performances of power through which it evolves. The ornament is an accumulation of refractions from myriad cultures, and these 'borrowings' are possible because of encounters that have occurred as a result of demonstrations of social and cultural power.[11]

Huxtable's creative process for the performance approaches the very tenets of the ornamental as a form, inasmuch as it 'rarely undergoes development to the point at which it loses resemblance to its original in nature so long as the latter has a magic or traditional significance or symbolism, or is common and familiar in fact'.[12] Further, her approach follows the ways in which 'an originally natural form undergoes such ornamental development as to lose its objective resemblance, it is an indication either that the original significance and symbolism have been lost or that the form is a foreign one which has been borrowed in fashionable emulation by a people for whom it has no significance or existence other than as a purely ornamental motive'.[13] This move to displace the certitude of history and cultural references, notably in Huxtable's tracing of humankind, national historical icons and symbols, as well as their afterlife in the digital realm, mimics the ornament's abstraction in its general usage and visual and textual qualities. The artist traverses one epoch to the next, divulging how the ornamental, in its proliferation and circulation, becomes a generalisation of its earliest incarnation, which is not to say that it is a reduction of the 'original'. However, the ornament's performance, and by extension Huxtable's as well, is one of luxuriant excess, lavish surplus, and exorbitant nimiety – kewt.

While the fetish, like the ornament, arises from the intermingling of societies and their culture (and also has an extensive and diverse discourse), it is most useful to turn to the historical paradigm in which the fetish emerged. Anthropologist William Pietz describes the origins of the fetish, which evolved in 'the cross-cultural spaces of the coast of West Africa during the sixteenth and seventeenth century'.[14] What is appropriated in the ornament and abstracted over time is a result of political and military dominance of one culture over another. While the fetish circulates within a similar power dynamic, it does so differently, which in Huxtable's commission manifests in references to queer life, Egyptology, and black nationalism. The fetish is a perception, a manufactured projection of extreme otherness, which, rather than subsume an image or object, is a profound negation of it. The fetish is of a 'sinister pedigree', deriving from the encounter between 'radically heterogeneous worlds… triangulated among Christian feudal, African lineage, and merchant capitalist social systems'.[15] Huxtable's art is imbued with and expresses its own internal power, a radical, vibrant matter. The performance is a container for her will, motives, and aesthetic choices.

In the context of psychoanalysis, Huxtable departs from Sigmund Freud's analysis of fetishism[16] through Elizabeth Grosz's writings on lesbian fetishism. In this instance, disavowal works as a refusal to accept a subordinated status such that social change becomes possible because of a negation of social reality through the subversion of play.

For example, *There Are Certain Facts that Cannot Be Disputed* directly mirrors the very mode and means through which we incessantly use the digital. It is the scene/screen portal for our self-indulgent will. We navigate and access the live event with the same individually directed, solipsistic desire. In this private-yet-public encounter, the performance becomes more than an extension of the self, it is relished and beheld as *of* the self, a self-producing, self-affirming armature that works both ways for the artist and for the viewer/consumer.

The ornament, though having a sexual dimension like the fetish (in psychological discourse, at least), lacks the overtly sinister, deviant characteristics attributed to 'fetish'. However, the ways in which the ornament functions as a visual reproduction of power and dominance, through an absolute absorption and incessant circulation of the image, both articulates and enacts social and cultural norms. In this configuration, the vexing evolution of décor approximates itself more closely to the fetish, seeming and being made to seem malevolent because its reproductive quality is embedded with the potential, and therefore the capacity, to circulate norms and accumulate their impressions.

Huxtable reveals how the ornament and the fetish indicate an inherent magical power in their images and objects. However, in the context of its performance in relation to 'traditional significance and symbolism', the ornament can have it both ways. On the one hand, as I have already mentioned, the ornament's accumulation of 'magical power' is possible only to the extent that it remains relevant to a society. On the other, the ornament, which has fallen out of favour or retains no use value as a magic object, becomes an abstraction. This is the quality that gives Huxtable's performance incredible levity. It is an assertion of power, or more precisely a Nietzschean will to power, that asserts a claim through complex asymmetries and violent ruptures, swerving history into the contemporary moment in a tale of sublime recognition. The performance is the moment when vulnerability or an offering up of the self makes such recognition possible, if only to foreclose the possibility of destruction, a likely outcome of unchecked consumption. This is especially imperative in a space/time where blackness and queerness embrace, and their amalgamation necessitates unbound imagination, determined perseverance, and unlimited support for someone who has been sent by history to stake a claim of her own in the now.

1   Audre Lorde, *Sister Outsider: Essays and Speeches by Audre Lorde* (Berkeley: Crossing Press, 2007) 38.

2   'Minor aesthetics' references principles that concern, guide and operate differently, meaning often outside of, the normative formulation of beauty in philosophical discourse on art. Following Gilles Deleuze and Félix Guattari's concept of becoming-minority, which reveals its emergence through affect, 'minor' marks, first, the will to identify with, or more precisely, to be in relation with, a particular collective of beings, and, second, an ethical imperative to possess and exert the right to create expressions capable of marking such relations and the conditions through which they evolve and with which they must contend in asserting their value. See Gilles Deleuze and Félix Guattari, *A Thousand Plateaus: Capitalism and Schizophrenia*, trans. Brian Massumi (Minneapolis: University of Minnesota Press, 1987) 469–71.

3   [Footnote 10 in source] American scholar Joseph Nye's political analysis defines the concept of soft power as a method of persuasion that leverages allure, attraction and appeal rather than force, violence and coercion.

4   [11] Sianne Ngai, *Our Aesthetic Categories: Zany, Cute, Interesting* (Cambridge, MA: Harvard University Press, 2012) 67.

5   [13] Ibid., 87.

6   [14] Lorde, op. cit., 36.

7   [15] Ibid.

8   [16] Ngai, op. cit., 58, 60.

9   [17] Ibid., 59.

10   [20] Ernst Bloch, *The Utopian Function of Art and Literature: Selected Essays*, trans. Jack Zipes and Frank Mecklenberg (Cambridge, MA: MIT Press, 1987) 102.

11   [21] William M. Ivins, Jr., 'The Philosophy of the Ornament', in *The Metropolitan Museum of Art Bulletin*, vol. 28, no. 5 (May 1933) 94.

12   [22] Ibid.

13   [23] Ibid.

14   [24] William Pietz, 'The Problem of the Fetish, I,', *RES*, vol. 9 (Spring 1985) 5.

15   [25] Ibid., 6.

16   [26] Freud formulates the concept of the sexual fetish as a distinctly male phenomenon that arises at the moment of recognition of the mother's lack of a penis, and thus the recognition of the possibility of castration. The male who does not adjust – that is, does not overcome the fear of female genitalia and make it an object of desire – seeks substitutes, a repetitive act that marks the desire to overcome the threat of castration and protection from it, as well as a memorial for the perceived loss of the mother's penis.

Adrienne Edwards, extracts from 'Relishing the Minor: Juliana Huxtable's Kewt Aesthetic' (2015), an essay published by The Museum of of Modern Art, New York to accompany the performance *There Are Certain Facts that Cannot Be Disputed*, co-commissioned by The Museum of Modern Art and Performa on the occasion of Performa 15 (www.moma.org/d/pdfs/W1siZiIsIjIwMTYvMDEvMDUvOWF2 bGY1dGlheF9NUDAxOTEyOF9KdWxpYW5hX0h1eHRhYmxlX0ZJTkFMLnBkZiJdXQ/MP019128_ Juliana_Huxtable_FINAL.pdf?sha=c7926cb946ae0a60).

Lauren Berlant and Lee Edelman
Sex, or the Unbearable//2017

Lee Edelman […] [We] both see sex as a site for experiencing this intensified encounter with what disorganises accustomed ways of being. And as Lauren and I both want to suggest, that encounter, viewed as traumatic or not, remains bound to the non-futural insistence in sex of something non-productive, non-teleological, and divorced from meaning making. In this sense sex without optimism invokes the negativity of sex as a defining and even enabling condition. Gayle Rubin reminds us in 'Thinking Sex' (1984) that 'Western cultures generally consider sex to be a dangerous, destructive, negative force', to which we might add: if only sex lived up to such press more often![1] If only, that is, the Panoptimism that rules us, even (or especially) in our denial of its hold, did not so often lend value to sex through the world-preserving meanings imposed upon it to repudiate its negativity. One need not romanticise sex to maintain that it offers, in its most intensely felt and therefore least routinised forms, something in excess of pleasure or happiness or the self-evidence of value. It takes us instead to a limit, and it is that limit, or the breaking beyond it, toward which sex without optimism points.

Lauren Berlant […] This leads me to our archive. After all of this Lee and I looked at what we could possibly use to exemplify our views. He wants to think about the subject's radical negativity. I had thought I would want to show sex at the extremes, since no doubt the first definition of 'sex without optimism' in the imaginary OED of the appetites would be bad sex, sex without pleasure, sex that was manifestly or tacitly coerced, forced or compulsive, sex that disappoints or that turned out to be beside the point. But in my current scholarly work I am focusing on the non-melodramatic affects that have come to saturate some sexually queer narratives, so that an optimistic structure might not sound like optimism at all […] I decided on an exemplary scene from [*You and I and Everyone We Know*, (2005)] to demonstrate encounters with the sexual that point to the sexual limit (of self-knowledge and of world-building potential) in ways that are enigmatic. Lee chose a photograph by Larry Johnson. It was then kind of shocking for us to realise that, after all this talk of negativity, we had both tapped for our examples the archive of the adorable.

Edelman Doesn't this exemplify in miniature how the 'shock' of negativity operates? It displaces what we thought we knew or could reliably predict and reveals the presence of something else at work in the decisions, desires and acts we think of as our own. We may smile at this striking convergence in such an unexpected archive, but the amusement doesn't fully displace the Wordsworthian 'shock of mild surprise' at something that seems to have 'enter[ed] unawares into [our] mind[s]'.[2] That the jolt here should come in response to our common recourse to 'the adorable' at the moment we seek out objects to illustrate the concept of sex without optimism enacts the sort of irony – the rhetorical figure of non-sovereignty – that the negativity we're focused on always carries in its train.

Perhaps, though, the very disturbance that the negativity of sex can induce makes it logical that sex without optimism would seek the shelter of adorability, invoking the familiarity, the recognisability of its aesthetic. Among the things to which sex refers is the prospect of an encounter with something much closer to the sublime than to the beautiful – which doesn't, as most of us know to our sorrow, mean that sex is always sublime, nor that it can't be conceptualised as beautiful, but rather that it trenches on an economy of danger where shifts of scale can at any moment reorganise value or empty it out, articulate new meanings or dislocate the subject of meaning altogether. Sex, then, may be inseparable from the question of the aesthetic, but primarily because the aesthetic (that is, the ideology of the aesthetic as opposed to the specificity of the work performed by aesthetic objects) can shield us against what threatens to undo and displace us in sexual encounters. That, of course, is why Lacan could describe the beautiful as the final barrier before the field of radical desire and as an outpost, along with goodness, against the disorganisations of jouissance.[3] The adorable, which almost seems to have wrested this privilege from the beautiful, can domesticate the riskiness that inhabits sexual encounter (consider, for example, the scenes of sexual intimacy in *Girls*) and so, as Lauren has put it, can work to 'neutralize how unsafe and close to the abject' sex can be. In that sense the archive of the adorable might be a treasure trove of negated encounters with the forms of negativity.

If the adorable is a dominant aesthetic mode of democratic modernity, invoking the reassuring privilege of a blandly harmonious normativity whose essence lies in its distance from the exceptionality of beauty or ugliness, then it also denotes what's expendable because so easily replaced, what refuses the burden of depth or the experience of emotional vicissitude. [...]

The adorable, in a related way, anesthetises feeling – or rather creates a paradoxical entity: an anaesthetic feeling, a feeling that aims to protect against overintensity of feeling and an attachment that can survive detachment from the particularity of its objects. [...]

Berlant The scene I am about to discuss, from *Me and You and Everyone We Know* (2005), is famous, if the 1,216,852 viewings of the scene on YouTube are any indication, in addition to the re-enactments of the scene that have proliferated. The scene involves transactions between two brothers (Peter and Robby Swersey) and a curator of a contemporary art museum (Nancy Herrington), who is the film's villain. The brothers – Peter is fourteen, Robby six – are exploratory and interested in sexually experimenting on the internet. Their parents have just divorced, and the mother is never far from the younger boy's mind, even when they're playing with sex talk online; in contrast, the older boy, manifesting sexual cynicism and genuine curiosity, is also exploring heterosex with his peers. Meanwhile the curator, Herrington, is established by way of her bad taste and aversive mien: she calls shallow things profound; she is liberally politically correct and humourless; she wears black as a badge of seriousness [...] and, most damningly, she is aggressively cold and verbally withholding to people who open their desire to her, face to face, co-workers and aspiring artists (like [director Miranda] July herself, playing 'Christine Jesperson').

In this scene the brothers have been sex-chatting online with the curator. Neither the filmgoers nor the children know that the curator is the sexual interlocutor whose fantasies the boys are soliciting. They do not even know that the writer is a 'she' because, as Peter points out, 'she's probably a man ... a fat guy with a little wiener', or something else, as 'everyone just makes stuff up on these things', these chat rooms. The curator-interlocutor does not know either that the 'man' is two biracial boys and underage. They do not know that she's white and cranky. How this or any non-knowledge matters matters not in the beginning of the relations that unfold in the film, where people fling themselves into things to become non-sovereign in a different way, as they must, at the beginning (if it is a beginning, that is, of a story), without a mutually agreed-on idiom of optimistic misrecognition like identity or love.

[...] But before there is a relation durable enough to become event there are the gestures of feeling out that are never fully absent from an intimacy's long middle. Robby gets curious. He wants to know if the woman likes baloney; Peter asks her if she's got big bosoms. They know some things about sex but not much: Peter pronounces 'bosom' like 'bozzum' [...].

The scene's drama intensifies when Robby insists that it's his turn to control the chat.

Peter: What should we write? 'I have a big wiener'?
Robby: I want to poop back and forth.
Peter: What? What does that mean?
Untitled: I'm wearing pants and a blouse.
NightWarrior: How's your bosom?
Untitled: I have a deliciously full 'bosom'.
NightWarrior: I want to poop back and forth.
Untitled: What does that mean exactly?
NightWarrior: I'll poop in your butt hole and then you will poop it back into my butt and we will keep doing it back and forth with the same poop. Forever.

[...] To figure the sexual fantasy of pooping back and forth, forever, that Robby imagines, he types in an emoticon-like ideogram. Later Herrington folds it into the title of an art exhibition ['WARM'] – and makes an icon of the age of a queered relation that adds to 'divestiture' a proliferation of scenes of care that might give fantasy *and* living some better options. Warm, digital, touch: to many political theorists, the dynamic flow of the fantasy –)) < > ((– is a structurally impossible achievement.[4] In *Me and You and Everyone We Know*, though, people of all statuses aspire seriously, intensely to become cartoon, to become billboard, to become comically iconic, to become lighter, to circulate, and to disperse the heavy comportment of their loneliness and structural exhaustion into a rhythm and a game.

Edelman [...] Like Lauren's example of sex without optimism, mine too engages the negativity of relation as making transformation possible. But where her text invokes a universe of people aspiring to 'become cartoon', mine involves a cartoon-like image that is 'unbecoming' itself. Larry Johnson's *Untitled (Ass)*, a colour photograph from 2007, offers a canny depiction of the touching, enforcing, and breaching of limits. Structured by the deeply ambiguous relation between the (photographed) sketch of the blissed-out donkey and the (photographed) 'reality' of the human hand (with a pencil as its prosthesis), the image mobilises differences in representational status and degree of agency (not to mention identification by species, colour, and apparent dimensionality) in order to approach the encounter with what (to paraphrase the old Blackglama ad) unbecomes us most. In doing so, it positions the donkey (with its 'humanly' expressive face) and the hand of the man with the pencil (presumably the artist who created it) in the intimacy of an illegible act taking place at the ass' asshole – or, at least, that's where it *would* take place if the ass had an asshole here. For the asshole is what the eraser at once erases and points out. Expunging from visibility what it directs the eye to take in, the eraser here enacts the intertwining of encounter and relation, negativity and attachment, which is why it can be seen as variously penetrating, concealing or erasing the asshole, and with it, the donkey's ass, and, by extension, the donkey itself *as* ass.

[...] If it's striking that our examples of sex without optimism, selected independently, bear similar traces of the adorable, it's equally striking that what's adorable in each should aestheticise the asshole. Both Robby's vision of 'butt hole[s]' open to the endless exchange of 'poop' and Johnson's picture of the effacing of the asshole as implicated in the asshole's insistence engage a back-and-forth movement reminiscent of the Freudian *fort/da*. Fittingly, therefore, in both of our images the asshole retains its libidinal associations with the assertion and undoing of control, the control to which, in one reading of the game, the play of *fort/da* aspires. On the basis of its association with such a discipline of self-governance, Guy Hocquenghem argued the centrality of the anus to capitalism's intersecting logics of privacy, property, and subjectivity and offered his account of what he called the 'privatisation' of the anus, the practice that erases it from view.[5] If this privatisation makes the anus the prototype of capitalistic production, generating surplus value by mastering labour and controlling exchange, it simultaneously increases the charge of what it requires to be concealed, necessitating a mediated expression of the libido that the anus thereby magnetises.

Perhaps that explains why the ass so often figures in the adorable. The Coppertone girl might stand for a host of other, similar instances where the 'cuteness' of the ass, allegedly free of sexual associations, stands in for the paradigmatic relation of the ass itself to cuteness. […] Insofar as signifiers of cuteness (the cartoonish lineaments of the donkey and the chat-room references to 'poop') inflect the assholes in our images, they displace the anxiety about anal control and the correlative threat of non-sovereignty onto a past we can view as behind us now that we've put aside childish things. The aesthetic of the adorable thus enables the sublimation of the asshole by giving it visibility in the form of what has yet to achieve its form – a form that reaffirms the temporal movement toward the subject's self-formation. (No wonder the adorable ass is so often depicted in diaper ads.) Robby's computer-graphic image of his fantasy is adorable because its iconic formulation sublimates a more graphic anal desire; similarly Johnson's image of the donkey with the eraser at its ass is adorable in ways that Robert Mapplethorpe's *Self-Portrait with Whip* (1978) could never be. The teleology implicit in the adorable, the dialectical determination of its unformed quality by the temporality of disciplinary formation (and hence of regulation, privatisation, and the regime of normativity) returns us, then, to the optimism that negativity could be erased. […]

1   [Ed. note] Gayle Rubin, 'Thinking Sex', in *Deviations: A Gayle Rubin Reader* (Durham, NC: Duke University Press, 2011) 148.

2   [Ed. note] William Wordsworth, *Selected Poems* (New York: Penguin Books, 2004) 238.

3   [Ed. note] Jacques Lacan, *The Ethics of Psychoanalysis, 1959–1960: The Seminar of Jacques Lacan, Book VII*, ed. Jacques-Alain Miller, trans. Dennis Potter (New York: Norton, 1992).

4   [Ed. note] Franco Berardi, *Precarious Rhapsody*, eds. Erik Empson and Stevphen Shukaitis, trans. Arianna Bove, Michael Goddard, Giuseppina Mecchia, Antonella Schintu and Steve Wright (London: Minor Compositions, 2009); Michael Hardt and Antonio Negri, *Declaration* (New York: Argo-Navis, 2012); Jodi Dean, *Blog Theory: Feedback and Capture in the Circuits of Drive* (London: Polity Press. 2010).

5   [Ed. note] Guy Hocquenghem, *Homosexual Desire* (1972) (Durham, NC: Duke University Press, 1993) 96.

Lauren Berlant and Lee Edelman, extracts from *Sex, or the Unbearable* (Durham, NC: Duke University Press, 2017) 11–12, 14, 15–17, 20–24, 29, 32–3.

Marilyn Ivy
The Art of Cute Little Things: Nara Yoshitomo's Parapolitics//2010

[…] Nara's art works with the intimacies of the cute and the ghastly, but in ways more intimate than [Takashi] Murakami's explosive fusions and bluntly didactic foregrounding of the unmitigated horror of the *kawaii* in its Japanese incarnation. They produce undeniable effects of fan devotion. Nowhere is this seen more clearly than with his groundbreaking exhibition at the Yokohama Museum of Art in 2001 entitled 'I DON'T MIND, IF YOU FORGET ME', which established Nara as a major contemporary artist in Japan. Nara had recently returned to live in Japan after some ten years in Germany, and the exhibition represented a homecoming for him, a return to the land of his childhood. This exhibition explicitly produced the museum as a theatre of childhood, and it did so by producing new fans and enticing old ones to participate in what came to be known as *Hamapuro* (the 'Yokohama Project'). The *Hamapuro* entailed putting out an open call through the Nara Yoshitomo fan Web site Happy Hour (now defunct) for volunteers each to sew a stuffed doll-toy (what the Japanese call *nuigurumi*) of one of Nara's figures. In a reversal of the commercialised trajectory in which one of Nara's eminently copyable *kyara* ('characters') becomes licenced out to toy companies and made into purchasable plush toys, Nara incorporated his fans in an enterprise that was outside the commodity circuit: make your own hand-sewn Nara plush toy and then donate it for use in the exhibition. Imagined as a way to produce a fan collectivity, as an 'action' that would incorporate the energies of fans in the exhibition itself, the Yokohama Project drew on the immense longings and identifications of the Nara fans to share his world. In attempting to move out of the commodity circuit – Nara increasingly uses volunteer labour to erect his museum installations – and to reframe the star-fan relationship as one of gift exchange, Nara works to produce the sensation of a shared emotional and aesthetic community.

What provides the basis for fans' participation in something as elusive as an artist's work? (Nara doesn't have a rock band or baseball team, as of yet). The Yokohama exhibition revealed the outlines of this project. At the entrance of the museum visitors saw – spelled out in huge, hollow, clear acrylic letters – I DON'T MIND, IF YOU FORGET ME. Massed inside those letters [were] hundreds of the stuffed Nara-figures made by his fans – there were some 1,500 figures in total – [which] redefined, in the process, what it means to be a 'stuffed toy'. Lined up on shelves below these letters were vintage toys, Nara's own collectibles, not all of them *nuigurumi* but all of them childhood toys. In another section of the museum was installed an enormous, room-spanning mirror with the words YOUR CHILDHOOD imprinted across the middle. And there, on the floor in a most promiscuous pile, were hundreds more fan-made stuffed dolls, heaped in profusion. Walking into the room, visitors confronted their own reflections in a mirror entitled YOUR CHILDHOOD, which reflected as well the sea of stuffed toys piled on the floor.

The art critic Sawaragi Noi thinks through the relationship of the *kawaii* to the *bukimi* [uncanny] (he explicitly remarks a relationship of equation between them) in an essay that compares the tried-and-true coupling of Murakami and Nara to the American one of Jeff Koons and Mike Kelley in the 1980s: Koons with his monstrous pink panther balloons and stainless steel rabbits, the shine and gloss of the commodity form and its sheen of glossy technical achievement contrasted with Mike Kelley and his defaced, re-stitched, stuffed animals, discarded objects unfit for the 'adult' space of the museum.[1] Here, the commentary on art – high/low, museum'd and otherwise – is paralleled with the place of childhood objects and of subcultural refuse. Sawaragi is interested in how not only toys but stuffed toys have functioned in aesthetic theory and practice. In thinking, then, about the place of the *nuigurumi* in contemporary art, Sawaragi deftly refers to them as 'transitional objects' (*ikō taishō*). What, indeed, are stuffed animals, plush toys, doing for all those two-year-old kids? They are, in the thinking of the psychoanalyst D.W. Winnicott, objects that help the child move away from the Mother by operating as substitutes for the maternal presence. They are loved fiercely, and, in the strongest instances, they never leave the child, even to the point of the disintegration of the soft object itself (one remembers *The Velveteen Rabbit*). At a certain moment, however, they must be overcome, discarded, expelled from the household and from the physical attachment and love of the child, if the child is to transition into the world of the adult, so object-relations analysts contend. Yet what becomes of the discarded transitional object? What happens when one does not give up the transitional object? Then we might find the perpetual child, the one who transfers transition, who defers transition, from one beloved object to the next. (This deferral of transition could describe a dimension of perversity.) Is this description so different from the obsessive otaku fan, the Nara groupie, or even the modal addictive consumer of late capitalism?

What Nara thematised so forcefully in 'I DON'T MIND, IF YOU FORGET ME' was the place of this transitional object, its place as remnant, as refused and as refuse, as leftover and excess. By virtue of this leftover quality, the abandoned *nuigurumi* powerfully embodies and evokes the child as past, and the past as the child. What is engaged is the place of the child as itself objectified as transitional, commodified in the work of art and imagistically available for purchase in any number of Nara stuffed toys (for adults as well as for children). The child is always and ever in transition, and it is only by a process of abandonment that one can provisionally give up the fixated version of childhood to which one clings. In visually fusing your childhood with the abandoned *nuigurumi*, visitors were invited to reflect – literally – on an irrevocably past but still potent identification with the child.

For anyone who has been to Japan and visited Buddhist temples, the sight of figures of the bodhisattva Jizō, the protector of pregnant women, children and the dead, standing over heaps of material objects given in remembrance of deceased loved ones is familiar. Jizō has come to be the patron saint, if you will, of aborted foetuses; women who have had abortions (along with women who have lost a child) often give offerings to Jizō, many of which consist of dolls, toys, stuffed animals, items of clothing: all the material signifiers of childhood, now given away and alienated as offerings. To see heaps of purposefully abandoned *nuigurumi* is inevitably to evoke the deathly resonances of Jizō offerings.

Nara is from the prefecture of Aomori, where the sacred Mount Osore is known for its yearly summer festival in which blind female spirit mediums call down the dead. [...] As such, then, the excess of these dolls, these toys, at the Yokohama exhibition evoked a kind of 'horror', according to one critic, a horror connected both to the death of childhood through the abandonment of toys and to the palpable death of actual children evoked by a number of dolls heaped on the floor. The dolls functioned as stand-ins for the dead: dead children, the death of the child's time, the dolls themselves as corpses.[2] As 'stranded objects' that can no longer be used to help the child transition into maturity, they evoked a particular melancholy and morbidity. [...]

Yet these stuffed toys were constructed to be exhibited, constructed to be abandoned in this overtly theatrical way. They were not, precisely, the abandoned, dirty 'lovie', with button eyes missing and ears ripped off. These were new, handmade dolls – faithfully portraying or evoking Nara's signature figures – that were given up by fans to be exhibited and then used to stage the scenario of the abandoned transitional object. The peculiar nature of these *nuigurumi* is disclosed by the letters from the Hamapuro fans to Nara the artist, many of which were published [...]. The fans referred to each other as 'brothers and sisters' (*kyōdai*); what is more, they refer (as did Nara himself) to the dolls (*ningyō*) themselves as brothers and sisters, or alternatively, as their 'children' (*ko*). Take this message from Nanao: 'First off, I was deeply impressed by how the exhibit was put together [...] Seeing so many brothers and sisters, filled with loving care, I was so happy I could hardly stand it. No matter how many there were and even though there were so many of them, I thought they were all works familiar to me in their innocence. (I had a weird [*fushigi na*] feeling when I saw myself reflected in the mirror.) I thought it was really wonderful that I could participate. When I found my child [*ko*] in the exhibition hall, I thought, "It really did arrive in good order!" and I started to cry a little.'[3] Another one: 'When I saw them in photographs, they appeared extremely individualistic taken one by one, but when I actually saw them at the exhibition, they became one work, and it was really moving. I searched for my sibling [*kyōdai*] with all my heart, and I found one that looked like it was the one. It was great that I could participate in such an awesome [*suteki na*] project.' And another: 'I was transfixed by forms that exceeded my imagination. Once again it came home to me how amazing Nara-san is. Really, going to look for my sibling was such a joy.' Repeatedly, the messages express their appreciation (*kansha*) to Nara, their feelings (*kanjō*), and their happiness at being part of the 'project' in which they communed with 'brothers and sisters' fictively produced as coparticipants and as intimately produced dolls (which also took on the status of children). The back jacket of the exhibition catalogue responded to the title I DON'T MIND, IF YOU FORGET ME by proclaiming 'Because, You Never Forget Me. I Never Forget You.' If we can move through the oddities of these phrases (including the punctuation), we might imagine (as Sawaragi does) that the subject here, the 'I' (*boku*) of the enunciation stands in for the abandoned child within, who had to be given up along with the beloved *nuigurumi* as well as childhood itself. The addressee must be the adult viewer, those who through this exhibition can reencounter the lost land of childhood and the lost child there. The child, the child of the past, the lost child, and the thrown-away transitional object fuse here in a movement of prosopopoeia (the movement of personification, which Ngai says is always at stake with the 'cute' object and its relation to its owner or viewer: one thinks of dolls and the ventriloquism of their child owners). The dead child and the abandoned doll are given voice in Nara's titles, and what is creepier than the undead (child, doll) speaking? The voices are from beyond the grave or the trash heap, saying, 'I don't forget you' ('Because, You Never Forget Me'). In a reversal of the title of the exhibition – 'I DON'T MIND, IF YOU FORGET ME' – the rejoinder on the back of the catalogue reminds us that there is an 'unforgettable' dimension to the relationship of child and transitional object, adult and inner child. Here is where the therapeutic dimension of Nara's exhibition is encountered: not unlike 'inner child' therapies in the United States and elsewhere that would enjoin the adult to use finger paints or to draw with the non-dominant hand in order to go back to the state of childhood, to recover the missing 'inner child', Nara's work solicits viewers to attend to an inner world of affect that had been repressed in an attempt to transit to adulthood.[4]

Sawaragi has argued that along with this potentially therapeutic dimension of Nara's staging for viewers is perhaps a more persuasive interpretation: that in contemporary Japanese consumer society, everyone is in thrall to commodity fetishes in the guise of *kawaii mono* (cute things), mass cultural figures, icons, and internetted experiences, such that the transitional object is never relinquished; the dependency on the object that keeps the Mother near is merely transferred from one form to another, keeping Japanese (or Japanese consumers) in a state of perpetual childhood. Adulthood is indefinitely postponed, and a dimension of unending fetishism and perversity is fundamentally inscribed into everyday life as it is. On this view, Japanese institutional structures of adult order and symbolic force are profoundly complicit in reproducing this system of childishness. As such, most viewers of Nara's exhibition probably did not experience anything like a therapeutic catharsis through the reminders of childhood traumas of abandonment; they merely, as Sawaragi proffers, turned toward Nara's iconic 'characters' in a movement of desire and attraction (*kyara moe*), as his works engage the intimate entanglement of iconic 'characters' from mass culture and older forms of portraiture.[5]

Yet it is clear that Nara's fans – fans largely drawn from a certain recognisable stratum of shōjo or post-shōjo girls and women – are subjects who do register some sort of cathartic encounter with childhood in viewing his works, and particularly in a form of community that was enabled by the Yokohama Project. Nara himself muses on this fan relationship in an interview:

> In Japan my fans are people who don't often go to galleries and museums. They just like my pictures, I don't really know why. Most of them are teenagers, some in their twenties, and a few in their thirties. In the beginning I was afraid that they were too young to follow my work, but their reaction to it led me to realise that they understand correctly, and deeply, what is expressed in my paintings. They spend no time on the surface of the work. I can verify this from the overwhelming flood of fan letters that I receive. The publisher of my last book enclosed a small readers' survey card to fill out, and whereas in most cases people don't take the trouble to pick up a pen, we received thousands of replies, many of them quite detailed. It meant that the majority felt personally addressed by my work; in Japan there are hardly any kids who haven't experienced the things I have or shared the same feelings.[6]

While Sawaragi believes that Nara's work follows the movement in postmodern Japanese art from an emphasis on the artist and the work of art to the lure of the *kyara*, Nara instead seems to mediate between an older sense of the artist and a serial logic of *kyara* proliferation (indeed, Nara denies that there is any seriality in his work whatsoever, although an intensive repetition of motifs and forms is obviously at work). His multiple paintings of virtually identical child figures – each one, however, entailing a crucial aesthetic difference – make homely and unhomely the serialised modalities, however enthralling, of kyara production. Indeed, Nara personalises seriality while keeping it recognisable and leaving it open after the fact to mass cultural recuperation (just look at his plush toys on the market, wherein his figures become 'characterised'). His child paintings operate as generative nodes of filiative identification with his fans: they literally operate as children and siblings for fans, and arguably, for Nara. This sense of filiative identification binds his fans into networked affiliations, often notated in the language of kinship.

Nara draws on this inchoate loneliness of the young in recessionary Japan, refunctioning loneliness as the basis for community itself: the loneliness, one might say, of the subject who has given up the transitional object but finds adulthood lacking. What might seem to be an aestheticisation of the (potentially) political – the cutification of the raw sentiments of rebellion and dissatisfaction among capitalist youth – is here changed into a version of the politicisation of the aesthetic – or at least what I would call a parapoliticisation. Nara never calls for overt, public political action as such. Yet his group endeavours produce a mode of politics 'beside' public politics; not simply personal, this parapolitics is based on shared affects and affections and generates forms of association and communality difficult to establish in late capitalist Japan.[7] His mobilisation of volunteers for his installations, his ongoing contact with his fans, his published diaries, his blogs and writings, his globe-spanning art projects can all be seen to form a parapolitics based on a zero degree of community: the fact that we've all been children. [...]

1   [Footnote 19 in source] For a lucid discussion of the notion of *kawaii* and its historical transformations, see Shiokawa Kanako, 'Cute but Deadly: Women and Violence in Japanese Comics', in *Themes and Issues in Asian Cartooning: Cute, Cheap, Mad, and Sexy,* ed. John A Lent, (Bowling Green, OH: Bowling Green State University Press, 1999) 93–125. See also Sharon Kinsella's discussion in 'Cuties in Japan', in *Women, Media, and Consumption in Japan,* ed. Lisa Skov & Brian Moeran (Honolulu: The University of Hawaii Press, 1996) 220–54.

2   [20] Sianne Ngai, 'The Cuteness of the Avant-Garde', *Critical Inquiry,* vol. 31, no. 4 (Summer 2005) 81.

3   [21] Ibid., 846.

4   [24] Ibid., 816.

5   [25] Ibid., 816–7.

6   [36] Nara Yoshitomo, 'My Superficiality Is Only a Game: A Conversation between Stephan Trescher and Yoshitomo Nara', in Nara, *Lullaby Supermarket,* 103–10 (Nürnberg: Institut für moderne Kunst Nürnberg, 2002).

7   [37] I realise this use of 'parapolitics' is quite to the side of standard uses of the term, which range from theoretical analyses that attempt to think about politics that transcend conventional political forms to perhaps its more common usage in referring to covert or illegal political forms and actions, forms that are often repressed. I aim to use the term literally, to indicate a form of unrecognised politics 'existing parallel to, or outside, the sphere of mainstream politics' (*OED,* s.v. 'parapolitics'). The formation of fan communities around Nara's art – and Nara – works as a form of (para)political

action, one that works to produce forms of solidarity resistant to right-wing politics, the justification of war, and neonationalist movements in Japan (and elsewhere).

Marilyn Ivy, extracts from 'The Art of Cute Little Things: Nara Yoshitomo's Parapolitics', *Mechademia*, vol. 5 (Minneapolis: University of Minnesota Press, 2010) 3–28 [some footnotes omitted].

Rosemarie Garland-Thomson
Seeing Disability: Visual Rhetorics of Disability in Popular Photography//2001

[…] If the spatial rhetoric of wonder positions the disabled figure above the viewed, the spatial rhetoric of the sentimental places the disabled figure below the viewer in a position of supplication or impotence. Whereas the wonder mode makes its subjects the capable if exceptional agents of climbing, eating and hammering, the sentimental mode makes its objects helpless, most often by presenting the disabled figure as a child or a woman so as to invoke other complementary stereotypes that will intensify the equation of disability with diminishment, vulnerability, dependence or incapacity. The sentimental is a hallmark of the rhetoric of charity and commerce alike. Most representations of disability promote the exchange of money, whether it is commerce or charity, buying or giving. Disability sells, for different reasons at different times.

The rhetorical element that charity introduces into the conventions of wonder is the sentiment of sympathy. Sympathy literally diminishes the wonderful, replacing awe with pity or the delight of the 'cute'.[1] The cute was a popular Victorian convention, as witnessed by the remarkable popularity of General Tom Thumb whose 1863 wedding, orchestrated by P.T. Barnum, was one of the major society events of New York City in the nineteenth century. Sympathy, which was largely absent from freak rhetoric, does not sell show tickets. But sympathy did flourish in the sentimental literature of nineteenth-century fiction, which often featured disabled characters intended to move their readers to political action or religious benevolence. The pathetic, the impotent, and the suffering confirmed Victorian bourgeoisie status by arousing their finest sentiments. As the increasingly empowered middle class imagined itself capable of capitalising the world, it began to see itself as responsible for the world as well, a stewardship that launched humanitarian and reform movements that today's telethons are heir to.

The rhetoric of sentiment found an effective home in the photographic conventions of the charity poster child of the mid twentieth century. The 1946

March of Dimes poster child clearly echoes Tom Thumb's spunky cuteness, but where the delight inspired by Tom Thumb was in his replication of adulthood in miniature – he is, after all, a 'general' – this poster choreographs the boy's childlike vulnerability by showing him propped up in a corner of his crib in a before-and-after format. The poster child is the quintessential sentimental figure of twentieth-century charity campaigns. To catalyse the adult middle-class spectator to whom the photo addresses itself, this March of Dimes poster presents disability as a problem for the rescuer to solve, an obstacle to be eliminated, a challenge to be met.

Such a logic transforms disability from an attribute of the disabled person to a project that morally enables the rescuer. The viewer's dimes, the poster suggests, will literally catapult the little boy who is unhappily trapped by his braces in the corner of his crib into a smiling and spirited little fellow striding determinedly toward the viewer. In this scene, disability becomes an occasion when the viewers' own narratives of progress, improvement or heroic deliverance can be enacted.

Not only does the poster pack in the benevolent rescue and the overcoming narratives, but it suggests as well what is often called the cure-or-kill approach to disability. The logic of 'cure or kill', accompanied by today's faith in technology, posits that if the disabled body cannot be normalised, it must be eliminated. If it does not respond to being improved, if it refuses to register the success of the rescuer's moral or technological efforts, the disabled body becomes intolerable, a witness to the human inability to perfect the world. This aspect of the relationship between the disabled and the non-disabled has led to such contemporary practices as aborting disabled foetuses, emphasising elimination rather than accommodation of disability, and the sometimes excessive surgical procedures that normalise disabilities. By thwarting the narrative of heroic redemption, the permanently disabled body testifies to the impotence of its failed rescuer, a reminder that the body is ultimately not fully under the control of the human will. The disabled body moves from opportunity to rebuke if it will not be rehabilitated.

Thus the poster child of the 1940s and 1950s introduced two new elements into the rhetoric of sentiment that disability photography inherited from the nineteenth century. The first is that cure replaces suffering as the motivation for action in the viewer. Whereas the earlier sentimental literature accentuated suffering to mobilise readers for humanitarian, reform or religious ends, the poster boy's suffering is only the background to his restoration to normalcy that results from 'your dimes'. Sentiment here, then, replaces the intensity of sympathy with the optimism of cure, testifying to a growing faith in medical treatment and scientific progress that developed as modernity increasingly medicalised and rationalised the body in the nineteenth and twentieth centuries. The second new element is what Paul Longmore describes as the self-serving opportunity that charity provides the giver for 'conspicuous contribution'.[2] What is clearest is that this rhetoric of sentiment diminishes the disabled figure in the interest of empowering, enhancing and enlarging the viewers' senses of themselves. [...]

1   [Footnote 21 in source] Lori Merish, 'Cuteness and Commodity Aesthetics', in *Freakery: Cultural Spectacles of the Extraordinary Body,* ed. Rosemarie Garland-Thomson (New York and London: New York University Press, 1996) 185–206.

2   [22] Paul Longmore, 'Conspicuous Contribution and American Cultural Dilemmas: Telethon Rituals of Cleansing and Renewal', in eds. David Mitchell and Sharon Snyder, *The Body and Physical Difference* (Ann Arbor: University of Michigan Press, 1997) 134-60.

Rosemarie Garland-Thomson, extract from 'Seeing Disability: Visual Rhetorics of Disability in Popular Photography', in *The New Disability History: American Perspectives,* eds. Paul K. Longmore and Lauri Umansky (New York: New York University Press, 2001) 352–6.

Michael Moon
Warhol and Queer Childhood//1996

[...] Warhol's early Pop Art derives much of its energies from its contradictory emphases: one a fascinated devotion to sexuality at its most flagrantly phallic, and the other a no less marked concern with 'marginal', non-phallic erotics (for example, the infantile erotics of withholding and releasing urine and faeces, which I shall discuss a little further on in relation to [...] Warhol's early Pop paintings). The revisionary queer power of much of his Pop cartoon work proceeds from its ability both to evoke and to a considerable degree to celebrate the phallic and also to subvert it comically and to disperse it across the range of abjected erotics I shall discuss in relation to a number of his early Pop paintings of cartoon characters.

[...] Infantile eroticism bodes large in [a number] of Warhol's initial Pop experiments: *Nancy* (1960) shows approximately a frame and a quarter of (presumably) a three- or four-frame sequence of the Ernie Bushmiller cartoon character. In the upper, 'full' frame, Nancy, standing in front of her house, holds herself and shivers, 'BRR MY SNOW SUIT ISNT WARM ENOUGH – I'LL PUT ON A SWEATER TOO'. In the lower partial frame, all that is visible are the words 'BRR IM STILL'. To understand the relation of this early Pop painting to the process of gay male encoding I have been analysing, one might begin by recalling that 'nancy' was (along with 'fairy') one of the most common terms in circulation at the time of the painting's production, both inside and outside gay culture, for an effeminate and therefore presumptively homosexual man. In considering the range of sexualities the painting might represent, we should bear in mind the prevailing climate of homophobia and misogyny manifest in some of the dominant psychoanalytic and psychiatric discourse of the 1950s and 60s. Take, for example, the widely cited work of such a prominent New York psychoanalyst of the period as Edmund Bergler, whose insistence on vaginal orgasm in heterosexual intercourse as an index of mental health in women ('Under frigidity we understand the incapacity of a woman to have a vaginal orgasm during intercourse', Bergler writes in his characteristically now-hear-this manner; a few lines later he foments, 'The sole criterion of frigidity is absence of vaginal orgasm'),[1] was as vehement as his parallel insistence on the necessity of psychiatric cure (what he calls 'destruction of the perversion') for homosexuals.[2] Bergler and other 'medical authorities' of his time took on what they saw as 'sexual neurotics' in single groups in some of their books and articles and across the board, as it were, in other publications, as the title of a 1951 book of Bergler's attests: *Neurotic Counterfeit-Sex: Homosexuality, Impotence, and Frigidity*. The book's procedure, accurately articulated in the title, is to equate with each other the members of various groups of men and women who fail to achieve what Bergler and his colleagues see as a 'healthy' and affirmative relation to heterosexual-male dominance. To deviate from this absolute standard is by definition to occupy one of the other positions, all of which are stigmatised as not only 'neurotic' but also 'counterfeit' (criminally false and deceptive) in the same gesture.

Besides those of the infantile pleasures we have already noticed, one of the other abjected positions Warhol explores in his early work – especially, perhaps, in *Nancy* – is that of the 'frigid' woman; in this image he represents a transitional scene of thawing between her position and that of the similarly abjected gay male 'nancy' and raises the question of whether there might not be strategic advantages in a gay man's energetically taking up the position of what may be the most misogynistic of twentieth-century psychiatric constructions, the frigid woman. 'Frigid people really make it' became one of Warhol's favourite mottos, and although 'frigidity' certainly admits of a wider range of meanings than simply 'sexual unresponsiveness' (such as 'habitually indifferent behavior' or 'frostiness of manner') , there is a sense in which this putatively feminine sexual characteristic remains the 'core' of the 'frigid' identity he embraced as one of his chief public personae.[3]

Nancy was one of the first of Warhol's early Pop works to attract the attention and admiration of Ivan Karp of the Castelli Gallery. According to David Bourdon, what 'grabbed' Karp about it on his first viewing was its 'interrupted narrative sequence and its implication that Nancy remains out in the cold indefinitely'.[4] Karp later spoke of the powerfully 'chilling' effect of Warhol's early cartoon paintings, praising them for their 'cold', 'bleak', and 'brutish' aspects – effects particularly conspicuous in *Nancy*, where the 'frigid' effects the artist was producing in much of his work of the period are literally thematised: 'outsider' Nancy tries to 'warm up' but fails to and 'stays frigid'.[5]

Karp became an instrumental figure in explaining and defending Warhol's Pop work to art dealers and collectors as well as to the media, but considerations of gender and sexuality played no part in his or, to my knowledge, any other critic's theory of Pop until years afterward. Yet what Karp immediately recognised as some of the most notable qualities of a painting like *Nancy* – its 'chilling' and 'brutish' appearance, its 'interrupted [ness]', its 'freezeframe' visual construction – all these characteristics require consideration in relation to the pathologised representations of feminine and gay male identity described above. As several lesbian and gay historians have amply demonstrated, gay people began 'coming in from the cold' in large numbers in the 1950s and 60s, began banding together socially and politically to reject the collective position that had been imposed on them of being officially 'frozen out' of common life.[6] In the figure of Warhol's *Nancy*, 'STILL' freezing or frigid no matter how many garments she puts on, we have not only a picture of a frigid woman starting to thaw or melt but also an emblem of sorts for a strategic repudiation of 'warm' models of gay male desire (of which the 'warm' nudes of Warhol's late 1950s sketches could be said to represent literal exemplars) and gay male 'community' and a similarly strategic embrace of an attributive femininity (or effeminacy) in its extremest (frigid) form [...].

Again, we may look to *Nancy* for a complex representation of some of the signs of infantile erotic desire and pleasure that I have discussed in relation to Warhol's *Superman*. [Ed. note: Moon points out that the hypermasculine character in *Superman* (1960) is depicted in a surprisingly childlike fashion, in which his 'trunks look more like a diaper or infant's rubber pants than like tight-fitting briefs over muscular adult-male buttocks'.] Most of the left three-quarters of the painting (showing the exterior of Nancy's house) is what one might call a 'muddy' or 'urine' yellow, while the upper right-hand quarter of it is a cool 'ice blue'. This dual colour scheme is interrupted two-thirds of the way down the canvas by the horizontal bank of 'snow' in which Nancy stands, a patch of paint that extends from one side of the painting to the other and ranges in colour from off-white to a dingy brownish white (significantly, the two speech balloons are painted in the same way the snowbank is). The three large patches of colour that make up the painting are brought into particularly tense relation to each other in the figure of Nancy herself, who stands hunched stiffly forward from the shoulders, her knees flexed and held tightly together in a way that suggests she not only might be cold but also might have to pee; the ice-blue pants of her snowsuit heighten the subliminal effect of the pose of 'frozen' discomfort, and their 'puffy' and 'stuffed' appearance suggests the similar appearance of the trunks did in *Superman* – that an infantile urethral erotics may be in play here. Superman is energised by the 'mighty puff' of 'super-breath' that also looks like a flood of water (or urine) loosed from on high; the energy of *Nancy* is withheld or held in in the crouching figure of Nancy, although the field of 'urine' yellow that surrounds her hints at a release of energy and tension – from urethral retention – of a kind that doesn't do any 'work' (as the 'mighty puff' of 'super-breath' does). I have been arguing that the cartoon figures in Warhol's early Pop are 'symbolically saturated' ones , and here in a sense is a picture that is on one level all about saturation, of the literal kind everyone experiences in infancy and early childhood (and sometimes later, although the experience of 'wetting oneself' as an adult is so highly stigmatised as hardly to make it into discourse except as a sign of intense abjection).[7] In the mid to late 1970s, Warhol made what he informally called 'Piss Paintings' – later exhibited and sold as *Oxidation Paintings* – on canvases that had been specially prepared to register permanently the streams of urine directed onto them by the artist and some of his assistants, but an early Pop painting like *Nancy* experiments with literalising urination in less direct fashion.

[…] It is notable that the way the painting represents the expression of intense concentration and resolve on Nancy's face is through a configuration of punctuation marks: her brows, the wrinkles of concentration between them, her eyes, nose and mouth form a kind of typographical pun on a determined face, composed entirely of parentheses, quotation marks, hyphens and periods. It is as if the missing punctuation from the sentence in the speech balloon over her head had migrated to her face, which registers for the viewer as a kind of complex exclamation mark.

This figure of a child's body, eroticised in terms of an infantile erotics that is subliminally represented as potentially dissipating its energies in a puddle of urine and/or thawing slush, is instead arrested, 'frozen', and focused at a threshold moment of increasingly intolerable discomfort. The painting as a whole, like others of the early Pop work, itself functions as a kind of complex, hypergraphic punctuation mark, like the stars-inducing 'punch' of the mighty first in *Saturday's Popeye* (1960) and *Popeye* (1961) or in the aforementioned cyclonic 'PUFF!' of Superman. The affective burst that *Nancy* enacts is perhaps more rather than less powerful than Popeye's and Superman's 'super'-virile actions because it is deferred indefinitely ('IM STILL'), represented as simultaneously being contained and becoming uncontained, like the thawed water emerging from the snow or the urine (already colouring most of the scene) threatening to escape from the body.

As we have seen him doing in the painting *Nancy* and as I believe we see him doing in much of the Pop painting of the early 1960s and in his writing and other kinds of production most closely related to it (for example, his films), Warhol derived – from the most hieratic and highly stylised gestural moments ('the frozen moment') of operatic and balletic performance, of highbrow and middlebrow tragedy, of middlebrow melodrama and lowbrow cartoons – a cool, mechanical, anti-tragic, anti-grandiose, anti-self-sacrificial moment of a kind that had a powerfully disruptive effect on the cultural pieties that underwrote much female and gay-male oppression and self-oppression in post-war culture.[8]

If 'feelings' and 'style' of some kinds do get eliminated from Warhol's early Pop work, other kinds of 'feelings' – commonly despised ones, infantile and other kinds of proscribed ones – play lambently around the margins and, as we have just seen, sometimes at the centre of his transformed practice. What Warhol spoke of at the time as the total elimination of 'style' from his work is rather an elimination of what was generally considered to constitute style in mid century United States: carefully cultivated technique employed in the painstaking transmission of a highly refined body of artistic conventions. In attempting, beginning about 1960, to rid his art of all conventional signs of the 'piss-elegant' style he had pursued so fervently and single-mindedly in his pre-Pop art, Warhol discovered in the process of re-engaging with the comic strip style and the comic-strip erotics of his childhood a field of representation that, however far removed from the explicit pre-Pop drawings of male nudes, is nonetheless valuable precisely for the ways in which it complicates and enriches notions of what constitutes queer artistic production. [...]

1   [Footnote 16 in source] Edmund Bergler, quoted by Robert Anton Wilson, 'Attitudes toward Sex, Modern', in *The Encyclopedia of Sexual Behavior*, ed. Albert Ellis & Albert Abarbanel (New York: Hawthorn, 1961) 190; emphases Bergler's.

2   [17] Edmund Bergler, 'Homosexuality and the Kinsey Report', in *The Homosexuals: As Seen by Themselves and Thirty Authorities*, ed. A. M. Krich (New York: Citadel, 1958) 233.

3   [18] See, for example, Warhol's discussion of this motto in his *Philosophy*, Andy Warhol, *The Philosophy of Andy Warhol* (New York: Harcourt Brace Jovanovich) 98.

4   [19] David Bourdon, *Warhol* (New York: Harry N. Abrams, 1989) 82.

5   [20] Of the terms in the first part of this sentence, 'cold' is quoted in Bourdon; the rest of the terms are quoted from the interview with Karp in the British documentary on Warhol.

6   [21] Among the key texts in the recent historiography of gay and lesbian social and political movements 'before Stonewall' is *Before Stonewall*, directed by Greta Schiller and co-directed by Robert Rosenberg (1986) videocassette; Allan Berube, *Coming Out under Fire: The History of Gay Men and Women in World War Two* (New York: Free Press, 1990); John D'Emilio, *Sexual Politics, Sexual Communities: The Making of a Homosexual Minority in the United States, 1940–1970* (Chicago: University of Chicago Press, 1983); Elizabeth Lapovsky Kennedy and Madeline Davis, *Boots of Leather, Slippers of Gold: The History of a Lesbian Community* (New York: Routledge, 1993); Stuart Timmons, *The Trouble with Harry Hay* (Boston: Alyson, 1990).

7   [24] 'Saturation' is Sandor Ferenczi's term for infantile sexual pleasure, in contrast with the cyclic and climactic qualities that characterise adult sexuality. See his essay 'Confusion of Tongues between

Adults and the Child' (1933), reprinted in Sandor Ferenczi, *Final Contributions to the Problems and Methods of Psychoanalysis*, ed. Michael Balint (New York: Brunner/Mazel, 1980) 156–67.

8   [25] Peter Brooks has written compellingly about the history and effects of 'the frozen moment' of melodrama in nineteenth-century literary and theatrical culture in *The Melodramatic Imagination: Balzac, Henry James. Melodrama, and the Mode of Excess* (New Haven: Yale University Press, 1976).

Michael Moon, extracts from 'Screen Memories, or, Pop Comes From the Outside: Warhol and Queer Childhood', in *Pop-Out: Queer Warhol*, eds. Jennifer Doyle, Jonathan Flatley and Jose Esteban Muñoz (Durham, NC and London: Duke University Press) 86, 92, 95, 96–8.

Kanako Shiokawa
Cute but Deadly: Women and Violence in Japanese Comics//1999

[…] 'Cute' has been in the domain of the girlchild subculture for decades. At first, it described the girls themselves in the traditional sense of those who would inspire compassion, and then, later, it became an exclusive term used by girls in order to express certain acceptable or favourable qualities among themselves. If something is 'cute', then it is good. This usage seemed very much a marker for being part of the in-group. Growing up in the 1960s and the 1970s, girls always had 'cute' things around them. They adorned their personal belongings, from school supplies to their drab school uniforms, with 'cute' (and often 'little') things, and enthusiastically adored 'cuteness', or the variable things and persons that represented this quality. Knowing what was and what was not 'cute' worked as a silent membership to many girl-child cliques in the 1970s. It was a shared culture, an unspoken communication. A woman who grew up in these decades in Japan knows exactly what constituted 'cute' in her immediate environment.

How, then, did this expression and its referents suddenly multiply and make a leap from the confined realm of good little girls? I believe the development of gender-specific comic books, a uniquely Japanese phenomenon, holds the key. In this instance, the emergence of *shojo manga*, or girls' comics, is the first and foremost contributor to the present-day mass consumption of anything 'cute'. Moreover, it has eventually led to the abundance of indestructible, but still very cute, action heroines today.

Girls' comics, aka *shojo manga*, is a commercial category. These are comic books, especially story comics, specifically aimed for girls, written chiefly by women, who are, in short, grown-up girls. Over the last few decades, it became an established and rather lucrative market. The success of the genre then encouraged the emergence of numerous thematic and stylistic sub-genres within. The idea that boys and girls are inherently different and therefore require different education and entertainment is a traditionally held view of neo-Confucianism, which was the official philosophy during the Shogunate Era. This attitude led to founding separate schools for boys and girls when modern education was introduced in Japan. When magazine publications began in the late nineteenth and the early twentieth centuries with the advent of modern printing technologies, magazines devoted to children were the last to arrive, and they usually had boy readers in mind. However, as single-sex education became the norm, magazines that aimed specifically for girls arrived as late as the 1920s and the 1930s, and in the late 1950s, comics magazines for girls finally emerged. Their debut was several years after their male counterparts. Publishers saw a market value in female readership and proceeded to found girls' versions of their successful boys' magazines.

In this early stage, however, the feature stories were mostly illustrated stories, usually penned by male writers and artists who customarily wrote for boys' magazines. Writing for girls' magazines was, evidently, something that they did to please the publishers. When girls' comics finally arrived, their subject matter varied little, with much of it taken from the pre-modern, illustrated reading materials that were considered to be 'for girls and women'. These stories featured tragic heroines, often orphaned princesses, in search of their true mothers. To put it simply, the girls' comics stories written by men (and later women writing under the strict supervision of boys' magazine publishers) depended on the classic notion of *kawaii*: the woe, the helpless.

Then, in the transitional period between the 1950s and the 1960s, girls who read the girls' illustrated stories and comics described above grew up, and some became comic book artists themselves. The conventions and stereotyped aesthetics for girls' reading materials set by male predecessors were at first dutifully followed by these young female writers. However, as more and more girls' comic magazines were introduced, aesthetical preferences of readers became distinct, thus producing devoted fans of specific magazines featuring intrinsically varied contents and styles. With readers' support, women writers were able to develop their own styles and conventions in the latter half of the 1960s. Stories were diversified in terms of their themes, subject matters, and settings, in spite of men's derisive comments that all girls' comics looked the same. Thus, finally, a specific convention known as *shojo manga* (girls' comic) style emerged .

The most significant feature of this particular art style in the late 1960s was the overwhelmingly large eyes of just about all the characters, many taking up nearly half of the faces. Masubuchi points out that the stylistic evolution of this particular feature headed toward even bigger eyes and more rounded faces during the height of its popularity. Specifically (and often derisively) known as *shojo manga* eyes, characters in such girls' comics had huge eyes made of enormous, dilated orbs of black pupils filled with numerous stars, sparkles, and glittering dots. And if one was uncertain as to who the main character was, the ground rule dictated that she was the possessor of the largest and the starriest eyes. These large-eyed girls were always accompanied by highly stylised drawings of blooming flowers that crowded the background. These flowers were so abundant and so consistent in girls' comics that their presence became the signature feature, an icon, of the girls' comics style.

Another significant feature of the girls' comics style in this period was its nearly complete avoidance of secondary sexual features, especially breasts. Almost every close-up frame of the heroines featured large, complex bows, twirling ribbons, and frilly laces, which were all strategically placed to cover up the chest. These items of artful cover-up came in various shapes and sizes, but their usage was formulaic. In full body frames, which were inserted often in order to fully articulate the costumes, the girl-heroine's breasts were only implied by simplified (and often fainter) curved lines if the design of the costume could not fully cover that particular region. This particular convention, similar to the popular Rika-chan™ dolls that were first introduced in the same period, only hinted at the presence of the girl-child's barely budding sexuality. Even full-grown female characters, with the exception of 'nanny' types, were depicted in this convention, with predominantly prepubescent figures. One must remember that this was also the time when Twiggy had made a worldwide sensation. The desired atmosphere to which all these stylised features in girls' comics contributed was *kirei*, pretty and neat (often considered 'gaudy' and 'gothic' by the uninitiated).

Kawaii, on the other hand, was a prerequisite for the girl heroine of these story comics, for girls were 'cute', and 'cute' was good. These heroines were most certainly not women-yet. When the heroine ever became an adult (a rare occurrence, in fact), then she would become *kirei*.

As mentioned earlier, the story lines of early girls' comics supported the notion of 'cute'. The traditional idea of fragility and sensitivity had a firm ground in the pictorial representation of cuteness then.

However, as more women writers crowded the girls' comics arena, a subtle change began to take place in the personalities depicted in the heroines. It was a transformation from the passive, tragic heroines of the earlier era, mainly developed by the male writers, to more active and tenacious characters. They held various occupations and positions, often in glamorous, exotic settings. Japanese school girls during this period identified themselves with the 'cute' heroine as she survived adverse situations by means of endurance, good humour, and not considerable luck.

Because of the rising popularity of the genre, numerous girls' comics magazines were founded one after another between the 1960s and the 1970s. The stories and characters, not to mention styles, of these new magazines, thus diversified in order to survive the competition, and in this free-for-all atmosphere, tenacious and strong, yet still very 'cute', characters emerged. Romantic and 'gothic' stories predominated, but the situation in which the ultimate romance had to be won also diversified. The adversary of the heroine's objective also became varied, and the hardships which the heroine had to conquer multiplied, although explicitly sexual situations were still rare. As a result of this boom, themes and topics in girls' comics further diversified, and quite a few very high quality works were written, attracting older women as well as men. Indeed, the 1970s was the golden age of *shojo manga*.

Girls' comics became very lucrative business in the seventies, lasting well into the eighties. Many new publications were issued, and more and more writers were in demand to fill the thick books of roughly 300 to 500 pages on weekly and monthly bases. This led to a further diversification of the genre's narrative and artistic expressions, and much refinement was made in the genre-specific formulas, such as the use of floral backgrounds and unique page layouts.

One important change in girls' comics in the seventies was the introduction of the competitive formula, especially in the context of sports. This element, especially combined with much action and violence, had been an established, sure-hit theme for boys' comics for quite a while. Thus, heroines in girls' comics of the seventies began to face severely competitive scenarios in order to achieve their goal, which invariably was happiness, although its forms varied somewhat. The common goal (with few exceptions) was the traditional, knight-in-shining-armor formula, but career-oriented goals began to emerge as heroines started to dabble in various athletic activities popular among girls, including (but not limited to) tennis, figure skating, volleyball, ballet, and swimming. Not all girls' comics stories had happy endings, but when the heroine did win her game, she usually got her boy as a matter of course.

This competitive framework necessitated worthy opponents for the heroines. The harder the rivals were to beat, the higher drama the heroines presented as they attempted to win. […]

In this competition-based story formula, the heroine was invariably very 'cute' (*kawaii*) in the convention of girls' comics of the 1960s and the 1970s, whereas her nemesis was infallibly stunning and beautiful (*utsukushii*, rather than just *kirei*). They were usually in the same age group, but the latter's physical features were those of a mature woman with full breasts. Although individual artists had their own drawing and storytelling styles, this formula was so successful that it soon became a golden rule. The 'sports(wo)manship' quickly expanded into other, nonathletic, but typically feminine fields such as acting, fashion design, hair dressing, photography, and broadcasting. The heroine, regardless of an innumerable offering of glittering stars in her eyes, was supposed to be 'cute' but in a rather ordinary (or even plain) fashion. In fact, she was very ordinary in just about every aspect with the exception of either her athletic or artistic potential or the strength of her character. Her rival was always extremely beautiful, intelligent, rich, and gifted in the same field as that of the heroine. Their paths crossed again and again. As they competed, often their intense rivalry evolved into tension-filled camaraderie based on mutual respect. But inevitably, in the most significant event for both of them, the heroine would win by sheer virtue of that one quality that she possessed. Her victory then set everything right, and she achieved the state of happily-ever-after-if, indeed, the story had set out to be a happy one. For the tragic hero/heroine-dies-in-the-end stories have also been very popular among the Japanese for centuries.

This particular formula implicitly leaves a message that being 'cute' is a virtue and, in an oddly paradoxical way, strength. However, cuteness in this instance is not in direct opposition to ugliness or neatness. It is clear by the characteristics of the heroine's nemesis, that cuteness in the girls' comics convention battles against 'beauty', that is, perfection and maturity. Masubuchi Soichi analysed this particular notion in detail and concluded that 'beautiful' (*utsukushii*) is an unequal condition based purely on luck, a hand dealt by fate, similar to wealth and genius – everyone wants these qualities, but only the select few can ever possess them. Such lucky few are targets of much envy by the plain, the common, and the mass. Masubuchi argues that physical beauty is a fatefully determined state of perfection, unlike the states indicated by such expressions as *kirei* (pretty, neat), *suteki* (dashing), or *kakko ii* (cool, good-looking). These categories, he argues, can be achieved by personal efforts of self-improvement, similar to cleaning up a room to make it look neat. In other words, even conventionally 'ugly' or 'plain' persons, as many girls' comic heroines are supposed to be, can make themselves 'cute' by working hard at it.

Interestingly, the term *kawaii* may have lost its concrete reference to the notion of helplessness; however, 'cute' heroines in the golden age of girls' comics usually receive appropriate and often crucial help in times of dire need, whereas the reverse is true with their nemeses, who are perfect in every other aspect. 'Cute', in other words, has become a strategic advantage in a girl's struggle for happiness. [...]

Kanako Shiokawa, extracts from 'Cute but Deadly: Women and Violence in Japanese Comics', in *Themes and Issues in Asian Cartooning: Cute, Cheap, Mad, and Sexy*, ed. John A. Lent (Bowling Green, OH: Bowling Green State University Popular Press, 1999) 98–107 [footnotes ommitted].

Sharon Kinsella
Cuties in Japan//1995

Cute Handwriting and Slang

[...] The emergence of the modern term *kawaii* in the early 1970s coincides with the beginning of the cute handwriting craze and childish fashion. In 1974, large numbers of teenagers, especially women, began to write using a new style of childish characters. By 1978 the phenomenon had become nationwide, and in 1985 it was estimated that upwards of five million young people were using the new script.

Previously, Japanese script had been written vertically, using strokes that varied in thickness along their length. The new style was written laterally, preferably using a mechanical pencil to produce very fine even lines.[1] Using extremely stylised, rounded characters with English, *katakana*,[2] and little cartoon pictures such as hearts, stars and faces inserted randomly into the text, the new style of handwriting was distinct and the characters difficult to read. In middle and high schools across the country, the craze for writing in the new style caused discipline problems. In some schools, the writing was banned entirely, or tests which were completed in the new cute style would not be marked. The new style of handwriting was described by a variety of names such as *marui ji* (round writing), *koneko ji* (kitten writing), *manga ji* (comic writing) and *burikko ji* (fake-child writing). Through the 1980s magazines, comics, advertising, packaging, and word processor software design (Macintosh) adapted the new style. Yamane Kazuma carried out two years of research into cute handwriting (between 1984 and 1986) which he officially labelled, 'Anomalous Female Teenage Handwriting'.[3] Arguing against the common view that cute handwriting was something young people bad mimicked from the lettering in comics, Yamane furnishes evidence that in fact the craze for rounded lettering pre-dates its use in comics, which relied on the later invention of photo composition methods in order to be able to use the round characters. Instead, he concludes that teenagers 'spontaneously' invented the new style. Results of Yamane's survey carried out in 1984–5 amongst middle and high school students showed that the older students were, the more likely it was that they would use the childish hand writing. 22.5% of eleven to twelve-year-old female pupils, 55.3% of twelve to fifteen-year-old female middle school pupils, and 55.7% of fifteen to eighteen-year-old female high school pupils used the cute writing style. Amongst young men, 10% of twelve to fifteen-year-old middle school, and

17.5% of fifteen to eighteen-year-old high school pupils used the cute style. Its increasing incidence amongst older students illustrates that cute handwriting was a style acquired with maturity and exposure to youth culture rather than the result of any adolescent writing disability. Yamane asked some of these young people why they used the round band writing style and was unequivocally informed:

> 'It's got a kind of cute feel.'
> 'I think it's cute and it's my style.'
> 'I think these letters are the cutest.'
> 'Cute! They are hard to read but they are so cute I use them.'[4]

It is interesting that cute style did not start in the multi-media which are frequently criticised for originating all the trends of youth culture, if not exercising a virtual mind control over young people. Rather, it began as an underground literary trend amongst young people who developed the habit of writing stylised childish letters to one another and to themselves. Cute handwriting was arrived at partly through the romanisation of Japanese text. The horizontal left to right format of cute handwriting and the liberal use of exclamation marks, as well as English words such as 'love' and 'friend', suggest that these young people were rebelling against traditional Japanese culture and identifying with European culture which they obviously imagined to be more fun. By writing in the new cute style, it was almost as though young people had invented a new language in which they were suddenly able to speak freely on their own terms for the first time. They were thus able to have an intimate relation with the text and express their feelings to their friends more easily. Through cute handwriting, young people made the written Japanese language – considered to be the lynchpin of Japanese culture – their own.

The spread of cute-style handwriting was one element of a broader shift in Japanese culture that took place between the mid 1960s and the mid 1970s in which vital popular culture, sponsored and processed by the new fashion, retail, mass-media and advertising industries, began to push traditional arts and crafts and strictly regulated literary and artistic culture to the margins of society. [...]

The Fancy Goods Industry

Cute culture started as youth culture amongst teenagers, especially young women. Cute culture was not founded by business. But in the disillusioned calm known as the *shirake* after the last of the student riots in 1971, the consumer boom was just beginning, and it did not take companies and market research agencies very long to discover and capitalise on cute style, which had manifested itself in manga and young people's handwriting.

In 1971 Sanrio, the Japanese equivalent of Hallmark Cards, experimented by printing cute designs on previously plain writing paper and stationery. Sanrio began to produce cute-decorated stationery and fancy diaries for the dreamy school students hooked on the cute handwriting craze. The success of this early prototype of *fanshi guzzu* (fancy goods), inspired by cute style in manga animation and young people's handwriting, encouraged Sanrio to expand production, and its range of fancy goods proliferated. The company established a firm monopoly in the fancy goods market and during 1990 sold ¥200 billion worth of goods, whilst the fancy goods business as a whole reached an estimated turnover of ¥10 trillion in 1990. Typical fancy goods sold in cute little shops were stationery, cuddly toys and gimmicks, toiletries, lunch boxes and cutlery, bags, towels and other personal paraphernalia.

The crucial ingredients of a fancy good are that it is small, pastel, round, soft, loveable, not traditional Japanese style but a foreign – in particular European or American – style, dreamy, frilly and fluffy. Most fancy goods are also decorated with cartoon characters. The essential anatomy of a cute cartoon character consists in its being small, soft, infantile, mammalian, round, without bodily appendages (e.g. arms), without bodily orifices (e.g. mouths), non-sexual, mute, insecure, helpless or bewildered. Sanrio invented a large cast of cute proprietary characters to endorse and give life to its fancy goods: Button Nose, Tiny Poem, Duckydoo, Little Twin Stars, Cheery Chums, Vanilla Bean and, most famous of all, Hello Kitty and Tuxedo Sam. Not only do these cute characters inhabit cute-shops; they have also worked hard selling under licence the goods and services of over 90 Japanese companies. A large number of these are financial institutions such as 23 banks, including Mitsui, Sumitomo, Sanwa, and Mitsubishi; fourteen stock companies, including Yamaichi, Daiwa and Nomura; and seven insurance companies, including Nihon Seimei, Sumitomo Seimei and Yasuda Kasai. [...]

1   [Footnote 4 in source] In the same years that the new handwriting cult spread, the mechanical pencil industry made record profits producing strong, thin leads and a plethora of cute mechanical pencils for young writers to choose from. Between 1969 and 1979 sales of mechanical pencils doubled, and between 1979 and 1981 trebled again.

2   [5] There are two syllabaries in the Japanese language. *Hiragana* is the alphabet used most frequently for all nonnal purposes, and *Katakana* is a special alphabet used originally for Buddhist texts and then for military purposes and foreign words, but now also used to give emphasis to particular words, and in advertising.

3   [6] Yamane's research involved examining visitors' books in tourist temples and love hotels where young people left signatures and personal messages, and a questionnaire survey in which

3021 school students nation-wide participated. See Yamane Kazuma, *Hentai Shōjo Moji no Kenkyū*, (Tokyo: Kodansha, 1986).

4   Ibid., 132.

Sharon Kinsella, extracts from 'Cuties in Japan', in *Women, Media, and Consumption in Japan*, eds. Lise Skov & Brian Moeran (Honolulu: University of Hawaii Press, 1995) 222–4, 225–6.

Sasha Archibald
Feline Darlings and the Anti-Cute//2015

In reply to online cat videos Carolee Schneemann's *Infinity Kisses* (1981–7) arrives like a missive from the past. The piece comprises a 9 x 7 foot arc of Schneemann kissing her cats, 140 times, in close-up colour photographs. These are not sterile pecks on the cheek, but full-throttle French kisses, the kind that distend the neck and leave glistening saliva all around.[1] The kisses are framed by pillows and bedclothes, intimate objects on a night table, and Schneemann's mussed-up hair. *Infinity Kisses* landed with a silent thud in the art world, seemingly too eccentric and repulsive to warrant attention.[2] The piece proved an heir to the cautious repugnance relegated to cat women, those self-elected pariahs who have exchanged human company for feline and carry the moult to prove it.

Schneemann, the creator of the infamous *Meat Joy*, a 1964 performance involving animal carcasses, and the 1975 *Interior Scroll*, in which she read from a manuscript extracted from her vagina, has always had a knack for intuiting the point at which contemporary art's tolerance for transgression shudders and snaps. And yet on the surface, *Infinity Kisses* seems hardly so outré as these earlier works: no vaginal fluid and no raw meat, only methodical documentation of a cat's belovedness. In fact, like Schneemann, we love our cats, kiss our cats, and film our cats. Cats play an outsize role in our emotional lives. The puzzle of *Infinity Kisses* is not that it is a paean to cat devotion to which we can't relate, but a paean to cat devotion that thoroughly evades the aesthetic of 'cute'. Cute is the affect cat photography tends to produce nowadays, and it is certainly the lingua franca of the online cat video. Schneemann's piece results rather in a squeamish gulp. Like a musty tropical fruit or a beloved cat in heat, *Infinity Kisses* tips the line between delectable and revulsive.

A handful of writers and critics have recently turned their attention to the cute, plumbing it with the sort of gravitas usually reserved for the beautiful or the just. The provocative sum of these analyses is that the characteristics of cute belie its true essence. Appearances to the contrary, cute is neither petite, sweet, nor vulnerable, but bombastic, evangelical and sadistic. William Burroughs wrote about control as having an inherent quality of boundless propagation, such that exercising control has the paradoxical effect of begetting more control. Cuteness shares this tendency toward explosive proliferation. As a visual experience, it has the characteristics of addiction; looking at cute things breeds the desire to look at more cute things, such that icons of cute are pasted on points of constant contact: calendars and screensavers, refrigerator magnets and bulletin boards. Moreover, the apex of cuteness is a flexible point, spiralling out further and further. Eyes grow bigger, features rounder, texture more uniform, colours more soft. There is always one critter cuter than another, such that cuteness implies an interminable search and a contest for the ultimate cute, albeit a contest of biased judges who unabashedly proselytise.[3] The highest level of praise in the cute lexicon – 'Isn't it cute?' – is a judgment disguised as a question, to which there is only one acceptable answer. Devotees of cute coerce agreement, thrusting their cell phone before your eyes, chirping in a sunny way that silences dissent. [...]

By positing a cat with agency enough to consensually kiss, Schneemann's photographs refute cuteness, whereas the ordinary online cat video stokes its fire. The cutest videos are those that depict a cat in a predicament, just as the most beautiful women are those, according to Edmund Burke, who 'counterfeit weakness, and even sickness'.[4] The index of cuteness is the degree to which an object sheds its power. Nothing possessed of full sentience can be cute, at least not simultaneous to it achieving cuteness. The aesthetic brokers no autonomy; an objectified subject is prerequisite. No wonder cute's operational mode is so often photography and video.

How, then, did cats become the cute icon extraordinaire? Unlike Hello Kitty or Beanie Babies or Pillow Pets, not only are cats alive – already an impediment to cuteness – but they scratch and bite, use urine as a form of protest, and, perhaps worst of all, kill other cute things. They command attention and accommodation, shamelessly exerting control over an entire household. Cats are notoriously conceited, supremely confident of their dominance. When a cat deigns to offer comfort and companionship, the relationship remains of the cat's design, contingent on its capricious inclinations. As most cat lovers acknowledge, the cat's imperviousness is key to its charm. Knowing the object of our attentions will never be subjugated makes its pursuit enjoyable: In chasing the cat's exquisite not-need, we allow ourselves to need. The tension between human agendas and kitty self-determination lies at the very heart of feline devotion. In a cat-and-mouse-game of our own invention, we attempt subjugation, and the cat resists, over and over and over. With the online cat video, however, our attempts at mastery have acquired their most powerful arsenal to date. Camera in hand, the cat is forced to yield its dignity, abandon its claims to privacy, and finally acquire a reputation wholly counter to its ancestral roots. The ancient cats of myth, literature, art, and even early twentieth-century popular culture bear little semblance to today's big-eyed kittens. YouTube speaks a tale of catness thoroughly at odds with feline history.

The shift is recent. Even just two hundred years ago, cats were operative symbols of qualities antithetic to cute: magical metamorphosis, potent danger, sexual provocation, and impervious autonomy. Take for instance, the feline's long-standing association with feminine sexuality. Whereas cute suggests a virginal and yet available sexuality – the aesthetic is a placeholder for the eroticisation of succumbing to another's desire – cats were historically the indicator of women's self-determined sexual prerogative. The links between pussy the cat and pussy the cunt extend over centuries of folklore, a connective tissue that binds the contemporary Russian punk-protest group Pussy Riot with ancient Egyptian celebrations that honoured the cat goddess Bastet. In Herodotus' account of these festivals, thousands of women crowded onto barges and travelled down the Nile, wildly dancing and drinking wine (more wine, Herodotus noted, than at any other annual holiday). As the barge passed by men on shore, the women flipped up their skirts to reveal nothing underneath. To celebrate the cat was to tout the pussy.

The fairy tale cat is almost always a syllogism for pussy as a provocation. In a Romanian fairy tale, for instance, when a young woman refuses to yield to her lovesick suitor, he is so broken-hearted he commits suicide, and she is punished for his death by being turned into a cat.[5] Her feline form becomes a warning to other young women of the dangers of non-conformity; by threat of cat transformation, women yield their bodies. Just as a woman who refuses sex becomes a cat, so does a woman too eager for sex or a woman who seems to love cats more than sex. Or a spell might command that a young woman become a cat the day of her eighteenth birthday, the symbolic moment at which she could exercise her sexual autonomy. In the reverse, a man who demonstrates kindness to a cat might be surprised with a beautiful lover – a lover who may or may not retain the head of a cat.[6] So permeable was the boundary between feminine wiles and kitty cats that in the Salem witch trials, a woman wasn't considered completely dead until her pet was also murdered.

[…] The original online cat video is not a video, but a little-known art film, produced the same year kitty litter hit the supermarket: Alexander Hammid (née Hackenschmied) and Maya Deren's *The Private Life of a Cat* (1947).[7] In their 25-minute silent short, Hammid and Deren film their cat, Glamour Girl (or Gigi for short), giving birth and tending to five kittens. Gigi's cardboard box labour is as lowly and sublime as a biblical birth in a manger. She cosies up as her kittens spool out from folds of pink flesh, ectoplasmic bundles of slime. She licks them into life and their fur spikes up; they flop about, nosing for a teat. When a placard indicates two weeks have passed, Gigi carries each by the scruff of its neck to an unused fireplace, where the kittens learn to walk and climb and lap cream from a saucer. Deren is deservedly celebrated as the grande dame of avant-garde film, and even this whimsical piece is stately and honorific. The shots are beautifully framed-shafts of light in a Hollywood bungalow – and the editing is witty and charming. Yet, like its less-polished cousin films, *The Private Life of a Cat* projects a version of catness that has little to do with cats. In peeking in on the cat's interior self, Hammid and Deren find no trace of alterity, but rather the familiar saga of an idealised mother. For all its delight, *The Private Life of a Cat* trespasses the privacy of a cat to satisfy the vanities of a human. Coddled and cuddled and photographed ad nauseam, cats like Gigi will soon be pressed in the mould of *America's Funniest Home Videos*. Pray we don't return to a time when children are indulged in setting cats on fire. And yet, are the sticky moans of cuteness endemic to cat love? Are there other ways to treasure an animal?

It's a dangling question, unresolved even in regards to human babies, let alone cats. There is, however, one apropos suggestion by the late philosopher Jacques Derrida. The cat could be restored its dignity, he suggests, by occasionally reversing the spectral terms of the human-feline relationship. In a late lecture, Derrida analyses the primal scene of his adulthood: he is undressed, preparing to get in the shower, and his cat appears. The animal stares at Derrida's naked body, gazing like a sphinx, or 'an extra-lucid blind person'.[8] The cat's gaze induces a cataclysm of discomfit. Derrida feels mortification and shame, he writes, but also a sense of momentousness. The encounter stages a threshold. He and the cat are frozen in space and time, eyes locked in a quiver of interspecies communication.

'Something happens there', writes Derrida, 'that shouldn't take place.'[9] (Indeed, a similar scene, described in Edgar Allan Poe's 1843 story *The Black Cat*, is the stuff of horror. The narrator becomes so unnerved by his cat's gaze he savagely puts out its eye.)[10]

It is only when this moment dissolves, Derrida reflects, that he can visit animals in a zoo, or enjoy paintings of animals, or stroll through dioramas at the natural history museum, or read about animals in a book, or, presumably, gorge on online cat videos. Gazing into the cat's eyes holds in abeyance these other forms of looking, such that the cat is allowed, briefly, to be something other than a toy or a surrogate or entertainment, something more majestic, peculiar, and potent … something more cat. Henceforth, a new requirement: before producing or consuming a depiction of catness, one must first submit to the gaze of the cat. Assume the posture of 'a child ready for the apocalypse': naked, no camera allowed, ego tucked between the legs.[11] Don't be surprised that should the apocalypse arrive, the cat will take its vengeance on cute. Brace yourself for an interspecies French kiss.

1   *Infinity Kisses I* (1981–7) was followed by a second photo grid, *Infinity Kisses II* (1990–98), and by a video, *Infinity Kisses – The Movie* (2008), which incorporates images from the two photo works and is available online (www.youtube.com/watch?v= _m4wuJH4M8I).

2   *Infinity Kisses* builds on explorations Schneemann took up twenty years earlier with *Fuses* (1965–8), the premise of which, as Schneemann describes, was to visualise her sex life through the eyes of her cat, Kitch. Schneemann filmed herself with her partner at the time, composer James Tenney, and then assiduously marked the 16mm footage with heat, water, paint and ink. The final product is a sex film that lacks the hallmarks of a sex film – no fetishised nude and no drive toward climax – and instead captures the texture of lovemaking, rendered as a series of flickering affects. Human sex from a cat's perspective seems innocuous enough as a description, but for two decades *Fuses* outraged audiences. At a screening in Cannes, theatregoers ripped apart the seat cushions in disgust. At another in El Paso, Texas, the projectionist was assaulted and arrested. As recently as 1988, the film was cancelled from the programme of a film festival in Moscow.

3   Artist Nina Katchadourian's *Continuum of Cute* literalises this contest by arranging one hundred animals in a linear trajectory (least cute to most cute) and inviting viewers to do the same (http:// archive.rhizome.org/exhibition/montage/katchadourian).

4   [Footnote 8 in source] Edmund Burke, 'On the Sublime and Beautiful', in *Harvard Classics*, vol. 24, ed. Charles W. Eliot, LL.D (New York: P.F. Collier & Son Company, 1909) 29–137.

5   [9] This fairy tale is the subject of a book-length Jungian analysis by Marie-Louise Von Franz, *The Cat: A Tale of Feminine Redemption* (Toronto: Inner City Books, 1999).

6   [10] Sylvia Townsend Warner cleverly scrambles these fairy-tale motifs in her novel *The Cat's Cradle Book,* in which a woman stumbles upon a remote cottage inundated with cats and inhabited by an enigmatic man. To atone for a past sin – he was so irritated by his cat in heat, he dumped water on her head and she subsequently died – the man has taught himself cat language in order to study cat folktales. He makes love to his visitor (with a decidedly feline technique), and asks her to share the burden of his task.

7   [19] Hammid is credited as the director, but later said the film was Deren's idea and that they worked together. Deren is the sole author of an introduction to the film included with the with the DVD *Maya Deren: Experimental Films* (Mystic Fire Video, 2002).

8   [20] Jacques Derrida, 'The Animal That Therefore I Am (More to Follow)', trans. David Wills, *Critical Inquiry*, vol. 28, no. 2 (Winter 2002) 369–418. In the scene Derrida describes, he is frontally naked, and the cat, he emphasises, is not an abstraction or an archetype but a singular cat with a singular personality: his cat. Peter Trachtenberg writes about the exact same moment in his memoir, *Another Insane Devotion: On the Love of Cats and Persons* (Boston: Da Capo Press, 2012), describing it

as one of exquisite vulnerability. Stroking the cat while naked combines two postures – defensive protectiveness and demonstrative affection – that are otherwise inimical.

9   [21] Ibid.

10   [22] In several respects, Poe's story draws on real customs of seventeenth-century France, detailed in Richard Darnton's *The Great Cat Massacre* (New York: Basic Books, 1984). For instance, it was believed that the trick to disabling a cat's powers of sorcery was to maim it: 'Cut its rail, clip its ears, smash one of its legs, tear or burn its fur, and you would break its malevolent power' (92, 94). In the same period, live cats were bricked into the mortar of new homes, a custom believed to protect the hearth. Poe's feline character suffers an identical fate, except it remains alive, meowing from inside a wall to betray his master.

11   [23] Derrida, op cit.

Sasha Archibald, extracts from 'Feline Darlings and the Anti-Cute', in *Cat is Art Spelled Wrong* (Minneapolis: Coffee House Press, 2015) 107–11, 116–20.

Kevin Young
Triangular Trade: Colouring, Remarking, and Narrative in the Writings of Kara Walker//2007

[...] While the scale of Walker's writing [in *Texts* (2001)] invokes the smaller size of the *American Primitives* series – and the miniatures of the nineteenth century and earlier – the writing's medium of index cards invokes something else entirely. Such cards render the form both formal and informal, both as notes for a speech and shorthand for a case study. They also, for me, invoke the lined children's paper that fellow artist Ellen Gallagher uses for her deconstructions of the inherent (and even abstract) notions of race.

Here, Walker seems interested less in deconstruction than in reconstruction – in rebuilding a South that never existed, yet will never die. In her hands (and type), Reconstruction, the experiment of black power that was stymied by violence and disenfranchisement, becomes a fantastical redressing of grievances and an undressing of the South's petticoats and pretty fictions. Rumours of black violence, historically an excuse for white violence against blacks, become mixed together – the fantasy merged with the fact – in ways troubling and all too familiar. Anyone who's seen the typical postbellum postcards or stereographs of black folks – children, usually in the mouth of an alligator or treed by a tiger – has seen some of this marketed violence before. While it may seem useful to distinguish between rumours of (adult) black violence and the thrill of seeing violence visited on (black) children, in truth, the view of black children as 'gator bait' only permits and even predicts the violence, literal or figurative, visited on them later at the hands of a lynch mob or at the lunch counter. In Walker's hands, fantasy and fact and memory – or, if you prefer, race and writing and art – sit in a solution in the chemical sense, constantly acting and provoking reactions, but rarely resolved.

[…] Here are some of the disturbing things we can see if we just glance at Walker's art: banana breasts, goose-head penises, ugly ducklings, umbilical cord chains, footstool toddlers.

The index cards and other writings don't do as much, can't hope to. But they also don't get involved in the same illusion that the cut-outs do, which isn't about negative images, or negative space, but about narrative. Instead, the writings engage seriously with narrative in much the same way children's books do – particularly pop-up books.

Walker herself has written a pop-up book, *Freedom: A Fable* (1997), whose title page informs us is 'A Curious Interpretation of the Wit of a Negress in Troubled Times with Illustrations.'[1] In general, the pop-up book interrupts narrative even as it illustrates it; the pop-ups give readers a point in the story not to hear but to see (and not just to see but to interact with). This brings to mind, in Walker's case, the title of Gwendolyn DuBois Shaw's full-length study on the artist, *Seeing the Unspeakable*, for the way pop-ups force us to read the visual. We may also think of the 'talking book', a trope in African American writing and oral culture from slavery to Stevie Wonder, who has an album of that name. […] There's a kind of motion and childhood magic-wonder-that the pop-up still conveys that culture or history or adulthood cannot erase.

One of the books I have in my collection is a pop-up Little Black Sambo by Helen Bannerman, the original author of the Sambo tale.[2] Beneath the title on the front cover it reads, 'ANIMATED! ANIMATED!' as a kind of invitation and as a warning, it would seem, though I'm not sure to whom. Perhaps to Sambo himself, who crouches on the cover, surrounded by four tigers grinning back at him. The physical blackness of the characters in the book (not to mention Little's middle name, Black) belies the defenders of Bannerman's original story who claim it somehow isn't racist because it is set in India – as if that country's history doesn't also include white racism and repression and colonisation. Instead, much as in King Kong – both the original film and the recent remakes – the vagueness of the 'natives,' their being ur-natives incorporating types spanning from Africa to the Far East, their perfect, imagined Orientalism, is proof itself.[3] What's more, as with the stereoscope, the reader's trip to Sambo's home (or for that matter Sambo's journey from home) is not external but internal. Such is the similarity between viewing and reading; the visual implies travelling, or projecting in a way made literal by Walker's recent projections incorporated as part of her cut-outs and installations. But reading transports us in a different way, one the pop-up book makes literal: the Sambo in question orders us every few pages to 'MOVE!' the illustrations. Walker's writings urge us to do some of the same things, moving the cut-outs slightly, metaphorically.

Here I am using the term pop-up loosely: technically, the Sambo volume is animated by the reader; nothing pops up at us so much as shimmies and moves on (or within) the page itself. But these 'animations' enact the kinds of mutations that early film animation – of Mickey Mouse, say – makes literal when it makes a body that is endlessly flexible, distortable, even wounded, only to be reconstituted, reconstructed, later. Sambo's body – if he can be said to have a body, as that's all he has, just hunger and instinct – is not as flexible, or free. Instead, it is constantly, negatively remarked upon. Instead, only the tigers get to morph and change, even if it's only into butter.

Sambo can't change at all, much less grow up. The fear of the adult black male results in his being a 'boy' no matter how old he is. Meanwhile, the 'lost girl' of Walker's work threatens us because she isn't a girl at all, or is a girl both violent and innocent. Walker's archetypal lost girl may be a lot of things, but unlike Sambo, she's not a victim. Such virtuosity, especially when confused with Walker's own, can be threatening in and of itself. The stakes for childlike virtuosity are high – think of Langston Hughes's '*Nobody loves a genius child.*/Kill him – and let his soul run wild!' – but what of the grown-up playing the child, or putting the child in harm's way, animated or not? As Hughes asks, 'Wild or tame,/Can you love a monster/Of frightening name?'[4]

Before he was turned into the silent puppet and cash cow he is today, Mickey Mouse was also as virtuosic, high-pitched, and violent as the lost girl in Walker's work. Voiced originally by Walt himself, Disney's invention was read many different ways. Certainly Mickey's look, white gloves and black body, reminds some of blackface minstrelsy; what's more, apparently Hitler banned Mickey quite explicitly because of his morphing, reading him as threatening in terms of blackness and Jewishness. The Nazi icon for degenerate music – a stereotypical black figure with a saxophone, a Gypsy earring, and a Jewish star on his chest – identifies just how slippery, how mixed, how miscegenated the Nazi view was of the black body. It embodies everything, especially everything 'degenerate'.

It's a short trip from the degenerate to the regenerating energy of early Mickey. But we need not look to animation to see how the body's reconstituting and radical dismemberment may be one way of getting to what Toni Morrison, in her novel *Beloved*, names 'rememory' – for the morphing black body is a familiar trope not just for racists but also for black artists. One might even say that the static blackness of Sambo's body, of the stereotype, and even of the stereograph with its illusion of movement is downright deadly. In this context, Walker's use of fluid artifice may make more sense. Let us take, for example, Bill Traylor, the self-taught artist and former slave who first began making art, as far as we know, in the 1930s, at a late age. His various figures, though not strictly silhouettes, evoke them with their use of dark, outlined forms – forms that move easily between a black body and the vegetable or mineral. In Traylor's capable hands, the figures look almost African in their willingness to depict not a self but a mask, not a body but an idealised, radical form. We may also think of Aaron Douglas, whose use of silhouette for uplift graced the covers of many of the books and publications of the Harlem Renaissance. The cover of Arna Bontemps' novel *God Sends Sunday* […] appears to have had a direct influence on the forms found in Walker's *Freedom: A Fable*, as noted by my colleague Randall Burkett.[5] If not a direct influence, then Douglas's detailed, dark figures, even those in colour on the cover of Bontemps' book, provide a useful context for Walker indeed, here the background colour seems to give us a sense of memory, both particular and racial, as a couple cakewalks in the horizon. It is easy to see the churning (and, given the images, topsy-turvy) nature of uplift at work in Douglas's art, and its equivalent as outrage in Walker's. […]

1   [Footnote 10 in source] Kara Walker, *Freedom: A Fable by Kara Elizabeth Walker – a Curious Interpretation of the Wit of a Negress in Troubled Times with Illustrations* (Santa Monica, CA: Norton Family Foundation, 1997).

2   [11] Helen Bannerman, *Little Black Sambo* (New York: Dunewald Printing Corporation, distributed by E.P. Dutton and Co., 1943), with pop-up animations by Julian Wehr.

3   [12] Snead's *White Screens/Black Images* contains a brilliant set of chapters on KK and its sequels *Son of Kong* (1933) and *Might Joe Youn* (1949). See 'Spectatorship and Capture in King Kong: The Guilty Look' and 'The *Kong* Sequels,' 1–36.

4   [13] Langston Hughes, 'Genius Child', in *The Collected Poems of Langston Hughes*, ed. Arnold Rampersad (New York: Knopf, 1994) 198.

5   [14] Thanks to RB, curator of AA collections at Emory University, for noticing this connection and for initially showing me the copy of *Freedom: A Fable* as part of the extensive holdings in AA collections at Emory.

Kevin Young, extracts from 'Triangular Trade: Coloring, Remarking, and Narrative in the Writings of Kara Walker', in *Kara Walker: My Complement, My Enemy, My Oppressor, My Love* (Minneapolis: Walker Art Center, 2007) 45–7.

Nayland Blake
Oral History: In Conversation with Alex Fialho//2016[1]

Alex Fialho […] [So] before we look a little bit forward, I do just want to bring up bunnies as this motif that we haven't touched on.[2]

Nayland Blake [Laughs] Sure.

Fialho Maybe *Negative Bunny* as a way in for that as a work or overall.[3]

Blake Yeah.

Fialho I feel like I can't talk to Nayland Blake for many hours and then not bring in that theme. [Laughs]

Blake So, the bunny thing got its start, in part, because in the late 80s, I was doing these performances and the performances were me reading these texts that I had edited together. And usually the texts were pop culture novels and kind of rants. I mean if I'm being honest, they were very, very influenced by Kathy Acker, in terms of the texts. And the reading was me in some sort of a costume, usually a prom dress, and I was asked to do one of these performances in Los Angeles around, maybe, 1992. And I felt like the whole boys in prom dress thing was pretty played out at that point, so I was trying to figure out what I could use as a costume for this and I was walking down a street in Los Angeles and passed by this sort of costume rental/magic shop. And there was a rabbit costume in the window and I thought, 'Oh, okay'. Well, this text is all collaged together from stuff about witchcraft and devil worship, and all about magic so I'll wear the rabbit costume and it'll be, you know, rabbit out of the hat with the magician.

So I got the costume and I did the performance, and then I started to think about, okay, what about rabbits? Why did that suddenly seem so resonate to me? And I started doing some drawings and started to think about, basically where I had – well, I just started to think about sort of the cultural identity of rabbits. I made this zine at the time called *Bunny Butt* and I started thinking, rabbits, what are they known for? They're known for shitting a lot and they're known for fucking a lot, and, you know, gay men are associated with having a lot of sex, with being promiscuous, fucking like bunnies, and the sex that they're having is anal sex so it's sort of related to shit. So I started doing these drawings and pieces where the rabbits were kind of a substitute or a stand in for gay men. And then I started asking myself the question of, okay, but where do I kind of remember rabbits from? And in some ways it was two places. It was watching Warner Brothers cartoons and watching Bugs Bunny, and my grandfather reading to me Uncle Wiggily stories and Br'er Rabbit stories.

And so I started, thinking about those stories and this is the grandfather on my dad's side. And thinking about the Br'er Rabbit stories, which are essentially very much associated with slavery. Uncle Remus is this slave character who's in dialect telling these stories to a supposed younger white kid. And also then remembering that – so I started doing some research into that and thinking about the way in which it turns out those stories, the Uncle Remus stories, are actually West African folk tales. So Joel Chandler Harris, who wrote them, actually was…they're characters that come to the US with slaves. And then I started thinking about Bugs Bunny and thinking about, on one hand, Bugs Bunny is this grey rabbit, he's sort of in between black and white. He's often appearing in drag so there's a way that his sexual expression is kind of fluid, but also he's often singing songs and the songs that he's singing are 'Camptown Races', and 'Dixie' and stuff – songs that are basically minstrel songs. And there's a way in those cartoons of the 1920s, 30s and 40s, there was still a holdover from vaudeville and minstrel performance that was in the American performance vernacular and crept into those cartoons.

And so I started making work that was about the relationship between racial ambiguity and racial fluidity and the rabbit as a sort of expression of that, of an expression of a sort of dual blackness and whiteness. And the most concrete expression of that was a project for the Baltimore Museum of Art that was another one of these installation projects where I had this rabbit suit. I picked objects from the museum's display that were black or white. I went around in the suit with this kind of kit on my back and did drawings of the various objects, and then took those drawings and made them into wax surrogates of […] those objects. And then put all of those into a shrine that I built in one of the galleries and in with the shrine is a selection of objects from the museum's collection that are – that were based on a keyword search for the word rabbit. So there's things in there like nineteenth-century hunting paintings and African Dogon rabbit masks and a whole collection of things. This installation was working off of two texts: the play and film *Harvey* and Ralph Ellison's *Invisible Man*. And there's a moment at the climax of *Invisible Man* where the protagonist is being interrogated and he's being asked who are you, who are you, and he finally says, 'I am Br'er Rabbit'. And *Harvey* is this play from, actually, roughly around the same time about a guy who has an invisible rabbit companion. And […] it is a play that in many ways is about closeted homosexuality.

So this is […] what we call a very complex text. So here's this shrine. It's got these surrogates, you know, of objects from the museum. It's got this curated section from the museum. I also wanted to have pictures, family photos in the shrine. So the two that I described […] in *Black Male* were initially in this installation and I had remembered that there was a photograph of me with a stuffed rabbit with my parents. And so I was going through the family photos to try find that. While I was doing that, I found this other photo of me from the year before where I'd been given a live rabbit for Easter. And I remember that what happened with that rabbit is that it ended up killing itself. My grandfather built this hutch for it and it managed to wedge its head into an area and sort of strangle itself. So that whole big arc is to say that the rabbit, the bunnies, have ended up meaning all of these different things, but I didn't […] access that sort of traumatic memory until I had done all of this research and tracked the rabbit through all of these other locales.

Fialho Which you did after you initially involved it in your work in the first place.

Blake Right, exactly. So that idea about having – making the thing and letting the thing then… and then interrogating what I've made as a way of understanding where my thought actually is in relationship to stuff is the sort of engine of my work. It's not having an idea and then expressing that idea. It is, you know, making something and then applying all of those tools of research and reflection to the thing that was made. To sort of suggest what I actually think about something.

Fialho And then do iterations from that?

Blake Yeah.

Fialho Develop and then it unfolds?

Blake Yeah, and then it – and then it keeps going in these different directions.[4] The other thing that was going on in that installation that became then kind of important to me was an attempt on my part to think about myself as a sculptor and what it might mean to engage with African modes of making, as opposed to strictly European. So those surrogates that I made were based on Bowli, these sculptures that are made in Mali, and the next show that I did at Matthew Marks in 1997 [Ed. note: *The Black/White Album*] was very much about trying to pull together all of these different ways of making objects based on various types of African sculpture. And there's a sort of […] neo-Beuysian shamanistic thing, but then there's also the notion of what if you make a sculpture where the power that it…it's about the power that it contains and how you access it rather than what it actually looks like, that the thing might not look like much, but that its importance might actually be contained within in it and where it's positioned. […]

1   This oral history transcript is the result of a recorded interview with Nayland Blake on 25 and 26 November, 2016. The interview took place at the home of Nayland Blake in New York City, NY and was conducted by the Archives of American Art, Smithsonian Institution. This interview is part of the Visual Arts and the AIDS Epidemic: An Oral History Project.

2   [Note 1 in source, ed. note, by Selby Nimrod] As we learn from a curatorial statement for *No Wrong Holes: Thirty Years of Nayland Blake*, 'Blake debuted the *Bunny Group*, a series of eighty drawings, in *The Black/White Album*, a 1997 exhibition that explicitly foregrounded Blake's biracial background (the exhibition also featured a suite of works inspired by African vernacular sculpture, including *Ibedji [Quick]*, also on view).' *No Wrong Holes: Thirty Years of Nayland Blake* was organised by the Institute of Contemporary Art, Los Angeles and was curated by Jamillah James, Curator. The List Center presentation was organised by Selby Nimrod, Assistant Curator, MIT List Visual Arts Center.

3   [2] *Negative Bunny*, video (colour, sound) TRT: 30 min. […] [Jamillah] James: '*Negative Bunny* addresses the entanglement of fear and intimacy at the height of the HIV/AIDS crisis in the United States. Blake voices a stuffed bunny who repeatedly asserts their HIV-negative status in the hopes of having sex with the viewer. Over the course of the video, the bunny's initially cute and humorous rhetoric shifts to evoke existential feelings of rejection and desperation, giving "negative" a different meaning. The bunny's inability to assure the viewer of their negative HIV status engages the anxiety and fear associated with the early years of the HIV/AIDS epidemic, whose stigma was bolstered by lack of public education and misinformation, homophobia and political inaction. In 1994, when Blake created this video, AIDS-related complications were the leading cause of death for Americans aged 24 to 44 years old. Although treatment and prevention of HIV/AIDS has since advanced dramatically, the video serves as a potent reminder of its impact on LGBTQ communities and communities of color.'

4   [3, ed. note by Selby Nimrod] *Starting Over* (2000), DVD video projection (colour, audio) TRT 23 mins. […] For their 2000 performance, *Starting Over*, Blake takes on the dual subjects of relationships and identity. Dressed in a 147-pound white bunny suit, filled with navy beans, Blake relentlessly attempts to tap-dance to a Michael Jackson soundtrack that plays in the background. Visibly agitated and uneasy from the heavy, restricting suit, Blake takes instruction from an off-camera voice, calling out various steps. The voice is that of their former partner, the late performer and choreographer Phillip Horvitz, whose weight is the physical point of reference of Blake's large bunny suit. Although we never see Horvitz, his presence plays an important role in Blake's performance. Straddling the line between cooperation and conflict, Blake's guided actions point to the 'give and take' nature of relationships and how this can influence or curtail one's autonomy.

Nayland Blake and Alex Fialho, extract from 'Oral history: Interview with Nayland Blake', transcript from Archives of American Art, Smithsonian Institution (25–26 November 2016).

"WHY WOULD ANYONE WANT A SHRINK-WRAPPED PIECE OF RAW DOUGH WITH A [HUMAN] TEAR?"

THE MACHINE AND THE COMMODITY

Hsuan L. Hsu
Mika Rottenberg's Productive Bodies//2010

[…] [Mika] Rottenberg's video installations feature bodies performing tasks that range from the extraordinary to the mundane: a woman painstakingly crossing a frozen lake balanced on her bare hands (*Julie*, 2003); a bored cashier tapping her fingernails on the counter of a kitschy Chinese take-out restaurant (*Time and a Half*, 2003); a contortionist bending over backward until her head is between her feet and then exploding in a puff of dust (*Fried Sweat*, 2008); and a bodybuilder grunting and dripping sweat onto a hotplate, each drop of sweat evaporating with a fizz (*Fried Sweat*). In other works, dancers, professional erotic wrestlers, and a group of women with fantastically long hair are put to work in inventive, surreal re-creations of the industrial assembly line. Critics often underscore the motifs of labour and manufacture in Rottenberg's videos, invoking Taylorism, the 'sweatshop', 'a blue-collar work ethic', and 'the sense of claustrophobia induced by a dead-end job'.[1] 'In this world's often vertical, assembly-line-like compartments,' writes Smith, 'women are enslaved and enshrined, serviced and exploited.'[2]

Yet the specific relations between Rottenberg's assembly lines and the dynamics of industrial production remain unclear. Do her factory settings function as critical parodies that condemn the exploitation of workers' bodies or as utopian simulacra of factories in which alternative modes of labour are imagined and staged? Do they critique capitalism's constraints on the body, or do they allegorise – in the spirit of Matthew Barney's *Drawing Restraint* (1987–) studio experiments – the labours involved in artistic creation? While critics have commented extensively on the themes of manual labour and industrial exploitation in Rottenberg's corpus, they stop short of the most puzzling aspects of her simulacral assembly lines, which have to do with their striking differences from actual situations of industrial production.

What is being produced in these scenes of repetitive labour? In *Time and a Half*, the continual tapping of fingernails, juxtaposed with the title's reference to overtime pay and fair labour laws, foregrounds a labour process divested from any material product. Similarly, the bodybuilders featured in Rottenberg's videos maintain only the simulacrum of a working-class body: less the body of a worker than a body that is worked *on*. Although many of the artist's factory scenarios do yield manufactured products – scented towelettes, maraschino cherries, globs of dough, a block of cheese – even these products seem defamiliarised, distanced from both utility and capitalist circuits of exchange. As one reviewer puts it, commenting on the end result of one of Rottenberg's assembly lines, 'Why would anyone want a shrink-wrapped piece of raw dough with a [human] tear?'[3]

These invocations of industrial manufacture seem anachronistic given that the Western cities in which Rottenberg's works are most often exhibited have been characterised by deindustrialisation and a concomitant increase in 'immaterial labour'. What do the bodies and by-products that appear in the artist's videos and installations have to do with the post-Fordist decline of industrial manufacture and the emergence of new strategies for deriving profit from human bodies? The historical context of Rottenberg's assembly lines suggests that they function as metaphors rather than literal objects of critique or representation. This essay considers how her works dramatise the increasing capitalisation of biological life itself: not what labourers produce but what bodies consist of, grow, secrete and reproduce. Drawing on Michael Hardt and Antonio Negri's analysis of post-Fordist 'empire' as 'a situation in which what is directly at stake in power is the production and reproduction of life itself', I examine the roles of industrial labour, bodily by-products, race and geography in Rottenberg's stagings of gendered industrial production.[4] Rottenberg's works, I argue, do not critique industrial labour so much as they evoke the dissonance between industrial assembly lines and emergent forms of affective, immaterial or biological production. By exploring relations between immaterial goods and manufactured products, Rottenberg exposes divisions of race, gender, and geography that complicate efforts to forge transnational alliances against capitalist exploitation.

Body Machines

Rottenberg's factory scenarios begin with two video installations completed while she was in art school. *Mary's Cherries*, the artist's first direct treatment of industrial manufacture, is set in a vertical arrangement of three rooms in which muscular women (played by professional wrestlers) collaborate to produce replicas of maraschino cherries while seated on stationary bicycles. The woman in the top room – whose name tag indicates that her name is Mary – clips one of her long, painted fingernails and passes it down to the middle room, where a woman named Barbara smashes and pulverises it by hand. She then passes it down to the bottom room, where a third worker named Rock Rose carefully rolls the fragments into a cherry. This process – an elegant dramatisation of Karl Marx's observation that, in the industrial production line, 'the result of the labour of the one is the starting-point for the labour of the other' – is repeated over and over again, because a lightbulb powered by the stationary bicycles accelerates the growth of Mary's nails.[5] Eventually, the workers are fed with burgers that appear on a conveyor belt, also powered by their stationary bikes.

If *Mary's Cherries* presents the image of a total production line in which even eating and exercise are accommodated by the architecture of the workstation, *Tropical Breeze* (2004) introduces the element of racial difference. The video depicts two labouring bodies: a white woman on a stationary bike and a muscular, profusely sweating black woman seated behind the steering wheel of a truck. The first woman – played by a dancer named Felicia – picks up squares of fabric with her foot, dabs them with some chewing gum from her mouth, and passes them to the other woman by means of a mechanical pulley; the second woman – played by a professional bodybuilder – then wipes a drop of her sweat onto each towelette and hands it back to her co-worker, who packages the products into boxes of lemon-scented towelettes labelled 'Tropical Breeze'. The women fuel their own bodies by ingesting Stay Awake pills and an energy drink labelled 'Lemon Rush' which is also the source of the towelettes' lemon scent. As in *Mary's Cherries*, the women's consumption – from energy drinks to chewing gum – is incorporated into the machinery of production. Both videos were exhibited in installations whose size and shape approximated the factory spaces depicted on-screen, suggesting a continuity between the gallery space and the constrained spaces of manual labour. Yet the self-sustaining nature of these assembly lines, their simulacral products, and their enclosed spaces (both on-screen and of the installations) also resonate with what Yvonne Spielmann has called the 'reflexive' and 'nonrepresentative' nature of video art. Video, Spielmann explains, is unique in being an audiovisual medium whose 'signal can emerge from the circulation of electric impulses in the devices and requires no external input'.[6] At the same time that she presents claustrophobic images of women at work, Rottenberg's playful replicas remind us that video (in contrast with film) does not represent 'real' objects and processes so much as it presents continual electric signals.

Asked about the factory scenario of *Dough* (2005–6) – an installation purchased by the Guggenheim Museum – Rottenberg commented, 'I suppose it really was based, somewhat literally, on Marx's theory of labour and value, but as more of a joke about surplus and product.'[7] Rottenberg is referring to Marx's labour theory of value and implying that the slow, repetitive nature of the tasks she depicts dramatises the link that Marx establishes between labour time and surplus value. Her depictions of bodies enclosed in factory spaces also resonate with Marx's account of how the transition from handicraft to cooperative manufacture (characterised by an increasingly specialised division of labour) saps the vitality and individuality of workers. Manufacture, he writes,

> converts the worker into a crippled monstrosity by furthering his particular
> skill as in a forcing-house, through the suppression of a whole world of

productive drives and inclinations, just as in the states of La Plata they butcher a whole beast for the sake of his hide or his tallow. Not only is the specialized work distributed among the different individuals, but the individual himself is divided up, and transformed into the automatic motor of a detail operation, thus realizing the absurd fable of Menenius Agrippa, which presents man as a mere fragment of his own body.[8]

Even as it dramatically increases industrial productivity, the fragmentation of the labour process enervates the worker's intellect and reshapes her body in accordance with the requirements of the assembly line. Yet even under these exploitative conditions, the relation between capital and the body is filled with contradictions. As David Harvey notes in 'The Body as an Accumulation Strategy', 'Capital continuously strives to shape bodies to its own requirements, while at the same time internalizing within its *modus operandi* effects of shifting and endlessly open bodily desires, wants, needs, and social relations [...] on the part of the laborer.'[9] If industrial production attempts to shape labourers into fragmentary, mechanical bodies, it also thrives on their 'creative passions, spontaneous responses, and animal spirits'.

This contradictory relation between capital and the labourer's body helps account for the divergent responses that Rottenberg's representations of labour have elicited. For example, critics have described the quirky, absurd process of producing vacuum-sealed globs of dough in *Dough* as both a dignified, intimate vision of empowered women's bodies and a critical exposé of the collusion between video technologies and Taylorist factory surveillance. The video installation depicts three physically distinctive women (one weighs six hundred pounds, and another is seven feet tall and unusually thin) harnessing flower pollens, allergy-induced tears, energy from stationary bicycles, and air from a bellows to shape a viscous raw material into packages of dough. Although she acknowledges that 'their toil is yoked by industry', Chen Tamir argues that the three women in *Dough* 'are not your average assembly-line housemaids: they are freakish and empowered. Their strength and individuality defy objectification by the camera's gaze'.[10] The video provides plenty of evidence to support Tamir's assessment: the small-scale, intimate, and intricately choreographed nature of the cooperative production process shared by the three women, as well as nearly erotic interest in the women's hands, faces, and lips that appears to motivate the video's close-ups, alter the usual, objectifying dynamics of the gaze.

Claire Barliant, conversely, suggests that Rottenberg intentionally draws a parallel between the viewer's spectatorship and industrial surveillance: 'Are we being put in the position of managers scrutinizing them for lapses in attention?'[11]

In this reading, the camera's erotic interest could be viewed as invasive and abusively intertwined with the managerial gaze; the video's close-ups could index the claustrophobically small 'factory' space in which these unusually large women are enclosed; their unusual physical features – obesity as well as thinness – could be read in terms of class, not 'freakish' fascination; and the inclusion of two dark-skinned workers – like the prominent role played by the sweating driver in *Tropical Breeze* – could be taken as a reminder of the disproportionate exploitation and vulnerability of women of colour in factory work, particularly under contemporary conditions of globalised maquiladora production. The very medium of video art is implicated in the industrial process, not only because it employs technologies produced in factories but also because its temporality – the endless playback loop, the suggestion that the activity depicted is contemporaneous and ongoing – captures the repetitious nature of sweatshop labour.

Yet far from being diametrically opposed, these readings together highlight the contradictory demands of industrial manufacture as detailed by Marx: it requires the vitality, passions, and idiosyncrasies of labourers at the same time that these are suppressed by impulses to lower wages, maximise efficiency, and intensify the division of labour. The ambiguities of Rottenberg's scenarios, which register as both satirical critiques of capitalism and utopian attempts to imagine intimate and collaborative systems of production, reflect the extent to which the capitalist assembly line itself requires, exploits, and controls utopian aspects of production such as cooperation, creativity, and the individuality of workers. Rottenberg's simulacral factories both express this contradiction and [...] move beyond it by significantly departing from the material conditions of industrial production. Her works cannot be understood in terms of the assembly line alone because they are concerned with bodies and tasks that reference not only industrial capital but also the post-Fordist predicaments of our own era. [...]

1   [Footnote 3 in source] Barliant, 'Mika Rottenberg', *Artforum* (April 2006) 247. Available at www.artforum.com/print/reviews/200604/mika-rottenberg-43685; Chen Tamir, 'Mika Rottenberg: "Dough"', *C Magazine* (Summer 2006) 42; Trinie Dalton, 'Mika Rottenberg: About the Artist', Whitney Museum of American Art (2008) (whitney.org/www/2008biennial/www/?section=artists&page=artist_rottenberg).

2   [4] Roberta Smith, 'Mika Rottenberg', *New York Times* (17 February 2006).

3   [5] Tamir, op. cit., 43.

4   [6] Michael Hardt and Antonio Negri, *Empire* (Cambridge, MA: Harvard University Press, 2001) 24.

5   [7] Karl Marx, *Capital, Vol. 1*, trans. Ben Fowkes (New York: Vintage, 1977) 464.

6   [8] Yvonne Spielmann, *Video: The Reflexive Medium* (Cambridge, MA: MIT Press, 2008) 32.

7   [9] Ossian Ward, 'The Body Factory: Mika Rottenberg in Conversation with Ossian Ward', *db artmag* (October– November 2006) (www.db-artmag.de/2006/6/e/1/482.php).

8   [10] Marx, op. cit., 481–2.

9   [11] David Harvey, 'The Body as an Accumulation Strategy', in *Spaces of Hope* (Berkeley: University of California Press, 2000) 115.

10   [12] Tamir, op. cit., 42.

11   [13] Barliant, op. cit., 247. Video artists such as Bruce Nauman (*Performance Corridor*,1968–70), Peter Campus (*Interface*, 1972), Dieter Froese (*Not a Model for Big Brother's Spy Cycle*, 1985), and Julia Scher (*Security by Julia*, 1988–) have long engaged with the intersections between video technology and different forms of visual surveillance. For a discussion of video artists' treatments of surveillance, see Michael Rush, *Video Art* (London: Thames and Hudson, 2007) 27–38.

Hsuan L. Hsu, extract from 'Mika Rottenberg's Productive Bodies', *Camera Obscura*, vol. 25, no. 2 (74) (September 2010) 41–8.

Mika Rottenberg
In Conversation with Julia Bryan-Wilson//2019

Julia Bryan-Wilson The sound in your new video, *Spaghetti Blockchain* (2019), consists of two main frequencies. A group of women perform traditional Tuvan throat singing, vocalising in a guttural chord that echoes across the Siberian landscape; that sound chimes with the hum of a server in a large antimatter factory. How does this pairing work for you conceptually?

Mika Rottenberg The main connection, as you point out, was through sound. I was really interested in the way Tuvan throat singing is designed to travel great distances through space, as far as possible, riding forces of nature and physics and generating soundwaves through the vast landscape. It really helps to visualise the sound as wave, as thing-energy. I also really liked how Tuvan throat singing extends the singer's physical space and at the same time very clearly marks her position. It connects back to something I've been obsessed with in all my work: the visualisation of one's actions and their cause and effect, or where the self ends and the world begins – if this separation has to exist.

I was thinking about technology, the internet, and this energy travelling through fibre optic cables laid across the planet. I thought it would be interesting to work with that too. Plus, the frequencies of the singing and the servers are almost the same; the sound reminds me of an analogue dial tone. I liked how one very bodily sound, from the bottom of your belly, and the other, the sound of technology – mainly the sound of the fans cooling the servers – connected so well together, and how they connect to this other 'body of sounds' I produced in the studio.

Bryan-Wilson Both the throat singing and the server resonate in the body to create similar somatic feelings. There is a third component to the soundtrack as well: ASMR sounds, such as the sounds of melting, sizzling and slapping. These sounds trigger ASMR tingles, an uncontrollable response that can be pleasurable. For you, what brings these things together?

Rottenberg I've been watching these 'most satisfying' video complications on YouTube for hours – in general, YouTube is a big influence for me – these videos are all about matter and materiality and manipulating materials: cutting, melting, sorting, crushing... . Yet the device they are meant for, the screen, is not at all tactile. It confuses your expectations of touch; you virtually touch so many 'things' but everything feels the same, like cold glass. The videos are somehow meant to compensate, using so many materials in various textures and bright colours to trigger your body to physically react. These videos had so much of what I was trying to do in my work and how I film materials and textures and record and manipulate sounds, that I really wanted to create my own ASMR factory...

And then there are the other two locations: CERN, the world's largest particle physics laboratory, on the border of Switzerland, France, and Italy, and a potato farm in Maine that uses the latest picking technologies. Actually, the ASMR 'factory' I created in the studio was inspired by my visit to CERN and this piece is inspired by particle physics – although I don't really understand much about it. I hope all these locations create interesting feedback; so many visual similarities accrue while filming.

Bryan-Wilson Some of the images in *Spaghetti Blockchain* are stimulating and deceptively disturbing. What looks like blood congealing or boiling plastic, which seems toxic, turns out be edible, like cotton candy or Jell-O; there's a friction between danger, risk and delight. The video also progresses via a logic of formal similarities, as when footage of a hand scoring parallel lines into clay jumps to the parallel lines of plowing potato plants. The spatial logic of congruency appears when a hexagram connects things together.

Rottenberg Right, it was a nice surprise when so many visual similarities accrued! The elements connected for me conceptually in thinking about humans' relationships with matter and about matter having agency and intelligence – nothing is actually inanimate. The video's logic is based on a hexagon; there are six main elements that play off each other, but I never expected so many visual parallels. When the Tuvan singer Choduraa's dress matched the colour of the Large Hadron Collider and the melting cotton candy, that was a great surprise. As you point out, there are many moments like that, when visual similarities take you from one place to another.

Another visual narrative is the move from small to large: you're looking at something tiny or in extreme close-up and then the video cuts to something gigantic. I wanted viewers to respond physically, so this expansion and contraction of space will also happen in viewers' bodies, kind of like ASMR triggers. I tried to play with two cinematic logics, one more linear logic of special connections and synthetic continuity, making disconnected locations appear linked, and then the other is more of a structuralist film logic, where the cut from A to B creates new meaning. […]

Bryan-Wilson So much of your work is about proximity and intimacy, when what seems distant is suddenly living with you or is on your skin. One phrase that's been used to talk about your work is 'social surrealism'. To me, that describes the condition of capitalism: how did this thing from halfway around the world get into my mouth? It is extremely surreal.

Rottenberg Yes, but it's also very real. This collapse of geography is something we experience more and more with technology. Your voice is able to travel across the world with a click of a finger. I'm also interested in blockchain as a kind of organic system with no centre and no hierarchy, governed by its own perpetual movement and growth.

Bryan-Wilson One irreverent moment occurs when you're literalising this blockchain made of spaghetti and baby marshmallows that are then singed and crushed. It's a comic, almost slapstick element.

Rottenberg I find it really satisfying as slapstick, but also the crushing of the dry spaghetti sounds so nice and scary, like crushing bones or the sound potato chips make when you chew – I actually heard that they make potato chips sound like bones being crushed to trigger this satisfying physical response in the consumer, so we're back to ASMR…. There's a friction, as you mentioned, in something that is both satisfying and menacing, like the cutting of the Jell-O: there are these beautiful, feminine hands, like those of a perfect host serving a cake, holding a giant knife and cutting this long, tube-shaped object. It's violent but also inviting and seductive.

Bryan-Wilson Right. It's a highly schematised roll cake that does not look appetising because the colours are so artificial. Your use of colour is always striking – it is really saturated, dense, even unnerving. The colours resemble nursery colours, like children's blocks or candy, yet they're so bright and flat that they read as chemical to me. How does colour structure your work?

Rottenberg It relates to the tension between seduction and repulsion or danger, which is the dynamic of capitalism, too. It makes you want things so badly. I also use colour to compensate for the lack of physical interaction. Watching an art video is a screen experience and not a tactile experience, so the overuse of colour compensates for the lack of touch.

Bryan-Wilson Your use of sound is so vivid that it becomes tactile, especially the way that viewers feel the throat singing in their bones. Sound turns to touch... . Some of your previous video works have been installations in which you have choreographed or sculpted the viewing experience. Is *Spaghetti Blockchain* also an environment?

Rottenberg Yes, you go into a corridor where ceiling fans are in slits on the sides, repeating the circular server ventilation system. The sound of the video travels through the corridor.

Bryan-Wilson *Cosmic Generator* also had an extensive viewing apparatus when it was shown at Skulptur Projekte Münster. Your work toggles between shininess – a sort of preternatural Teletubbies shininess – and dustiness or antiquatedness. These different surfaces register as different yet always overlapping temporalities of capitalism; one is perpetually renewing itself in a plasticky way and another has hinges, manual levers, and creaking mechanisms.

Rottenberg It's like the shield or the skin as opposed to how things actually work inside the machine or the body – the guts and the messier parts.

Bryan-Wilson [...] Do you do research on materials, such as experiments with what melts best or how things slice?

Rottenberg When I researched ASMR videos, I really got into it. As a video maker, I found it really challenging to compete with these compilations with millions of views, sometimes made by kids or teenagers... . I want to see if I can make my own channel... .

Bryan-Wilson I have wasted many, many hours watching ASMR videos. There's this one where someone's squeezing an orange plastic purse. That is all that happens, but it's mesmerising and you crave it like a drug.

Rottenberg I thought, 'Oh, it will be easy to come up with a million videos'. It wasn't so easy. People that make ASMR videos for YouTube are professionals. They try many kinds of slime until they get the right one, and the aesthetics of the filming and sets are really thought out. I was so interested in the slime and in all the different textured materials with no purpose beyond triggering a fake tactile feeling in the viewer – it's so artificial, and I find artificiality so interesting.

This book called *New Materialisms* (2010) – the editors, Diana Coole and Samantha Frost, have also contributed to this exhibition catalogue – was an 'Aha!' moment for me in terms of thinking about matter and materialism in relationship to my work, and how it connects to Marx and materialism under capitalism. If Marx talks about 'dead labour' and an energy or vitality that's trapped in everything, *New Materialisms* is about the material itself having agency. This is not a new idea; it's basically animism.

I was talking to Samantha Frost about plastic, saying it seems like a sad, hijacked material. And she said that's actually true because plastic is made from oil products, so it's decomposing organic matter that can't go back to the earth to continue decomposing – it's trapped! In a sense, it is hijacked.

Bryan-Wilson One of the criticisms of new materialism is that some versions of it can be very masculine and white, which brings me to another observation about your work: some of it, interestingly, draws parallels between seemingly unlike spaces, such as China and Mexico, that do not travel through and are not triangulated in terms of a Euro-American 'centre'.

Rottenberg It's funny, because I think of new materialism as being so feminist; all the books I've seen are written by women.

Bryan-Wilson There are many versions and schools of thought within new materialism and one of them is object-oriented ontology, which is dominated by white male philosophers. But the version that I find most interesting is indebted to indigenous epistemologies and other worldviews that have long posited that something like a rock might be alive.

Rottenberg For me, working remotely with the throat singers in Tuva was interesting because they practice a kind of singing that stretches one's voice through nature. In a way, it is like the internet, which also expands how far one's 'voice' can travel. This kind of singing, Khoomei, is also so fascinating because of the super high and super low frequencies that the body learns to perform simultaneously.

Bryan-Wilson You've created a totally different origin point for the internet. That's why the moment in the video when the servers are suddenly in the yurt makes perfect sense. In *Squeeze* (2010), you juxtapose a latex forest in India and lettuce farming by migrant workers in Arizona. In the past, people would have called this a Third World alliance, and your work suggests connections in which the Global North is not the main organising principle.

Rottenberg Yes, maybe it's decentralised, which links back to the blockchain idea…

Bryan-Wilson An astonishing sequence in *Spaghetti Blockchain* involves an aerial view of farmland being ploughed. A machine rakes over the land and deposits perfectly picked potatoes. How many people did that one machine replace?

Rottenberg A lot, but then there are all the people who have to fix it, because half of the time it doesn't run smoothly.

Bryan-Wilson Was it was hard to get access to film the Large Hadron Collider, which is the largest machine in the world?

Rottenberg Access to CERN was relatively easy; they have a great art programme. But there was no interest from potato farmers. Funnily, 'Spud-nick' is the name of the machine. I contacted the company, but heard nothing. Then a friend of mine, the artist Jacqueline Goss, said, 'My cousin in Maine works at a potato farm'. So I had an in, but it was hard to actually get access. It's just the difficult business of farming. They've invested millions in these machines and the crop is in season and they don't have time.

Bryan-Wilson What would you have been if you hadn't been an artist?

Rottenberg Particle scientist. As if I could do that!

Bryan-Wilson Do you have that kind of mind?

Rottenberg No, but at CERN, I thought, 'These people, the physicists that lead the experiments, are like artists. It's not applied physics, so it's all pure experiments and observations…looking at stuff. There's no direct use value; it's pure experimenting and observing.

Bryan-Wilson Right, it's theoretical. Regarding your sculpture and its status in your practice, are there different thoughts that go into and then get resolved in sculpture in contrast to the videos?

Rottenberg I work on the videos for a year or two and they contain many, many sculptures. I think of the sculptures in a kinetic, chance-driven way, working with forces like gravity and heat. Also, they're very cinematic, and the cinematic is sculptural.

Bryan-Wilson What was your relationship to popular culture and television when you were growing up? The televisual feel of your videos is very sophisticated, with a distinctive aesthetic, in part because it is kind of retrograde, like you're entering a 1970s TV show.

Rottenberg I never thought about it, but growing up in Israel there was only one channel. It was the national public channel, and there were no commercials, perhaps because at the time Israel was a little more socialist. Instead of commercials, there were milk ads from the Association of Milk, for example. There was only one milk producer in the country, so it was a commercial for milk, not a brand or a company.

Then from five to seven there was Arabic TV, and on Fridays there were always movies from Egypt. Because TV in Israel was government-run at the time, it was trying to create a picture of this ideal country. I do think about those commercials. There's something Eastern European about the aesthetic, and something of the culture of the kibbutz. When I was working on *Tropical Breeze* (2004), I was really interested in Soviet product design, which relates to the products and commercials I grew up with.

Bryan-Wilson You get asked a lot about your use of people with unconventional bodies as the talent in your pieces. They are often people who make money or are valued for how they look or what their bodies do. I am interested in how you build trust with them, especially because sometimes you meet them online and then they introduce you to others from their world.

Rottenberg It's something that's changing in my work. In the older work, it was very much a business transaction and framed as a discussion of empowerment and ownership of one's body. With *Spaghetti Blockchain*, I worked with

Choduraa Tumat, the singer from Tuva, and the members of her group, Tyva Kyzy [Daughters of Tuva], trying to explain to her what the piece is about, and her questions were difficult to answer. She said that she didn't understand the connection between the Large Hadron Collider, the potato farm, and Tuvan singing. It was the first time I really had to articulate these connections in writing. This is usually the case; the first time I have to explain myself and the work is to the performers over email, and that helps me progress with the work as well as build trust.

It was a little different when I was filming the pearl sorting factory in China. The boss agreed to the filming but I didn't know if the workers all did. I used a translator to tell them a bit about it and to say that if anyone didn't want to be filmed, they wouldn't be. It's possible that their boss said that they had to be filmed, although I had no reason to think that; it is more likely that they simply didn't ask. An ethical question comes up for me in situations like these, but in this case, I decided to do it. I don't take for granted that it's okay. Maybe it's for viewers to judge.

I do think there's power in visibility and that there's something beautiful in the way the workers sort the pearls, their skill and speed. At the same time, I see the women as confined by their work, with their bodies treated as machines. I really wanted to pay respect to the work they do by filming it with the best cinematic tools, showing the beauty and cruelty of it all. I was exploiting them too, in a way, to generate my own cultural capital, though I do think I ultimately gave the participants agency.

Bryan-Wilson It seems like the whole work is trying to theorise the complexities of that exchange.

Rottenberg Yes, in part. In *Cosmic Generator*, I asked the women in the stores directly, so it wasn't up to their boss. I gave them a couple days' notice so they could prepare and dress up, and they were clearly excited. There is certainly a difference between their lives and my life, but looking at my daughter's room with all these plastic items, and thinking about how they are used or whether they end up in piles of trash, I see a connection to my life. Maybe the work is about the complexity of the situation.

Mika Rottenberg and Julia Bryan-Wilson, extracts from In Conversation, from *Mika Rottenberg, Easypieces*, ed. Margot Norton (New York: New Museum, 2019) 21–30.

John Roberts
Dean Kenning's Kinetics//2019

Kinetic art and animatronic sculpture have until recently been mostly condescended to in critical art theory. This may have something to do with the fetishised opposition between technological 'failure' and captivation by technical adroitness that machines in art tend to succumb to, in a kind of binary embrace. The first position invariably identifies machine-technology with an attack on technological progress; the second position with the fluent insertion of art into machine-technology as an extension of art's post-aesthetic use-values – art needs to remind itself that its relationship to the new lives in the same world as technology. The first position under-identifies with technology (mostly through irony and hyperbaton), the second position, over-identifies with technology, in the hope of art exiting from modernist negation into a newly positivistic world of art and science. Despite, the pitfalls of both positions (the crowd pleasing and quirky, and the sleek and imposing), it is the first position that continues to have the greater scope for critical inventiveness. Building or utilising machines that 'don't work' or 'work badly' – resulting in outcomes that are adventitious or strangely hybrid – allows some light into the understanding of technology as an ensemble of social relations. Building machines that 'do work', not only obviously bypasses this, but attaches the rationalisation of art's outcomes to the belief that art might have a part to play in reordering or humanising technological reason and progress. This is why the dream of such machine-builders is to move out of art all together, in the way computer programmers, technicians and engineers have left their specialist scientific domains to find a common home in the games industry and techno-sphere generally. Both positions are involved in 'world-building' in this sense, but these two worlds are very much chalk and cheese: the latter sees machines and technological knowledge in art as part of 'cultural production', the former wants nothing to do with this, and sees old and abandoned technologies and old machines as a space for reflection on what technology carries along with it, like a virus: imminent death, violence and the loss of reason.

In this sense, this salvaging is not strictly anti-technology, but anti-historicist, and functions precisely as a ghost-practice in which old technologies form a revenant landscape of lost or diminished use-values. This approach subjects old technologies less to a sense of an 'ending', than to a deflationary re-imagining on the basis that technology never truly arrives at its destination: the rational distribution and organisation of human needs. This is why much of this work, with its refunctioning of redundant machinery and parts, taps into DIY, eco-conservationist mode. This refunctioning of old machines, or the making of new machines from old parts and components, allows the artist to open out the possible part that art (as non-instrumental technique) might play in a new mode of production; a mode of creative non-growth.

But, if the deflationary logic of these DIY ghost-practices appeals to 'failure' as the subfusc truth of technological progress, this sense of loss also enables the artist to draw significantly on another sense of loss, the relationship between technology and (surplus) jouissance: that is, the notion of technology – in its deathly passing – as a dead realm of desire, or more generously, trapped desires unable to attach themselves to new drives. It is precisely this sense of ghostliness that Dean Kenning has been concerned with in his own kinetic refunctioning of old machines and machine parts. His investment in 'moving art' more broadly is less the result of idiosyncratic eco-tinkering, than a re-assimilation of machines as things that were once drivers of surplus-jouissance and, as such, things that had not just a functional, but an imaginary, hold over lives. This is strikingly evident in his large kinetic 'musicological' installation *The Origin of Life* (2019, shown at Beaconsfield, London, March–April 2019). A number of motion sensors placed inconspicuously around the gallery floor triggered one or two thick, white, silicon rubber 'fingers', to play twenty-one small electronic keyboards (including one analogue synthesiser) from the 1970s, 80s and 90s (Bontempi, Korg, Casio and Yamaha), repeatedly striking the same notes in a kind of manic persistence. Moving quickly around the work, navigating various routes, you could trigger all the 'fingers' simultaneously creating a cacophonous overlapping of clusters of repeated notes. When the cacophony dissipated, invariably there would be one or two 'fingers' that would have switched off in the act of depressing a key and so certain notes persisted longer than the rest, as if they were urging the other keyboards to continue. Indeed, this forlornness is what remained most distinctive about the installation, particularly when the sound of one keyboard faded to be replaced by another and then another, in a kind of desperate and diminishing chorus of sonic assertion. The human-aided discontinuity or broken temporality of the sound, consequently, produced a distinctive user-work relationship. Rather than 'turning on' a pre-set system, the triggering of the sensors produced a strange intersubjective relationship with the 'fingers', as if the visitor was less the audience, than the 'other' of the 'fingers' desire. It felt as if you were giving life to the 'fingers' in order that they could persist in their slightly demented need to make a noise at all costs, before blackness and silence descended again. This is why the forlornness of the solitary 'fingers' banging away for all they were worth, felt like a kind of pleading from inside the death-drive of technology, as if the 'fingers' were the last bodily remnants of a jouissance barely recognisable as jouissance, given that desire in this fragmented state was now embodied in the non-human and thus unable truly, fully to attach itself to its own autonomous drives.

This interface between the non-human and human gives the kinetic dynamic of *The Origin of Life* its peculiar force and wild, anxious 'subjectivity'; machine and rote, mechanised desire are brought to repetitive, frustrated, splenetic life by the unconscious sadism of the visitor ('play, play, play'; 'entertain me'); and, as such, what appears to be given life 'intersubjectively', is in the end, sustained by non-reciprocity. The visitor brings the 'fingers' to life, but only, as a repetitive exercise. This is why the imputed musicological content of the piece is perhaps misleading; even if the structure of the work owes a formal debt to a post-Cageian, aleatoric aesthetics, the 'aesthetic' outcome of the sound patterns is incidental to the staging and impact of the 'fingers' ghostly jouissance. Indeed, the 'fingers' announce their fading desire not just as the amnesiacal and broken recovery of lost musical horizons and pleasures (of good times, spent in the presence of ecstatic 'repetitive beats'; of clubs now closed and deserted), but as a kind of self-brutalising libidinal entrapment; that is, the frenetic and repetitive outbursts appear to 'reason desire' back into the 'same', rather than give up the desire of desire for one moment. And this of course is where the disenchantment, repetition and pain of jouissance under capitalism intersect, at their most intense, with the utopian; or at least its dulled memory.

This relationship between the uncanny and unexpected life in the inhuman human-like body-fragment is well known. Getting robot-like machines or machine parts to perform human-like actions, is denaturalising in precisely this uncanny way; and Kenning's keyboards as broken 'desiring-machines' do this beautifully: the pleading, 'forgetful' repetition of the sounds appears unbearably close to a call for love, insofar as the mechanical 'fingers' mimicry of (barely functioning) human drives demands from the respondent an immediate, affective response. Indeed, the response to this call is the basis of the work's uncanny technological-sadistic relation: 'I'm still lovable, look what I can do'. 'Talk to me' says the talking doll. 'Play me, play me, I haven't forgotten,' say Kenning's keyboards. Getting Kenning's 'fingers' to move then is 'irresistible' to the visitor, precisely because the stomping of feet gets us to take a pleasure from the hubristic overcoming of the past, at the same time as the 'fingers' ask us to listen to the fragile but persistent 'voices' released by the superseded technologies. And this is why ghost-kinetics and the charms of physical, machinic animation in art remains such an uneasy, even queasy, affective experience; the broken DIY machine wants you to be its friend, so to speak – to get you to see through the technological sadism of the 'new' – even when, as in the case of Kenning's sad, floppy 'fingers', all you want to do is punish it for its sickly pleading presumptuousness and run a mile from its demand for love.

We also see this intersection between fascination, revulsion and violence in Kenning's *Untitled (Rubber Plant)* (2019) which is very different in formal structure and animating logic than the *The Origin of Life*. Nevertheless the pair of slightly malign, sparring rubber plant-figures, requires the spectator to find a point of understanding with them as believable sentient-like presences, as they angrily feint and dodge, as opposed to seeing it coldly as a kind of clunky fairground attraction, worked by hidden hands. If *The Origin of Life* stages the fading of jouissance as a kind of melancholic non-human remnant, imposing the sadism of surplus-jouissance (embodied in new technology) over the deathly passing of old technologies and desires, here desire takes a sentient non-human form that challenges the very boundaries of human desire as such. Here new life as a human-created 'second nature' – synthetic Life 2.0 – comes out fighting: two synthetic plants, square up to each other or dirty dance for territory and perhaps for sexual dominance, like Victor Hugo's fantasy of 'murderous plants in subterranean combat'. Whatever the slightly quixotic nature of this image, the overriding effect is deeply unappealing and threatening. In this respect, this is not just a commonplace image of vegetable 'second nature' gone rogue or 'super-smart', familiar from the outer-reaches of popular science and contemporary science fiction film. Rather, as in *The Origin of Life*, Kenning uses machinic animation to bring desire and science into alignment with freedom and non-reciprocity.

One of the key axioms of current ecological thinking is 'solidarity' with the non-human, on the basis that the human and non-human coexist, indeed are indivisible. But what if the sentient non-human is indifferent, even antagonistic, to this solidarity? In a future world of thinking and self-organising plants and self-organising life-forms, non-reciprocity will be a matter of life and death with non-human desire and the threat of sadism. And perhaps, this is the key to Kenning's underlying attraction to kinetics: it not only allows the artist to create revenant and heteroclite desires from dead technological remnants, allowing us a relationship with machines that provides us a little breathing space from the death-drive of technology, but also enables him to produce strange, fictive, living, aggressive forms, that sharpen the limits of our understanding of reciprocity and human solidarity with the immanent violence of the human-indifferent human-created non-human. On this basis, Kenning's kinetics are not, exactly, dystopian; the denaturalisation of nature here is not a mourning for a lost 'first nature' or 'human values', but a recognition that the creative biogenetic refunctioning of nature does not mean that solidarity with the non-human will be a violence-free process. Post-anthropocentric humans, as a condition of their freedom and therefore their exit from necessity will be forced to release themselves from the solidarity with this new nature – to kill what plans to kill them. There is no harmony with nature waiting for us, even if we get through this current global ecological crisis. Indeed, this is because the development of 'second nature' is part of the emancipatory solution to this crisis itself and will bring with it inevitably its own pathologies and reciprocal limits, unless humans in their post-anthropocentric penitence truly do take the critique of human 'egoism' seriously and willingly offer themselves up in solidarity to the needs of these new non-human lifeforms – as foodstuff. Then the problem of non-reciprocity and surplus-jouissance will certainly be solved – at least for human life.

John Roberts, 'Dean Kenning's Kinetics', an essay written for the exhibition 'Dean Kenning *Psychobotanical*', Matt's Gallery, London, 8–30 June 2019 (www.mattsgallery.org/artists/kenning/KenningPoster.pdf).

Norman Bryson
Cute Futures: Mariko Mori's Techno-Enlightenment//1998

When it comes to thinking through the relations between high and popular culture, historians of art have for a long time had recourse to a certain fable, which might be called the power-comes-from-below thesis. Historical examples are abundant. In *ancien régime* France, painting had been quietly stagnating for thirty years when, suddenly, [Jean-Antoine] Watteau introduced a quite new kind of image. How? The power-from-below explanation is that Watteau's work re-connected the etiolated art of painting to the most vital and robust energies of the popular culture of his day – the vulgar and street-wise *commedia dell'arte*, the boom in luxury goods (*The Sign-board of Gersaint,* 1720–21), the vogue for masquerade (which lies behind all Watteau's *fêtes champêtres* [garden parties]). How did [Gustav] Courbet manage to dismantle the academy's formulae for composing a history painting? By keying the image to the crudest and least composed kind of popular print, thereby tapping into the political culture of the urban masses. The high arts, so the thesis runs, are prone to a particular deterioration or fatigue that comes from their tendency to over-discipline the image, to force it to renounce anything resembling instant gratification. The most radical shifts in style occur when the enfeebled, mandarin drills of high art are unexpectedly injected with the energy that flows through visual culture at large. It is then that we see the emergence of a [Michaelangelo] Caravaggio, a [Jacques-Louis] David, a [Andy] Warhol.

All I would note about this thesis is that it is much easier to endorse when the case in question is historically remote. But what would a project look and feel like that sought to embrace power-from-below in the late 1990s? What kind of image would result if the aim were not simply to let the 'influence' of popular visual culture creep in at the edges, or in the guise of irony or allusion? What if the image were deliberately built in order to withstand the competition from the most intense kinds of imagery circulating in the popular sphere? Clearly a few quotations from advertising or from Hollywood folklore would no longer be enough. Popular visual culture has come a long way since Warhol, or since Cindy Sherman's *Untitled Film Stills* (1977–80).

Just consider what the competition is now like. An image-system that genuinely sought to release power-from-below would have to match in intensity MTV, as well as the fashion industry at all its levels, from costume design to still photography to the catwalk extravaganza. It would have to equal or outstrip the new computer games (Riven), the old computer games (Myst), as well as the velocities and saturations of IMAX, and the web. It would have to be born knowing that if you place a person next to a TV monitor on which that person appears, the eye spends more time with the video image. In terms of scale it would need to move beyond the homemade, let's pretend games of Sherman or [Yasumasa] Morimura, and frankly aim for Cecil B. De Mille, with a considerable supporting cast of couturiers, prop-makers, make-up artists, Photoshop editors, lighting technicians, and on-location cameras. In short, the project would soon come to resemble Mariko Mori's luscious and meticulously assembled tableaux.

That Mori's intention is to rival or surpass the forces mobilised by the contemporary image-stream is confirmed, I think, by the distinct sense of queasiness that her work is able to provoke – as if the concessions she makes to the image-stream had gone altogether too far. One is constantly on the lookout for signs of criticality, as though discovering these would save one from the awful fate of being truly plunged into the image-stream without protection, stuck on some nightmarish theme-park ride where galaxies and planets whizz past as you start to feel increasingly nauseous. Indeed signs of criticality exist, especially in Mori's work from the early 1990s, which typically depict a creature from the image-stream suddenly manifesting in the real world: on a subway car, in an amusement arcade, in an office building. These works sound the note of high criticality loud and clear: you see precisely where and how the psychic investments in the image-stream fit into the larger social-economic picture. The icons of the futuristic figure in *Subway* (1994), the Sailor Moon cutie in *Play With Me* (1994), and the pixified office lady in *Tea Ceremony III* (1995) grow directly out of their respective social milieux, as components of a corporate, urban, salary-man centred imaginary that is as much a part of the real social fabric as

Japan's transport system, its corporate architecture, or its workplace hierarchy. It is probably true that by Western standards Mori was not doing enough to place a distance between herself and her various roles: Shouldn't she have done more to disown these icons, through parody or irony? But the opposite argument could also be made: that by making so wide the gap between the fantasy-image and the real-world milieu that engendered it, Mori ensured that we would understand the work in a critical sense. We would take it in the spirit of a cultural-materialist analysis of how the social imaginary actually operates: on one side, the social actuality of the male-dominated corporation, or the programmed leisure of the pachinko parlour, or the blanked-out anomie of the subway car; on the other side, the fantasies which, arising from these specific milieux, work to keep the dominant forms of subjectivity lubricated and turning in their designated social slots.

With Mori's *Empty Dream* (1995) one could still keep a 'criticality' case going – though with some difficulty. The scene is Ocean Dome in Miyazaki prefecture, the largest aquatic theme-park in the world, complete with artificial sky, clouds, beach and waves. Mori's appearance as a synthetic mermaid grows out of this high-consumerist setting as organically and surely as the futuristic protagonist of *Subway* grows out of the Manga imaginary of the Tokyo subway. But the strategy has clearly shifted: Mori is not so much commenting analytically on the brittle plastic delights of modern Japan, as incarnating the social field in her own, versatile body. To draw a rather crude distinction: *Subway*, *Play With Me* and *Tea Ceremony III* were in a social-realist mode, which used the disjunction between the fantasy figure and the social-technological milieu that had engendered the figure as the basis for viewing and understanding the work. From *Empty Dream* onward, Mori has pursued a rather different goal that might be called symptomatic personification: Mori conjures up a body and a scenography for that body that are no longer tied (as in her social-realist mode) to any determinate social milieu. *Nirvana* (1997), *Burning Desire* (1996–8) and *Kumano* (1997) are works concerned with the structures and pressures of the imaginary as a force field in itself. The gain is that Mori no longer appears as the knowing sociologist, neatly mapping the articulations between the social and imaginary fields. The risk is that her recent work will be read as having been completely swamped by the imagery and the aims of contemporary mass media, as capitulating to capitalist narcissism on a truly cosmic scale, in a Madonna-style self-deification.

In Mori's work since 1996 the contours and shaping pressures of the contemporary image-stream are explored less by way of the classical-modernist strategy of distantiation and analysis than by impersonation: she uses her body as a lens that captures the light of the contemporary image-stream, and through certain enhancements and exaggerations makes it clear what the image-stream really wants of us. In the first place, it appears keen to eliminate any residual sense of the historical: allusions to Mayan, Indian, Egyptian, Greek and Chinese art are laid out on the same flat plane, floating weightlessly in the molten electronic mix. In the second place, the image-stream intends to be rid of whatever residual humanism might interfere with the smooth interlocking of the human being and the machine. In the Western twentieth century there has been a long tradition of thinking about the human/machine interface in gothic terms: in Berlin Dada or in Fritz Lang's *Metropolis* (1927) the image of machine parts replacing body parts has conveyed a sense of dread at the imminent loss of the human; and that tradition is still alive and well in Hollywood, where horror at the human-turned-machine suffuses a whole gallery of cyborg monstrosities, from *Star Wars* to the *Terminator* series to *Star Trek*'s spine-chilling enemy, the Borg. But Mori builds on a different, pacific conception of the harmony between man and machine, whose first fully developed expressions were perhaps the Astro Boy and Phoenix cartoon books of Osamu Tezuka. From the point of view of Astro Boy, to imagine some fearful antagonism between the energy-being that is man and the energy-being that is the machine, seems merely a parochial Western prejudice, a product of some antiquated, Cartesian pre-history of the modern. In Mori all the cyborgs are as sweet and harmless as Hello Kitty. The implication is that we already live in a world where the machines are on the whole more colourful, lively and interesting than the people. What we should do, then, is forget our differences from machines and focus on the resemblances, become more like them.

To expedite this process, the image-stream may have to work overtime to subdue whatever dissident, wayward and generally antisocial impulses that the techno-subject may still be harbouring in its Luddite breast. It is vital that no intimations of disharmony, or social or psychic unrest, upset the serene glidings of the techno-imaginary machinery. Neutralisation of sexuality becomes a high priority. Not the repression of sexuality: there is nothing austere or puritanical about the libidinal economy that Mori presents in her work. On the contrary, it is important that sexual energy be allowed to circulate freely within the visual system. But it must do so under the sign of a general blandness: a sexuality without raunch or risk, and with no grand, Tristan-and-Isolde climaxes; a sexuality that constantly moves toward the infantile – where the infantile is also the cute. Mori's imagery interestingly locates a potential for disharmony in the Western opposition between the supposedly presexual category of childhood, and the category of adolescence or adulthood where sexuality stands for whatever in the subject remains mutinous or wild. Mori's imagery undoes that opposition: On the one hand it sexualises the child, while on the other it infantilises the adult. Mori's avatars of feminine sexuality insist on a nursery world of pastel colours and round, huggable shapes: Barbarella and Bardot are vanquished by My Little Pony. In the general reconfiguration of the body that Mori's work performs, what has to be altogether abandoned is the idea of the body as creatural, as flesh and blood. In its place, Mori visualises the body as a set of radiant energies that sublimate the thing-of-flesh into a spirit made of (celluloid) light. The official cultural reference is to esoteric Buddhism, with its anatomy of chakras and energy-centres, and its conception of the 'rainbow body' of Enlightenment *(Burning Desire, Nirvana, Kumano)*. Yet there may be a more down-to-earth referent at work as well. From the historical advent of Taylorism onward, bodily behaviour in the twentieth century has been subject to analysis in terms of movement and energy flows. In a sense the whole global economy has been built as a system of flows with different velocities prevailing in each of its tiers or sectors – the slow-moving transport of raw materials and finished products, the middle-speed flows of urban populations (cars, subways, trains, the great Tokyo intersections such as Shibuya Crossing), and the highspeed velocities of electronic communication, media, and the stock market. Subjects under advanced capitalism may still wake up and discover in the mirror a creature of skin and bone; yet the moment they step out into the metropolitan field, they at once become a vector of flows and energies, of bodies, information and goods, as a commuter, as a worker, as a consumer. Mori's tantric vision of the body as composed of flaming energies and radiances may correspond to real conditions of the social economy, while at the same time presenting those conditions in a utopian light, as a transfiguration or *Aufhebung* of flesh and blood into subtle lights and energies. The image-stream may want more than to influence us with images of glamour; it wants us to know that, from its own perspective, we are streams of energetic movement already, that in the next era of industrial capitalism we are to feel ourselves as agile and spiritualised as angels, or bodhisattvas. I surmise that there may be a good deal of resistance to Mori's tableaux, often taking the form of an unspoken accusation that this is the work of a Sailor Moon princess utterly spoiled by the luxuries of her techno-toys. But there may be a rather different way to understand her strategy, which is to mime the process of capitalist production-consumption; to personify the energies of the current stage of the social formation; and by wholly yielding to popular culture's power-from-below, to give it intelligible outline and form, portraying the present psycho-social moment by occupying, not the place of the critical analysis, but the place of the critical symptom.

Norman Bryson, 'Cute Futures: Mariko Mori's Techno-Enlightenment', *Parkett*, vol. 54 (1998–9) 76–80.

Mary Ann Doane
The Desire to Desire//1987

[…] What we tend to define, since Marx, as commodity fetishism is in fact more accurately situated as a form of narcissism. Fetishism, in the Freudian paradigm, is a phallic defence which allows the subject to distance himself from the object of desire (or, more accurately, from its implications in relation to castration) through the overvaluation of a mediating substitute object. Narcissism confounds the differentiation between subject and object and is one of the few psychical mechanisms [Sigmund] Freud associates specifically with female desire.[1]

Having and appearing are closely intertwined in the woman's purportedly narcissistic relation to the commodity. Commodification presupposes that acutely self-conscious relation to the body which is attributed to femininity. The effective operation of the commodity system requires the breakdown of the body into parts – nails, hair, skin, breath – each one of which can constantly be improved through the purchase of a commodity. As Stuart Ewen points out, in relation to this 'commodity self', 'each position of the body was to be viewed critically, as a *potential* bauble in a successful assemblage'.[2] The ideological effect of commodity logic on a large scale is therefore the deflection of any dissatisfaction with one's life or any critique of the social system onto an intensified concern with a body which is in some way guaranteed to be at fault.[3] The body becomes increasingly *the* stake of late capitalism. *Having* the commodified object – and the initial distance and distinction it presupposes – is displaced by *appearing,* producing a strange constriction of the gap between consumer and commodity. The form of affect which embodies this constriction is also an affect aligned with the feminine – empathy. As [Walter] Benjamin points out, 'If the soul of the commodity which Marx occasionally mentions in jest existed, it would be the most empathetic ever encountered in the realm of souls, for it would have to see in everyone the buyer in whose hand and house it wants to nestle.'[4] Commodity and consumer share the same attributes – appeal to the eye and an empathetic relation to the other – and become indistinguishable. Just as the category of 'youth' has been expropriated by the commodity system and, as Guy Debord maintains, 'is in no way the property of those who are now young',[5] 'femininity' as a category is not the possession of women – it is not necessarily something we should strive to reclaim. The feminine position has come to exemplify the roles of consumer and spectator in their embodiment of a curiously passive desiring subjectivity. […]

1   [Footnote 88 in source] As Miriam Hansen has pointed out to me, the alignment of the opposition between distance and closeness with that between fetishism and non-fetishism does tend to reduce the dynamics of proximity and distance operating within fetishism itself. One could undoubtedly also argue that narcissism presupposes a similar dialectic, invoking the inevitable distance between the desiring subject and the mirror image. Nevertheless, my point is that fetishism ultimately enables the maintenance of a distance – for the fetishist, 'having' and 'being' are separable. The fetishist's relation to the object is always doubly mediated: through the constitution of a substitute object and the 'knowledge' that the woman 'really' does lack the phallus. Narcissism implies no knowledge whatsoever – rather, it signifies full investment in an illusion.

2   [89] Stuart Ewen, *Captains of Consciousness* (New York: McGraw-Hill, 1977) 47.

3   [90] Ibid.

4   [91] Walter Benjamin, *Charles Baudelaire: A Lyric Poet in the Era of High Capitalism,* trans. Harry Zohn (London: New Left Books, 1973) 55.

5   [92] Guy Debord, *Society of the Spectacle* (Detroit: Black and Red, 1977) section 62.

Mary Ann Doane, extract from *The Desire to Desire: The Woman's Film of the 1940s* (Bloomington: Indiana University Press, 1987) 32.

Theodor Adorno
Toy Shop//1974

Toy shop. – Friedrich Hebbel, in a surprising entry in his diary, asks what takes away 'life's magic in later years'. 'It is because in all the brightly-coloured contorted marionettes, we see the revolving cylinder that sets them in motion, and because for this very reason the captivating variety of life is reduced to wooden monotony. A child seeing the tightrope-walkers singing, the pipers playing, the girls fetching water, the coachmen driving, thinks all this is happening for the joy of doing so; he can't imagine that these people also have to eat and drink, go to bed and get up again. We however, know what is at stake.' Namely, earning a living, which commandeers all those activities as mere means, reduces them to interchangeable, abstract labour-time. The quality of things ceases to be their essence and becomes the accidental appearance of their value. The 'equivalent form'[1] mars all perceptions: what is no longer irradiated by the light of its own self-determination as 'joy in doing', pales to the eye. Our organs grasp nothing sensuous in isolation, but notice whether a colour, a sound, a movement is there for its own sake or for something else; wearied by a false variety, they steep all in grey, disappointed by the deceptive claim of qualities still to be there at all, while they conform to the purposes of appropriation, indeed largely owe their existence to it alone. Disenchantment with the contemplated world is the sensorium's reaction to its objective role as a 'commodity world'. Only when purified of appropriation would things be colourful and useful at once: under universal compulsion the two cannot be reconciled. Children, however, are not so much, as Hebbel thought, subject to illusions of 'captivating variety', as still aware, in their spontaneous perception, of the contradiction between phenomenon and fungibility that the resigned adult no longer sees, and they shun it. Play is their defence. The unerring child is struck by the 'peculiarity of the equivalent form': 'use-value becomes the form of manifestation, the phenomenal form of its opposite, value'.[2]

In his purposeless activity the child, by a subterfuge, sides with use-value against exchange value. Just because he deprives the things with which he plays of their mediated usefulness, he seeks to rescue in them what is benign towards men and not what subserves the exchange relation that equally deforms men and things. The little trucks travel nowhere and the tiny barrels on them are empty; yet they remain true to their destiny by not performing, not participating in the process of abstraction that levels down that destiny, but instead abide as allegories of what they are specifically for. Scattered, it is true, but not ensnared, they wait to see whether society will finally remove the social stigma on them; whether the vital process between men and things, praxis, will cease to be practical. The unreality of games gives notice that reality is not yet real. Unconsciously they rehearse the right life. The relation of children to animals depends entirely on the fact that Utopia goes disguised in the creatures whom Marx even begrudged the surplus value they contribute as workers. In existing without any purpose recognisable to men, animals hold out, as if for expression, their own names, utterly impossible to exchange. This make them so beloved of children, their contemplation so blissful. I am a rhinoceros, signifies the shape of the rhinoceros. Fairy-tales and operettas know such images, and the ridiculous question of the woman: how do we know that Orion is really called Orion, rises to the stars.

1   See Karl Marx, *Capital*, Vol. 1 (Moscow, 1961) 55.

2   Ibid., 56,

Theodor Adorno, 'Toy Shop' (1974), in *Minima Moralia: Reflections From Damaged Life*, trans. E.F.N. Jephcott (New York and London: Verso, 2005) 227–8.

David Robbins
The Ice Cream Social//2004

[…] The ridiculous is delicate as spun sugar. Staging it before the world's indifference demands from the manufacturer discipline and rigour, plus a seriousness of purpose which can itself reach the level of the absurd.

Although Mark's painting was to be a simple abstraction, and not particularly ambitious visually – a dot here, a dot there, what could be difficult? – its execution in fact turned out to be complicated.

Specifically, there was a content problem to solve. A big one. For when the pink and brown dots were removed from the context of the Baskin-Robbins decor, they became just that: dots, dumb, blank and empty. Only silly. Only vacant. Whatever other content had been in them was suddenly out like a light.

Reawakening their beauty required a kiss from the right lips; to communicate his intentions, the dots couldn't mean just anything. But what exactly were his intentions? Were these silly dots 'him' – that is, expressive of some interior state, neurotic or otherwise? Were the dots sublime emblems of the idyllic but synthetic America represented in the parlour's decor? Were they merely absurd decoration, darkly dispatched to assassinate meaning? In a gallery setting the painting couldn't help but invite readings such as these, traditional ambitions of abstract art. But he intended that his painting would extract from the ether another content altogether.

If as yet unsure of the precise body of that content, he did sense its outline: the painting ought to reference something public instead of private, something not so much inside people as between them.

Mark reasoned that the only way to ensure the reading he sought was by restricting the painting's imagination of itself. If that could be done, then particular interpretations could be locked in, others frozen out. Conditioning the painting's imagination would charge it with a specific valence of intention which it could never entirely lose, whatever its fortunes. To program the painting's memory, then – that was the key.

The idea yielded another: 'programming' could be accomplished by inaugurating the painting into public life in a place apart from the usual haunts of art, since a memory of that novel, 'inappropriate' context would necessarily be built into the painting's experience, and thus into the experience of encountering the painting afterwards.

Obviously, the most logical place to exhibit his dot painting in order to program its memory properly was a Baskin-Robbins Ice Cream Parlour.

Mark was as enthusiastic as a puppy about the idea. Renting a parlour for an evening and displaying his creation seemed the most natural thing in the world. Its meaning was inspecific, but as a gesture it was exceedingly precise. Carrying it out would amount to writing a line of autobiography.

Certain aspects of the painting's production were predetermined. The colours had to match those of the company's logo. The scale of the painting had to be small enough to fit on a wall likely crowded with cardboard posters promoting sundaes, shakes and ice cream cakes. In fact, in regard to the painting's appearance there was only one truly complex thing to be decided: the arrangement of the dots on the canvas.

Over this, though, Mark agonised. Why should any composition of dots be arranged one way and not another? There was, finally, no reason, so long as the dots' organisation was based upon taste. In pursuit of a more objective method of composition he used his Lapdog computer to randomly generate a series of dot patterns. All the dots were the same size, just as they were in the Baskin-Robbins logo. When the patterns were printed out, grey ink on white paper, some were nearly handsome, some nearly poignant, others almost funny.

None, however, answered a more fundamental question: did he really wish the dots to represent pure chance? After all, as an organising principle, chance was as flabby and arbitrary as personal taste. Finding neither subjectivity nor happenstance wholly satisfactory, Mark simply took a vacation from the problem, and stashed the printouts in a desk file.

Several months later, when enough life had passed to make him a slightly different person, he revived the painting project. During this second go-round he patiently re-examined each page. Eventually he selected the two strongest candidates. While pulling the pages from the messy pile, he happened to pass the two in front of his desklamp. Strong backlighting rendered both translucent, like pages of illuminated manuscript, and enabled him to read their patterns as one. Instantly he recognised that the pair in combination offered the solution. Not only was the visual design a strong, balanced composition but the method of its origination cut impersonal, computer-generated chance with a measure of humble human accident. Each 'system' of chance rested in composure against the other. Their partnership was perfect.

Partnership figured in the physical production of the painting, as well, since Mark wanted it to be carried out by another's hand. The Baskin-Robbins corporation sought through the decor and the designation 'parlour' to suggest the intimacy of a modest partnership, and he wanted to wire that same confusion – of the personal and the impersonal – into the painting's own imagination.

Finding a young painter in need of money is among the world's easier tasks. By putting out word among the staff at some of the local art supply shops Mark obtained the names of several struggling talents. After interviewing them he decided to hire a painter who employed the airbrush technique in her own work. Although not actually a skill required for the simple pink, brown and white painting, Mark thought it fitting to employ someone who'd already made a commitment to the dispassionate commercial surface.

After Molly the painter had agreed to his terms he handed over the clipped-together design, established the dimensions and colour choices, and paid her half her fee in advance in order to depersonalise the meeting. He was management, she labour. This was business.

Two weeks later, on the first snowfall of winter, when Mark came to collect the painting he was immensely pleased with the result. Flat pastel pink and brown dots floated in a calm white field. Painted in matte, uninflected acrylic, the painting looked matter-of-fact, blank but alert, an intelligence awaiting programming.

The painting completed, the next chore dropped into the chute: finding a suitable Baskin-Robbins in which to hang the thing. The room had to be large enough to accommodate perhaps two dozen people comfortably, and it had to feature enough undecorated wall space to afford an uncluttered view of the painting. Mark tramped through the snow to examine possibilities in the Laketown, Perrin Park and Winslet neighbourhoods, but only one parlour, on the corner of Dunlap and 23rd, between an Entertainment Recycling Center and a Sunset Liquor'n'Video outlet, met both conditions. Although far from beautiful the space was clean and in good condition.

The manager was a friendly middle-aged Cantonese named John Chin. Mr. Chin was tall, and as he listened patiently to the stranger he gazed down at him with placid brown eyes which had taken in stronger challenges. Mark made no attempt to disguise or misrepresent what he was doing, but instead told the proprietor exactly what he hoped to accomplish by installing a painting based on the Baskin-Robbins dots. To his surprise Mr. Chin agreed immediately. 'There should be more of this kind of innocent fun', said the older man. As Mr. Chin did not want regular customers to be scared away by the sight of some kind of private event, and Mark did not want guests to have to pay for ice cream, the two agreed to a fee of fifty dollars for the short period of time that the painting would be hung. Together they settled on a date for the event.

The crucial arrangements made, Mark turned his attention to promotion. He designed an announcement using the same P.T. Barnum font favoured by the Baskin-Robbins company, and photocopied it onto vivid pink paper.

    YOU are invited to an
    ICE CREAM SOCIAL
    January 3

8:30 pm
Baskin-Robbins at 23rd and Dunlap
FREE ICE CREAM!

It wasn't until he'd started stapling the small posters upon telephone poles and bulletin boards that he became aware of the absurdity of inviting total strangers to join him for ice cream in the dead of winter. He wondered whether anyone at all would bother to show up. But when Trace Weaver, emerging from a taxi on her way to a production meeting at a recording studio, spotted the pink announcement, an audience of at least one was guaranteed. Trace adored ice cream, and everything good was even better when free.

On the evening of the Ice Cream Social, Mark dressed in the understated costume he'd set aside: pink oxford-cloth button-down shirt, white jeans, brown shoes. He arrived at the Baskin-Robbins early in order to hang the painting. The parlour glowed cold white in the night.

'Nice painting', said Mr. Chin after the object had been unwrapped. 'You make that?'

'I caused it to exist. Yes.'

Mr. Chin helped him with the hanging. To avoid making any permanent marks in the wall Mark had brought two strips of velcro. That did the trick.

The arrival of the first guests transformed Mark into a host. 'How are you this evening? C'mon in. I'm Mark. Please be sure to have some ice cream. My treat. Just go up to the counter and ask Mr. Chin or his assistant Ling. Uh huh, any flavour you like, that's right. Hi. Thanks for coming. Notice the painting? Yup. Ice cream's free.' Strangers wandered in, singly and in pairs. White people and black. Latino and Asian. Children with their parents. People dressed in parkas and tweed topcoats, denim jackets and leather bombers. Some people carried cameras, video or still.

Everyone in the roomful of strangers moved about a bit timidly at first. One by one the guests made their way through the crowd and examined the painting. They looked at the painted dots, then they looked at the dots decorating the walls of the parlour, and again at the dots on the painting. Then they looked puzzled but not unhappy.

The tiny space soon became crowded. Bodies circulated. Mark buzzed about the room, flush with the confidence of the inventor. He encouraged any reticent party to enjoy some ice cream. No small number of guests needed encouragement.

'Is this the event?' asked a tall young woman whose short white hair and black glasses communicated 'art school'.

'Possibly you are the event', replied Mark in all sincerity.

'To be honest with you I can't quite locate where the event is', noted a middle-aged fellow attired in a grey business suit. He wore rubbers on his shoes, and wire-rim glasses.

'Oh?'

'Nope. Keeps shifting. Between your guests, the ice cream, the space, and the painting. It refuses to settle down.'

'Plus, there's my name.' Mark told the fellow his name.

'Interesting', said the grey man, nodding. 'Interesting.'

An unlovely man in his thirties joined their conversation. He wore a plaid flannel shirt and jeans. 'So what do you want us to be doing?'

'Doing?'

'Yeah. I can't figure out what's expected of me here', replied the man. 'I don't get it.'

'Nothing is expected of you', Mark assured him. 'The Ice Cream Social is just a reason to gather. You've gathered. Relax and enjoy it.'

The plaid man persisted. 'I know what to do at an art opening', said he, 'and I know what to do at an ice cream parlour but I don't know what to do with a combination of the two.'

Mark offered only a smile.

Occasionally, customers wandered into the store on their own, to purchase a cone or a pint.

'What is this, the ice cream convention?' laughed a young black woman sassily, on her way out the door, cone in hand.

Through it all, the painting acquired memory. Whatever additional meaning might come to be heaped on it in the future, the meaning of the painting could never be entirely separated from this event. Mark was thrilled to learn that it was possible to program art.

After allowing a few minutes more to pass, he judged the room ready and made his way behind the counter, where an obviously amused Mr. Chin shook his hand before receding to the sidelines. Mark stood for a moment looking across the counter at the eager faces expectantly gazing back at him. A roomful of strangers, united by a single experience. The hum of voices in the room quieted, and he addressed his guests.

'I've written a poem to commemorate the event.' With all eyes on him, he nervously plunged ahead.

Where the clock strikes 31
Players conspiring in the enjoyment of enjoyment
Unfurl the pink and brown of the Insupportable
Against animal virtue's blooded tribes
To savour the Ice Cream Social

Cold, licking-sweet, always melting and,
Empty of all save their pleasure in it, sticky enough.

Unaccustomed to having a love poem addressed to them, the crowd was a mosaic of baffled faces. Mark repeated the poem but did not elaborate upon its meaning, as he had to be mindful of the painting's memory, and the Ice Cream Social was not intended to be a commentary on experience but rather experience itself; explication would blur the clean line of the gesture. It was better that those in attendance work things out for themselves and determine their own relation to what they had seen and heard. Standing there behind the counter, Mark imagined that he knew something of what Dr. Frankenstein must have felt upon achieving the creation of life, purpose and outcome unknown....

He looked over the heads of the audience at the painting which, having taken on certain of the conditions of a mirror, now seemed to reflect the entire room.

'Thank you for coming tonight and being a part of our temporary community', said Mark. 'Hope you take a good memory along with you; I know the painting will!'

With that, the Ice Cream Social began to melt away. Some of the bolder guests came forward, cones blobby and dripping, to thank their host.

'That was very entertaining', said a woman who introduced herself as Trace Weaver, extending a business card.

Mark took the card. The Quid Pro Quo Company. Famed Quidco! And the woman was smiling at him!

'It was like TV without the TV', commented another woman with long sleek auburn bangs cut at an acute angle.

'Brilliant! I'll have to remember that!' said Mark.

'Yes', agreed Trace Weaver of Quidco, nodding. 'That is a good one.'

'Definitely post-media', commented a pale bookish-looking fellow.

Mark wrinkled his nose. 'Too severe, don't you think? Suggests rupture. Let's stress continuum. "Apres-media", perhaps?'

Everyone agreed that was much better.

In the weeks following the Ice Cream Social, thoughts about that evening surfaced in the minds of those who'd attended.

'Ever since the children arrived we've become so used to parties that take place in daylight. This was a nice change.'

'People came from all over to be together for such a short period of time. I liked that.'

'It was an experience with quotation marks around it.'

'Everyone was guarded and tense at first. There were so many cameras. Then they ate ice cream and became more relaxed.'
'At times I felt like audience and at times I felt like I was part of the performance, and that ambiguity made me feel uncomfortable.'

'It was innocent but in a sophisticated way. It made the conventional idea of hip seem passe.'

'I felt square, but I think the guy serving ice cream behind the counter felt hip.'

'It's hard to feel hip while holding a Very Berry ice cream in your hand. Ice cream has never allowed me to feel hip.'

'Like a yo-yo, the painting went back and forth from product motif to abstraction, and back again.'

'The painting was gratuitous and ridiculous, and that made it one of the most successful parts of the event.'

'Without the other stuff the painting wouldn't have been as funny, definitely.'

'Dots are always a little funny, aren't they?'

'I've always liked it when someone speaks after a meal.'

'Walking behind the counter was great. It was very political. Like he was letting us know why the meeting had been called.'

'I felt part of a community.'

'Making life heavenly for other people. One does want a position in reference to that.'

'I can't think of Baskin-Robbins any more without thinking of that guy's Ice Cream Social. It's like he owns the company now!'

Trace Weaver, too, had reflected on that evening's events. 'I think we may have something here', thought she. […]

David Robbins, 'Where the Clock Strikes 31', in *The Ice Cream Social* (Zurich: JRP Ringier, 2004) 31–47.

Leigh Claire La Berge
The Artwork of Children's Labour//2019

[...] *Haircuts by Children* (2006–19), by the artist collective Mammalian Diving Reflex (mdr), pays children to work as artwork. In his 'Childhood and Critical Theory', Paolo Virno argues that 'the meaningless and parasitic nature of wage labor becomes particularly evident in light of the game practiced in the preschool period in which the absence of a goal and an experimental inclination coexist'.[1] The collective seems to have accepted Virno's insight and transformed it into a kind of challenge: Can children not expose the wage, but play with it, and if so, will the wage retain its organising force? Will the child retain her playfulness?

Haircuts by Children has been staged globally over the course of ten years, and in each of its iterations children become – for a few days, anyway – wage labourers. In the performance, mdr collaborates with a hair salon and a primary school over a series of weeks to train a group of between twenty and thirty children in the skill of haircutting. After a series of workshops about the history of socially engaged art, in which they will soon be partaking, as well as vocational training with hair stylists, the participating children take over a haircutting salon for a weekend, during which they commit to four to five-hour staffing shifts.[2] Publicising their availability with hand-drawn posters, the children and mdr make available free haircutting appointments to an adult public who shows up and allows their hair to be cut by a group of children.

Like other socially engaged art that provides an encounter with difference, often along lines of race, class, nationality or geography, here an encounter with a different age structures the work.[3] Adults and children meet each other and the adults' appearances will be modified as a result. The collective selected hair for their object of practice because few aspects of our person are as easily modifiable (both to get rid of and get back) and as revealing of our own narcissism. Jenna Winter, one member of the mdr collective, recalls her early participation in *Haircuts by Children*. 'The first time I got my hair cut [by children]: I was like: oh my god! For artists [it's] ok, but for other people, they have to live in the world and go to their jobs.'[4] This risk or temptation that one might look weird could explain, in part, why certain adults consent to have their hair cut by children: that they too may be read as artists. Yet mdr reports that a substantial portion of their haircutting audience are senior citizens who might have to live in the world but do not have to go to work. If business gets slow the children resort to cutting each other's hair, a process that tends to result in 'a lot of crying'.[5] *Haircuts* is not simply about hair, then, but rather concerns itself with social risk, gendered risk, generational risk, and the self-transformation that might accompany the taking of each.

The piece is documented through photo, video and text, and – for a brief period, anyway – through the transformed appearance of the participants who allow their hair to be cut. In one of the collective's many videos that accompany the performance, salon owners and managers are interviewed as to why they would turn over their business to a group of 8 to 12-year olds. 'Publicity' and 'fun' are among the answers; 'working with artists' is also mentioned. Patrons, too, are interviewed as to why they would turn over their heads, their appearances even, to a group of recently trained children. Their answers are similar: 'fun', 'experience' and 'free hair-cuts'. The collective also interviews its own members: Why do they do it? Here, their message of social engagement comes to the fore. They understand child-adult interaction outside of circumscribed, usually familial, and thus racial contexts as exceedingly rare. If adults have children, then of course they interact with them and their friends. But most adults do not encounter different populations of children across the bounds of class and race, much less share a public space with them over the course of twenty or thirty minutes. And adults rarely touch nor are they touched by children other than their own or their family members. mdr understands this piece as an activist intervention into the boundary that separates adults and children into disparate populations. That intervention is structured through the art-based interruption of one of the definitional exclusions of the child in capitalist democracies of the Global North: children do not work.

Critics often locate socially engaged art on a genealogical map in a position that postdates Fluxus and that considers it as the inheritance of 1960s and 70s performance art. A piece such as *Haircuts by Children* can be easily compared to Fluxus artist Geoffrey Hendricks's 1976 piece, *Unfinished Business: Education of a Boy Child*, in which multiple acts of haircutting, beard-shaving and 'educational activities' were staged in New York over a several-day period with performers who included Hendricks' son, Bracken, as well as leading Fluxus artist George Maciunas.[6] Hannah Higgins has aptly, for this chapter at least, offered the term 'Fluxkids' to refer to the many children, including her, who dotted, if not motivated, various Fluxus performances. Its use of a similar demographic notwithstanding, *Haircuts* both borrows from and modifies a piece such as *Unfinished Business* by scaling up and depersonalising the act of cutting of hair. *Haircuts* is structured to include more participatory possibility and in that a repeatability. There is no equivalent of a George Maciunas here; there are many children, many patrons, many haircuts. The children are trained in a trade, they advertise their availability with their own drawings, they cut the hair, and they are paid to do so.

[…] *Haircuts* assumes a world of real subsumption in which we are all always already working. It makes this assumption over and against a logic of neoliberal self-capitalisation in which a subject's self-investment in human capital now might produce a return later. There is no deferred investment in the children; rather, their wage renders their labour a commodity in the here and now.

The collective does not assume that viewers, much less children, know the history of child labour prohibitions. Why, precisely, are children prohibited from working? David McNally has claimed that the plight of children's factory labour in nineteenth-century England may be understood as one of the 'first moral panics of capitalism'.[7] But we are surely a long way from the mills of Manchester. And indeed, worries about children's safety are today narrated in a quite different moral panic – namely, that of the child's premature sexualisation. To consider one moral panic, the piece will necessarily need to consider the other. Included alongside the installation's documentation is the text 'Protocols for Working with Children', authored by mdr collective member Darren O'Donnell. The publication functions as both an explanation of and justification for works such as *Haircuts by Children*. 'Protocols' might be read as a manifesto of sorts. It declares, 'In the future, every child will be given a pair of scissors and invited to shape our destinies. In the future, every child will be granted full citizenship rights; [they will be] encouraged to vote, run for office and drive streetcars. In the future, children will teach and adults will learn […]. In the future, children will be powerful creatures able to cross the street without looking both ways, and hold their breath underwater forever and ever and ever.'[8]

Scissors function as a metaphor for access to shape a collective social world through work. But they also cut hair, an action that is initially fun for them and that, through its repetition, might become a form of skilled trade. This literalising of social power through the refusal of a distinction between the toy and the tool also extends to the wage form as a refusal to distinguish between commodified and decommodified labour. Each child who participates in *Haircuts by Children* is paid for her labour. The children don't simply mimic work, they are compensated for working. Yet children cannot work. Thus their actions must be understood somewhere between mimicking and doing in art, a place where no one works. Finally, in returning to and questioning a historical capitalist moral panic that has become common sense – children do not work – the piece must confront a contemporary moral panic: non-related adults and children should not touch each other.

Thus mdr's public declaration of a methodology is particularly important for *Haircuts* because the piece confronts the two structuring prohibitions that, according to [Kathryn] Bond Stockton, in fact constitute contemporary childhood: the exclusion of paid labour and the exclusion of shared sexuality

– even if only non-familial touch – between children and adults. 'Childhood' as an invaluable and protected space depends on the circulation of the fictions and fantasies found in these prohibitions. To perform this work in places such as the United States, Canada and the United Kingdom is to trespass not only on laws against child labour but on forms of cultural normativity that define children as 'priceless' and fundamentally non-economic actors who possess little agency. Because they have no agency, because they are not sullied by the economy, they also have a certain 'innocence', which then, in a predictably Foucauldian dialectic, both invites and discourages their sexualisation by adults. According to Bond Stockton, these two prohibitions are not easily disentangled. And indeed she suggests through a series of novelistic readings that 'what may be children's greatest vulnerability [...] involves not sex but money. If children were to have more economic power, would they be less vulnerable to adults, in some contexts.'[9] In the genealogy that Bond Stockton, Zelizer and Ariès all trace, as children are deracinated from a wage labour that is itself becoming increasingly dominant, they become newly vulnerable, newly innocent, newly violable. Indeed, before Foucault's introduction of the repressive hypothesis in *The History of Sexuality* volume 1, [Phillip] Ariès had already noted that as childhood becomes more clearly defined over the course of modernity, adults' perception of children shifts from 'immodesty to innocence'.[10]

mdr confronts this knot of taboos directly: the collective pays children to work touching adults as artwork. Each child receives a wage of $10 for participating. Yet there surely exists a reason why all Western democracies outlaw child labour. No one favours a return to the days when 'little hands' were considered 'ideal for weaving', or when the future of the United States' economic growth and national character were narrated with the claim that 'the work of the world has to be done, and these children have their share [...] why should we place emphasis on prohibitions? We don't want to rear up a generation of non-workers, what we want is workers and more workers'.[11] Of course such a sentiment was hardly borne equally by all children; class and race have always had as much influence on whether modernity's children worked as did their age.

mdr must answer the twin questions of how one should work with children and why children should work. Their 'Protocol for Working with Children' borrows from a rights-based discourse. For example, it includes reference to the United Nations' Convention on the Rights of the Child. Children have the right to 'relax and play, and to join in a wide range of cultural, artistic and other recreational activities'. Because this treaty is global in reach and includes signatories in both the Global North and Global South, we also find in it an acknowledgement of children's work. 'The government should protect children from work that is dangerous or might harm their health or their education

[....] Children's work should not jeopardize any of their other rights, including the right to education, or the right to relaxation and play.'[12] *Haircuts by Children* exerts a certain sense of restitution, then. Children, in exile from so many adult worlds in the capitalist democracies of the Global North, are welcomed back into the public sphere that has always been, whether liberalism acknowledges it or not, at the same time a commercial sphere. The rights to play and to protection from work are not mutually exclusive; rather, they might be conjoined. In the Global North, that conjoining will appear in art where labour is already difficult to discern. In the realm of art, decommodified labour seems at home, and it is here that children's labour will be recommodified, as it were, as a site to critique the commodity status of all labour.

But in an unintentional demonstration of the soundness of Bond Stockton's argument in *The Queer Child*, to pay children, to enfranchise them through work, is to pass through the spectre of child sexual abuse. In demonstrating this consequence, the performance exceeds the rights-based discourse that it itself champions. Children, for their part, are told to be wary of 'stranger danger'. mdr uses this term repeatedly in its texts and discussions to indicate the pervasive fear to which children are instructed to adhere: adult strangers should be avoided. Conversely, adults are told to be wary of being perceived as too interested in children, lest that interest be perceived as sexual. [...] Each is taught to fear the other. This space of mutual, sexualised fear – the reverse command to see children as sexual through the policing of all interest in children as potentially sexual – is foundational to what James Kincaid calls 'the culture of child molesting' in his remarkable book with a subtitle of the same name.[13] *Haircuts by Children* is motivated by and must respond to the reality of such fears.

Foremost, the problem of 'stranger danger' is one that this work both invokes and distances itself from. In declaring that they will not be subject to this moral panic, the piece enacts what studies such as Kincaid's and Bond Stockton's can only insist on – namely, that 'strangers' are hardly the 'danger'.[14] *Haircuts by Children* risks an interaction between adults and children who do not know each other. And indeed, a haircut requires a specific engagement: the communication of wants, the vulnerability of vanity, and finally, repeated touching. During the performance's duration there transpires sustained physical interaction between adult strangers and the children who attend to them. These children place their hands on the adult's head, shoulders, perhaps even face. This is a haptic work, then, one whose medium is touch. It involves the mediation of individual and collective proprioception through its insistence on cross-generational touching, which is simultaneously artist-audience touching. [...]

Fittingly, a hair salon is a place of mirrors, where things are not only seen from one angle, or two, but from many, as mirrors reflect other mirrors. As the scissors offer the literal possibility of reshaping both hair and social relations, the mirrors offer multiple perspectives with which to see the present. A salon is a business, which will, at least for a few days, be run by children: appointments will be made and kept, reception will be staffed, floors will be swept, instruments will be disinfected. *Haircuts by Children* transforms the salon into what [Walter] Benjamin described as the Saturnalia-like environment specific to children's theatre. 'Everything is turned upside down, and just as master served slave during the Roman Saturnalia, so during the performance, children stand on stage and teach and educate their attentive educators. New Forces and new impulses appear.'[15] Children at play may be 'representatives of paradise' according to Benjamin, but their utopia is a delicate one. On the one hand, utopia may be found in the neighbourhood hair salon, a declaration of the imminent possibility of the transformation of social relations. On the other hand, the nearness of utopia is also fleeting, as the salon becomes a site of frequent breakdown: children refuse to rotate tasks, some avoid clean up and the maintenance work of running the salon, everyone desires to control the scissors.[16]

But these children working as art differ from Benjamin's children as representations of not working – or utopia. And part of that difference may be located in the decommodified labour that artists do and that children have, since 1938, been formal representatives of. Combing both of these historical variations of labour, the piece offers a critique of each. Children do not represent the possibility of art through play; rather, they are the art as they 'play at work'. The work that they play at is artistic labour, and that labour has been decommodified. Here a decommodified population of workers undertakes commodified labour in art.

[…] *Haircuts* refuses the play-versus-work dichotomy by refusing other dichotomies – namely, tool versus toy and children as commodified versus decommodified labourers. In *Haircuts by Children*, what Virno suggested was the 'meaningless' and 'parasitic' nature of wage labour – its repetitive temporality, its monotony of task, the inelasticity of the wage itself – becomes the site of play. It becomes fun. Furthermore, the absence of wage labour found in the child's world of immediacy and intensity is paired with the seeming mimicry of the wage itself: the children are paid to 'play at work'. Through the payment, the mimicry is refused. The piece refuses to let children function as or represent decommodified labour.

But if the prohibition on receiving a wage in part defines the boundedness of childhood, then its violation must have some consequence. Indeed, with its refusal of children's decommodified labour, with its redistribution of the wage within the piece, the piece suggests another form of potential redistribution – namely, of childhood as an affective state. Alongside a distribution of the wage to now include children – itself made possible by considering and dispelling the worry of 'stranger danger' – the piece then seeks to redistribute the affective density of childhood itself.

[...] In positioning children to undergird its critique of decommodified labour, how different *Haircuts by Children* appears from Tino Sehgal's or Carsten Höller's collaborations with children. In their recent works, either work or play predominates so as to easily criticise, and stabilise, its dichotomous other. Sehgal's *This Progress*, staged to great acclaim at the Guggenheim in 2010, involved the training and participation of children of all ages. (Adults underwent training to participate in the piece as well). As we would expect from Sehgal, *This Progress* orchestrated a series of conversations between the audience and the piece's child and adult 'interpreters', who were stationed throughout the museum's famous rotunda. In her reading of the piece, Shannon Jackson argues that the children's participation appears as though it is 'bent on proving that ephemerality cannot in fact resist commodification'.[17] In fact, the reverse is true – commodification cannot resist ephemerality. But regardless, it is not the children's presence but their labour that indexes the so-called ephemeral. We see clearly the importance of the children's labour in the *New York Times*'s feature on *This Progress*. [The] *Times* isolates the children's lack of wage and their overwork. It reports that 'the schedule could be grueling even for much younger interpreters, who, unlike their elders, were unpaid. (They did receive a hat, bag and a museum membership; adults were paid $18.75 an hour, teenagers $7.25 an hour.) Solomon Dworkin [...], who was one of the oldest children in the piece, said many of the younger ones had trouble with the pace of forty to fifty interactions a day, sixty to seventy on weekends. 'They had a workload breakdown', he said.'[18]

According to the *Times*, the commodification of labour is the piece's ultimate horizon: who gets paid, who doesn't, how much, and with what consequences. Children are paid nothing; teenagers, something; adults, more. *This Progress* is described in a language of pure work; children are present to insist that even work has an end. Even if, as they themselves insist, they are exhausted. The joke, of course, is that the children aren't really working both because they can't and because art isn't really work.

Carsten Höller's productions with children take the precisely opposite approach. Children occupy a site of all fun and no work, and conversely, his piece *Gartenkinder* (2014) has been interpreted as pure play. The *Financial Times* reports that 'children play at the opening of artist Carsten Höller's installation *Gartenkinder* in which he has transformed the Gagosian Gallery [...] into a children's playground'.[19] The British *Art Daily* explains the piece as 'a new form of children's playground with walls and floor in red, green, blue and yellow [...]

[which also] includes a large-scale dice that children can crawl inside [and] a giant mushroom that rocks like a roly-poly toy [...]. The installation emphasises the importance of play'.[20]

It seems that Höller has staged what used to be known as a playground. I do not make this comment dismissively. Rather, I want to suggest that critics do not yet have another language for the decommodified labour that they witness in Sehgal's and Höller's artwork. Without such a language, their pieces are interpreted as either all work or all play. With regard to Sehgal's expansion of work, children are used absolutely normatively to critique both too much work and to assure the viewer that even work ends. With regard to Höller's expansion of play, we should heed Weiss's reading of Adorno's own worries about the over-representation of play. 'If play attributes too much capacity to itself, [it] weighs down [...] its own development. If it conceives of itself as the sole avenue of relating to the world's disenchantment [...] play actually becomes closer to sport.'[21]

Conclusion

In accordance with our definition of 'the aesthetic', art remains a site where adults access play. Yet the meaning of such access has itself been modified, and the artists who populate this chapter seem less interested in adults playing like children and more interested in children working like adults. That work happens in artwork, within the realm of the aesthetic – in the gallery or museum – which by definition is a place of the suspension of work. [...] Children, as historically once and soon-to-be-again individual labourers, here are captured aesthetically at the moment of their non-utility and put to work. The child, defined in part as she who cannot contract to work, enters the gallery to represent work, while the adult, she who works too much and cannot access play, enters the gallery to suspend work. There their paths cross and in doing so, put pressure on the wage form. But what kind of pressure should be brought to bear? More work? More play? Or a refusal of the very difference?

There, at the moment when they cannot work, in the space where work itself cannot happen, children's arrival in the artwork must now be understood as one response to the decommodification of artistic labour. In every example but *Haircuts by Children*, children are asked to work without a wage so as to buttress a demonstration of economic inequality. Unsurprisingly, then, it is Mammalian Diving Reflex's 'Protocols for Collaborating with Children' that ventures to describe 'decommodified labor', even if that term is not used. It claims that 'we feel that it is important to point out that recent developments in the world of work and the locations where value is produced have put children at the centre of the work world, often in ways that are not yet acknowledged or, for that matter, fully understood'.

There is a certain irony here. Children stand as one of labour's major historical decommodifications, one that is historical and visible as well as deeply moralised, raced and gendered. In addition to that fact not being acknowledged or understood, the collective argues that 'this is a new frontier for the generation of value, and it's important that children are recognised as important content and, in turn, value providers, who remain uncompensated'.[22] They do not say that socially engaged art may be understood as both cause and effect of this frontier; they turn instead to 'creative' enterprises such as Facebook and other sites of 'playbor'. But certainly the fact that art offers both a seamless site of continuation and a possible site of restitution may be read as an argument in their work and in this book.

Of course, one cannot scale art – perhaps the physical manifestation of the unique ability of aesthetic judgment to think the particular under the universal – and the point is not to begin paying children to be children, something that certain neoliberals have in fact suggested (similar to basic income).[23] Rather, the point is to demonstrate that as artistic labour has been decommodified, artists have begun to incorporate populations of decommodified labourers into their work. Those incorporations have followed a range of strategies and tones – some critical, some celebratory, some polemical. This range of approaches to critiquing children as representatives and potential critics of decommodified artistic labour is crucial to understanding socially engaged art's relations to the economy.

1   [Footnote 69 in source] Paolo Virno, 'Childhood and Critical Thought', *Grey Room*, vol. 39, no. 21 (Autumn 2005) 6–12. Available at www.mitpressjournals.org/doi/abs/10.1162/grey.2005.1.21.6?journalCode=grey#.WQxtstwh5pY/

2   [70] All material and quotations about *Haircuts by Children* are taken from mammalian.ca (accessed February 2016) unless otherwise noted.

3   [71] As it is with their piece 'All the Sex I've Ever Had', in which a self-selecting group of 'elderly' people speak publicly about their individual sexual histories.

4   [72] In conversation with mdr member Jenna Winter, March 2016.

5   [73] Ibid.

6   [74] Hannah Higgins, *Fluxus Experience* (Berkeley: University of California Press, 2002) 101–3.

7   [75] Historical Materialism, 'Gender and Capital Panel,' New York City, April 2012.

8   [76] Mammalian Diving Reflex, 'The Mammalian Protocol for Collaborating with Children' (2011) (www.mammalian.ca/pdf/MDR%20Protocol6Dec2011.pdf/).

9   [77] Kathryn Bond Stockton, *Moving Sideways in the Twentieth Century* (Durham, NC: Duke University Press, 2009) 38.

10   [78] Philippe Ariès, *Centuries of Childhood: A Social History of Family Life* (New York: Penguin, 1960).

11   [79] Both quotations cited in Viviana Zelizer, *Pricing the Priceless Child* (Princeton: Princeton University Press, 1985) chapter 3.

12 [80] United Nations, chapter iv, 'Human Rights', '11. Convention on the Rights of the Child' (20 November, 1989) (https://treaties.un.org/pages/ViewDetails.aspx?src=IND&mtdsg_no=IV-11&chapter =4&lang=en/).

13 [81] James Kincaid, *Erotic Innocence: The Culture of Child Molesting* (Durham, NC: Duke University Press, 1998).

14 [82] It is, of course, family members and intimates, teachers, coaches and priests – those who are repeatedly in proximity to children – who are the danger; the closer the proximity, the greater the danger.

15 [85] Benjamin quoted in Susan Buck-Morss, *The Dialectics of Seeing* (Cambridge, MA: MIT Press, 1989) 264.

16 [86] Conversation with Jenna Winter, March 2016.

17 [91] Shannon Jackson, *Social Works: Performing Art, Supporting Publics* (New York: Routledge, 2012) 242.

18 [92] Alicia Desantis, 'At the Guggenheim, the Art Walked Beside You, Asking Questions', *New York Times* (12 March 2010). Available at www.nytimes.com/2010/03/13/arts /design/13progress.html

19 [93] Jackie Wullschlager, 'Frieze Art Fair: The Best Piece of Theatre in Town', *Financial Times* (14 October 2014). Available at http://blogs.ft.com/photo-diary/2014/10/carsten-hollers -gartenkinder/

20 [94] 'Carsten Höller Turns Frieze Booth into Children's Playground', *artdaily.org* (15 October 2014) (http://artdaily.com/news/73620/Carsten-H-ouml-ller-turns-Frieze-booth-into-children-s-playground#.WTlHCsm1vdQ/).

21 [95] Joseph Weiss, *The Idea of Mimesis: Semblance, Play, and Critique in the Works of Walter Benjamin and Theodor W. Adorno* (PhD diss., DePaul University, 2012) 187. Available at http://via. library.depaul.edu/cgi/viewcontent.cgi?article=1131&context=etd; Lambert Zuidervaart also claims this in *Artistic Truth*, (Cambridge: Cambridge University Press, 2010) 57.

22 [97] 'Mammalian Protocol for Collaborating with Children', op. cit.

23 [98] Laura Fitzpatrick, 'Should Students Be Paid for Good Grades?', *Time* (14 January 2009) (http://content.time.com/time/nation/article/0,8599,1871528,00.html).

Leigh Claire La Berge, extracts from 'The Artwork of Children's Labor: Socially Engaged Art and the Future of Work', in *Wages Against Artwork: Decommodified Labor and the Claims of Socially Engaged Art* (Durham, NC and London: Duke University Press, 2019) 186–92, 193–7.

CUTENESS AND PLASMATICNESS REPRESENT TWO COMPETING UNDERSTANDINGS OF ANIMATED FORM, ONE FRAMED IN TERMS OF DOMINATION, THE OTHER IN TERMS OF FREEDOM.

Peggy Ahwesh and Johanna Gosse, 'Cut to Cute: Fact, Form, and Feeling in Digital Animation', 2018

OUR ENDLESS CUTEMPORARY

Jennifer Doyle
Introduction to Difficulty//2013

Critics have limits. Our faculties break down when an artwork reminds us of something so painful, or makes us so mad, or is something we like so much we struggle to write about it. Or when we are tired and having a bad day. There are whole genres certain critics just don't get (for [Theodor] Adorno, famously, it was jazz). Critics can be tone deaf; we can miss the pleasures others take, ignore the irritation that others feel. We can be willful and stubborn, blind to the dwindling relevance of those artists we love and indifferent to the emergence of new practices we don't understand. We all have limits that look pretty uncritical from most angles, and we rarely know these limits until we encounter them.

I begin this chapter with a story about hitting my own wall. In the fall of 2007, I booked and then failed to make an appointment for a one-on-one performance encounter with the English artist Adrian Howells. I had also made an appointment that day at a beauty salon for a cut and colour, far too close to the timeslot I'd arranged to see Howells's performance. My hair was covered in a mud of dye and wrapped in plastic when I looked at my watch and realised that I needed to be across London in an hour, and it would take at least that to get there. I flipped through magazines, doing the math in my head. Anxiety rose like a tide in my throat as I realised that there was no way I was going to make it there. I dug the phone out of my purse and called to cancel, without, however, leaving enough time for another person to take my place.

It was a careless and ordinary mistake. But the nature of Howells's performance and my reaction to missing the appointment suggested that something more was in play. Howells's work maximises the possibilities of what he describes as 'accelerated intimacy'. He has explored the contours of confession and autobiography in performances that rehearse the most painful and embarrassing moments in his history for small audiences, and sometimes audiences of one. In *Held*, Howells invites his audience into three twenty-minute scenes. First, they sit at a table, drink tea, and chat. Then they sit together on a couch in front of the television and hold hands. Last, they go up to a bedroom, lie down together, and spoon. Participants respond to this performance differently. Some are ill at ease and on their guard; some make themselves right at home. One person fell asleep. When Howells stages a performance like this, he sees perhaps six people in a day. As one might imagine, these appointments are hard to come by. I felt the full weight of this; by screwing up the appointment, I prevented another person from seeing his work.

Later that day I went to the venue's address to meet friends who had honoured their appointments. I held in my hands a small gift of cookies, brought to convey my apologies to the artist. Howells had just finished up for the day when I got there. I wanted to be simply apologetic, but instead I found myself fighting back tears – and, worse, failing to keep them in check. We drank tea and ate the cookies. I was embarrassed and self-conscious that my affect risked expanding into a selfish display of abjection: shame mounted as a kind of counterattack.

Howells was sympathetic and warm. Looking at him through my tears, I felt even worse. My emotionality was well out of proportion to the circumstance. My friends and I walked back to the train station. As I listened to them talk about their experience of *Held*, I tried to come to terms with the fact that I'd subconsciously sabotaged my appointment. I'd been looking forward to it all week, had been careful to make sure I got the timeslot, and then scheduled a pointless event right over it. Clearly the whole idea of *Held* challenged me. Apparently I couldn't inhabit the structure of that encounter without being overwhelmed – by what, though?

I was afraid of what might happen, of how it might make me feel. I think too I was equally put off by its artificiality – not that my own feelings would be inauthentic but that they would be delivered within a temporary architecture of intimacy. What happens at the end of the appointment? I was attracted enough to the idea to schedule the appointment but disturbed enough that I made it impossible for me to honour it. In doing so, I subconsciously pre-empted the betrayal I expected, for the experience of *Held* would feel either very empty and disappointing or very full and disappointing. I had reacted badly to what Jon Cairns describes as the 'confusing context of "staged" intimacy' in which Howells works.[1] His medium is the affective density of the interaction between artist and audience, and even a failure like mine should be understood as part of the work's performative field. By failing to make the appointment, by failing to cancel in time to allow another person to take my place, and then by trekking down there anyway to solicit his forgiveness, I managed to extract the caretaking that Howells offered within the boundaries of *Held* but outside the boundaries of the event. I insisted on getting what I thought the artist had promised me, but on my own terms, and after blowing him off. (Of course, behind this self-analysis are years of therapy. The responsibility to each other's time is one of the first things one works through with an analyst, especially if one has missed an appointment or is habitually late.)

Until that day I had considered myself a seasoned spectator to some of the most challenging forms of performance. When we think about challenging performance art, we generally mean not the domestic normalcy cited by *Held* but what is often described as 'extreme' performance involving violence toward the body and sexualised forms of display. Familiar with this kind of work (e.g., the work of Ron Athey, Bob Flanagan, Franko B, Kembra Pfahler, Kira O'Reilly), I had come to assume that there was nothing I couldn't handle. I would say, in fact, that prior to this experience I was cavalier about my own limits and dismissive of others', as if it were a moral failing to be averse to the sight of blood or be uncomfortable with the idea of live performances engaging in acts that look (and sometimes are) sexual. Howells showed me how deluded I'd been: the mere idea of certain kinds of performance provoked in me a defensive need to assert control over my place in the picture. As a spectator to performance art, I might have a high tolerance for blood, nudity and noise, but I seem to have a lower tolerance for work engaged with more ordinary forms of relational intimacy, for the things that 'feel' like life and therefore cut too close.

[…] I was caught off guard by my reaction to *Held* not only because I am a regular at performance art events that people might characterise as extreme but because I am also an avid consumer of cinematic melodrama (*Stella Dallas* is one of my favourite movies) and nearly all forms of novels that demand emotional investment from their readers (from the sugary *Little Women* to the grim *Germinal*). In general, I love a good weepie like *Now, Voyager*, and I eat up the stark realism of a film like *Matewan*. Perhaps it's the professor in me (always looking for the teachable moment), but my reaction to the idea of *Held* made me re-examine how I thought about the emotionality of such work. Previously I'd approached emotion as something that cuts across mediums; for example, I thought of a sentimental pop song as like a sentimental novel or film, as if sentimentality were a thing in and of itself, which a text might embody and communicate.

The sentimentality deployed within Howells's performances has its own particular challenges. Much of his work has evolved around a feminine persona named Adrienne. In *An Audience with Adrienne* (2007), for example, Adrienne invites people to watch home movies with her and to talk about episodes from her life that participants select from a café-style menu. Audience members may be invited to share their own stories. Reviewing that work for *The Guardian*, Lyn Gardner explains that the 'unthreatening realm of the domestic' offers the viewer-participant 'a direct conduit to our own childhoods, the episodes we recall with pin-sharp clarity and those we bury somewhere deep inside and try to forget'.[2] The cosiness of the domestic space is a lure; as any student of sentimental fiction knows, homes are haunted. Howells invites his audience into a queer space of intimacy whose edges are shaped by failure and isolation. (What domestic scene isn't?) *Held* distills the autobiographical exchange of his other projects to the act of simply keeping company.

There is something jarring about the idea of Howells receiving visitors for *Held*, as if this home were a bordello offering not the sexual excitement of the mistress but the grounding companionship of the wife. He may use the innocence of domestic normalcy to frame your encounter with him, but this very slight shift in the most banal scene of intimacy (from that of a romantic couple to that of an artist and his audience; from that of straight romance to queer domesticity) exposes just how loaded, how overdetermined that scene of domestic intimacy is for many of us. Cairns therefore describes the artist as practicing an ambivalent form of intimacy – a fundamentally queer occupation of domestic, personal, feminine and reproductive scenes in which sites associated with privacy and safety become instead scenes of exposure. Lauren Berlant describes these kinds of spaces as 'intimate publics'; Tavia Nyong'o uses the term extimate to suggest how they can fail, leaving us feeling more alone than ever.[3]

If we expect such a performance to be easy on the spectator, it is because we've already coded these terms (privacy, domesticity, the personal) as well as the feminised labour that defines them (nurturing, supporting, caring) as such. My failure as an audience for Howells forced me to take notice of the contingency of difficulty and consider the place of affect and emotion in a conversation about what makes a work hard for one person and easy for another. Those contingencies pertain not only to the person (and his or her history) but also to that person's conditioning as a viewer, reader and audience member. [...]

Art criticism has aligned one form of difficulty (in which a work's meaning is not readily available to the viewer) with a regulation of affect (in which opacity, the difficulty of meaning, is packaged as cool, distanced and anti-emotional). Galleries, museums and magazines sell this marriage of the impenetrable and the unmovable as Art, as if those of us who go to galleries and museums (or become art historians) are doing so in order to be relieved of the burdens of an emotional life. [...]

Many of the artists most frequently identified as controversial and shocking – such as Jeff Koons, Vanessa Beecroft, and Santiago Sierra – don't make work that is actually all that difficult. Some controversial artists are, in fact, quite popular with curators and with the art press.[4] How difficult can Beecroft's work be, really, when even as we complain about its exploitative structures, reproductions of her work grace the covers of art magazines? Critical hand-wringing over the ethical and taste issues raised by the scandalous practices of gallery darlings like Koons and Sierra is a bit of a bad faith exercise. Writers love artists like these because they give us something around which we can rally: the expansion of the field of art-making, the defense of a sense of taste, the politicisation of the space of art consumption, the literalisation of the exploitative dynamics of art as luxury product.

If frequently exhibited and commercially viable work marks the outer limits of our conversations about art, what do we do with work so challenging to convention that it receives little or no institutional support – work that in most contexts is stubbornly unfundable, uncollectable, and impossible to curate for fear of offending politicians and donors? What do we do with artists indifferent to galleries and their cultures and to mainstream taste and values? What do we have to say about artists who aren't making art about Art but about the Mexico-US border, about intimacy and exposure, or in response to a culture of hate and fear?

This is why I find *difficult* a more productive critical term than either *controversial* or *obscene*. […]

1   Jon Cairns, 'Public Intimacies: My Audiences with Adrienne', paper presented at Performance Studies International 16, Toronto, June 2010.

2   [Footnote 4 in source] Lyn Gardner, 'An Audience with Adrienne', *The Guardian* (10 August 2007).

3   [5] Cairns, 'Public Intimacies', Berlant introduces the term *intimate publics in The Queen of America Goes to Washington City*. For Nyong'o's writing on 'extimacy', see 'Brown Punk: Kalup Linzy's Musical Anticipations', *tdr: Theater and Drama Review* vol. 54, no. 3 (2010) 71–86.

4   [22] For sustained discussions of art and censorship, see, for example, Meyer, *Outlaw Representation* (2002); W.J.T. Mitchell, 'Offending Images', in *What Do Pictures Want?* (2004), 125–44; Wendy Steiner, *The Scandal of Pleasure* (1995). The controversy of Kara Walker's work grows from its explicit dialogue with the racist imaginary, as well as from the challenges it poses to some members of the African American arts community who have found its popularity with the (white) mainstream problematic. Some of her critics balked at watching an African American artist play into the art market's demand for sensational, abject black bodies. This issue makes the work more difficult within the African American arts community than within the whiter spaces of the commercial galleries selling her work. As Gwendolyn DuBois Shaw explains in her writing on the artist, within the African American community, Walker's work can be harder to programme even though her commitment to confronting racism would suggest otherwise. Thus in some contexts, Walker's work is both controversial *and* difficult. See Gwendolyn DuBois Shaw, *Seeing the Unspeakable* (2004), especially the chapter 'Censorship and Rejection.'

Jennifer Doyle, extract from 'Introduction to Difficulty', in *Hold it Against Me: Difficulty and Emotion in Contemporary Art* (Durham, NC and London: Duke University Press, 2013) 1–4, 5–8, 15.

Ian Bogost
The Quiet Revolution of Animal Crossing//2020

In the midst of a pandemic, it's delightful to imagine doing whatever you like without worrying about making a living.

Many years ago, when my son was 5, he got upside down on a long-term loan in Animal Crossing, Nintendo's 2002 video game about running away from home to lead a prosaic life in an adorable animal village. The problem was familiar, although perhaps not to a kindergartner: He had spent his income on the trappings of consumer life – furniture, garments, accessories, even video games. But now he had no room for all that stuff, he explained to me. He also had no cash to pay off the mortgage, which the local real-estate tycoon, a raccoon named Tom Nook, had forced him to take out upon arrival. Until the note was paid, my son reasoned, he wouldn't be able to take out another loan – to fund a home expansion that would finally make room for all his purchases. 'What should I do?' he asked.

For years, I spun this story as an example of games' special ability to teach complexity. What the hell kind of video game consigns you to a mortgage when you boot it up? But Animal Crossing had taught my young son about the trap of long-term debt before he ever had a bank account.

Animal Crossing is back, and what a time for it to arrive. A new title in the franchise, New Horizons, launched in late March, just as many Americans were settling into quarantine; its players have since found comfort and relief in the game's cute pastoralism, a reprieve from uncertainty. The title has become so popular, in fact, that Nintendo Switch consoles have become about as hard to find as hand sanitiser. Amid social and economic chaos, with most people holed up inside, the days having melted into a shapeless slurry, Animal Crossing serves up unexpected consolation by offering surrogate habits – a structured, if fictional, alternative to normal life.

Read: You already live in quarantine.

Days pass in real time, and the seasons change too, along with the calendar. You can fish and catch bugs, plant trees or chop them down for wood. You can buy clothing, furniture and other goods, or do odd jobs for the animals who live in town. You can work off that infernal mortgage, of course, but you can also choose not to, and Tom Nook will never evict you. Instead, you might bury treasure on the beach, or just watch the stars at night. In summer, the crickets chirp at dusk. When spring blooms, as it is now, the wind makes cherry blossoms dance over the streams.

The whole time my kid with the video-game mortgage was growing up, I insisted in books and during lectures and on late-night shows that games like Animal Crossing could help people better understand other big problems, like climate change or even pandemic flu (a topic I later turned into a game, not that it made much of a difference). Today, my son is about to graduate from college and into the economic cataclysm that will likely become the coronavirus depression. He's back home now, because his school closed down, playing the new Animal Crossing with the rest of us. Its lessons don't seem so useful anymore.

Maybe I had it all wrong all those years ago. I had imagined Animal Crossing to be a game about the world, one that offered ingenious, if abstract, life lessons. But the players enjoying it in quarantine celebrate it for escapism, which any form of entertainment might provide. Neither interpretation seems quite right. Even though it can function as escapism, Animal Crossing isn't a fantasy-world replacement from real life, absent all its burdens. But nor is it a handbook for how to live in actual reality more effectively – the most distinctive aspect of mortgage lending, after all, is the crushing weight of compounding interest, which enriches lenders that get bailouts if they fail. None of that stuff appears in the game at all.

Instead, Animal Crossing is a political hypothesis about how a different kind of world might work – one with no losers. Millions of people already have spent hours in the game stewing on that idea since the coronavirus crisis began.

Sequestered at home on lockdown, the NYU Game Center professor Naomi Clark recently offered a compelling reading of Animal Crossing to her students and colleagues, many of whom probably have been playing it to pass the time. The game, she argued, is a nostalgic fantasy for the Japanese *furusato*, a pastoral hometown. Before industrialisation, a seaside fishing village or hillside paddy-field farm might have sustained a simple, deliberate life of basic subsistence and straightforward agricultural trade, much like the life the player leads in Animal Crossing.

Read: We need to stop trying to replicate the life we had.

But the size and economies of these villages were too modest even to sustain their basic familial and mercantile needs, so the villages would take on collective debt – to pay for fishing nets and supplies, say. But nobody would ever pay back the debt, Clark explained. They didn't have the money! Instead, it would bind the locals to their village – you owed something to the collective, so how could you ever leave? And so the community would persist, a tableau of Georgic calm sealed inside the bottle of a company town.

Nintendo is a traditional, Japanese company, so Clark's interpretation is convincing. The game has other distinctively Japanese elements that might not be immediately obvious to Western players, too. Tom Nook, for example, is not a raccoon but a *tanuki* (Tom Nook, *tanuki*, you get the picture), a Japanese raccoon dog with a long-standing folkloric history as both a trickster and a symbol of wealth, much like the fox in the West. Among other things, the *tanuki* has enormous testicles (but not Tom Nook; this is a family game). Many Japanese woodblock prints depict a *tanuki* kneading its testes into the shape of various objects, such as raincoats or fishing nets. The supernatural industriousness of Tom Nook, who can divine manufactured goods from thin air in the game, takes on another meaning when seen through the lens of *tanuki* mythology.

The *furusato* fantasy offers one view on the fusion of commerce and the countryside, but it doesn't really land in the West, especially in America. Here, capitalism and pastoralism are often seen as opposing forces. So, too, personal benefit and collective good.

This goes all the way back to John Locke, who held that individuals had a right to turn natural resources that belonged to no one into individual property for personal use, through labour. The Lockean idea justified all manner of accomplishments and violations in American history, including the colonial seizure of Native lands and the justification of resource extraction via the efficiencies of industry. In the nation that grew from those assumptions, the accrual of wealth became incompatible with a return to the land. Agrarianism forked into factory farming on the one hand or farm-to-table luxury on the other. And pastoralism never really got a foothold in America as it did in England or Japan: Land was so plentiful that its survival was taken for granted.

But according to the Tom Nook doctrine, pastoralism and capitalism coexist perfectly. You can fish for high-value red snappers and sell them to buy espadrilles for your character, or 1950s-diner furnishings for your house. Or you can fish for never-before-seen specimens, to donate them to the museum. Or you can cast a line just to enjoy watching the moon dance across the water. All of these activities are interchangeable and equally delightful. Animal Crossing sees no greater or lesser virtue in one than another.

This ambivalence extends to labour and commerce on Tom Nook's island. To make the game's economy operate, players can sell raw materials and manufactured items for currency (called 'bells'), which can be used to buy other goods. Nook's apprentices, Timmy and Tommy, run a shop that stocks a few things each day, but the two critters will also buy literally anything the player wants to get rid of: Fruit shaken off trees, insects snared from stumps, old cans or tires fished from the deep, lamps or tables fashioned from found wood and ore, garments that no longer spark joy.

Supply and demand still rule, with common items fetching fewer bells than rare ones. Some critics see Tom Nook as a capitalist oligarch, pressing players to become entrepreneurs who farm high-value tarantulas for big profits. But Animal Crossing players are mostly foragers, and Tom Nook doesn't seem that interested in capitalism. You can't become an investor or much of a financier; a 'stalk market' for turnip commodities is mostly a loser's game best avoided. Nook never seems to benefit from his profits; he seems more like a reforming ecological collectivist, working behind the scenes to maintain the village's fecund repleteness.

Price variation notwithstanding, Timmy and Tommy value any kind of effort the player wants to conduct as viable labour. Want to collect coconuts from the palm trees every three days? That's fine. Want to travel abroad to mine iron for crafting park benches? They'll buy those too. Want to catch butterflies? No problem. Every effort is valid, every accomplishment exchangeable for capital. Want to do no job whatsoever, but just sit on stumps and shake a tambourine?

That's fine too; there are no consequences for not earning 'bells'. Nobody cares in Animal Crossing. You are okay.

For Americans playing the game as coronavirus lockdowns produce historic spikes in unemployment, the idea that any activity might be seen as viable work is a comfort, and perhaps even an aspiration. Imagine if everyone had a job that they enjoyed, that they were good at, and that could sustain them. What if they could thrive with no job at all, a step well beyond universal basic income? Even a month ago, such ideas would have felt preposterous beyond the cartoonish shores of a video game. But now they feel like dreams worth dreaming. [...]

That said, the game has added some features that risk undermining Animal Crossing's careful balance of the market and the countryside. One is crafting, a video-game design pattern in which players must accrue raw materials and fashion them into more complex objects for further use. In New Horizons, crafting is an unending malaise. The player is forced to acquire sticks and stones to make axes or nets or fishing rods, but these basic tools break quickly after a few dozen uses. You end up using axes or shovels to mine rocks for iron, just to use that iron to build slightly less flimsy tools.

On first blush, crafting almost commands the player to see the island as a mere strip mine – not to mention neighbouring islands visited only for resource extraction and then forgotten forever. But though it is a toy world, the island is not a microcosm; its own resources are limited, and the greater the local population (eight human players can 'live' on one console), the more competition exists for those resources. Is it better to omit this truth, to pretend that resources are infinite, as many games do, or to force the player to contend with the scarcity and violence intrinsic to manufacturing? It would be disproportionate to conclude that merely representing the dynamic implies that the game endorses it. And yet, Animal Crossing doesn't decry the practice either. Instead, the conflict persists forever, like the island sunset chasing the horizon.

Another gut punch comes from the addition of an in-game smartphone, new to the series in this title. Tom Nook gives it to players to store crafting recipes and design custom clothing in virtual apps. There's also a loyalty-programme app, called Nook Miles, which doles out a scrip currency for player accomplishments, such as catching ten bugs or chatting with three animal neighbours in a day.

Here too, the game seems to undermine its own principles at first. Animal Crossing used to be self-directed, and players would often chat with the animal characters in order to be assigned favours to complete. But now the smartphone serves up infinite ideas: One completed task just spawns another in its place. Players are motivated to do specific things for extrinsic rewards rather than doing whatever they like for the sake of intrinsic pleasure, and knowing it will be valued.

And yet, isn't this exactly the trade-off that real smartphones demand, a constant lifeline to new options, all more or less the same in nature, judged valuable by how many likes or hearts they accrue? But remember, this is a video-game iPhone, not a real one. Smartphones are always deceptive, Tom Nook seems to warn, but maybe they can be used differently. Perhaps the problem with real life isn't the devices, but the hyper-employment that turns every activity conducted upon them into secret labour from the start.

Late one night recently, a barrage of texts blew up my phone. They were from my friend Frank Lantz, the director of the NYU Game Center, who also designs cult games.

'I hate Animal Crossing', Lantz's opening message read.

He and his wife and collaborator, Hilary, had sat down to play it, looking for the same low-key, cute cosiness that everyone else found comforting. 'It is the most boring, long-winded, repetitive, condescending, infantile bullshit we've ever seen.' After a few more invectives, he posed a question: 'Do people find comfort in tedious, bureaucratic, pandering authoritarianism?'

The answer, which Lantz knew before he asked, is: Of course they do. Americans in particular are addicted to bureaucracy's directed control even as they cry yawps of independence and self-actualisation.

But with coronavirus deaths soaring and the real economy tanking, Animal Crossing might inspire Americans to reclaim structure and routine, and to motivate it toward modest rather than remarkable ends. Nobody really wants to live a pastoral-capitalist equilibrium of humdrum labour – unless that's what everyone wants, actually, and not even so secretly. Civic life, after all, coheres not in abstract fantasies about politician-heroes, but in habitual practices that take place in real communities. All video games aestheticise busywork. But few make it feel like freedom.

Ian Bogost, 'The Quiet Revolution of Animal Crossing', *The Atlantic* (15 April 2020). Available at www.theatlantic.com/family/archive/2020/04/animal-crossing-isnt-escapist-its-political/610012/

Peggy Ahwesh
Cut to Cute: In Conversation with Johanna Gosse//2018

This conversation with film-maker Peggy Ahwesh focuses on three of her recent works, *Lessons of War* (2015), *The Blackest Sea* (2016) and *The Falling Sky* (2017), a trilogy of experimental films that sit at the intersection of digital animation, found-footage essay, and moving image installation. The films are comprised of animated CGI video that Ahwesh sourced from YouTube and then edited into original compilations. Their source material was produced by two Taiwanese news agencies, TomoNews US and News Direct, which specialise in CGI 'newsreels' that report on global catastrophes like war, the refugee crisis and climate change, to more everyday stories like politics, crime and celebrity gossip.

[…] The following conversation between Ahwesh and scholar Johanna Gosse considers the experimental uses (and dystopian mis-uses) of digital animation at a time of political, economic, and ecological instability. […]

Johanna Gosse Let's start with your source footage. Can you describe how you first encountered these Taiwanese news agencies? […]

Peggy Ahwesh I was researching re-enactment when I first came across the Taiwanese animators. Of immediate interest was the re-enactment of the Trayvon Martin killing in Florida as it was portrayed as animated news, a literal play-by-play retelling of the event with details that were available from the major news networks, and as reported on the major networks.

These details were presented without analysis, irony, or perceived point of view. It was frightening and cold as a story. The attempt to mimic the so-called objectivity of the mainstream news was amplified by the simplicity of the animation, in which the people are depicted with the slightest ethnic features and generic bodies. Since there were no pictures of the actual event, the clues and the police reports, the harrowing calls to 911 and the forensic crime scene data all had to be compiled in order to determine the sequence of events and how to narrate it. The look of the animation, its aesthetic style, makes it palatable to watch, since it leaves out the gruesome reality of the killing. To watch a story sandwiched between reportage and cartoons is a queasy and disconnected experience – like the uncanny creepiness of a happy clown. […]

Complicity and Labour Politics

Gosse Earlier, you spoke about your 'complicity' with the Taiwanese animators – a term that casts you as more of an accomplice or co-conspirator than a collaborator or co-author. [...]

As an act of complicity, your use of these animations points back to your accomplices – the anonymous crew of digital artists – and their relationship to the global economy. I wonder, is their labour considered high or low-skilled? Are these studios run like digital sweatshops? By appropriating their products, are you actually outsourcing your own artistic labour and further contributing to the workers' exploitation? What are the political implications of framing appropriation as complicity and collusion rather than collaboration and solidarity?

Ahwesh These are really good questions that always need to be considered when it comes to appropriation. In some way, the kinship I feel to the makers of these videos is similar to how an author uses a quotation in a text. It can be used to bolster the argument that the author is trying to make, it can be an incantation to add levels of meaning, and/or it can be a betrayal or a critical reading of the original. Perhaps there are more uses to quotation, but in my work, I try to hit upon these three. That said, these questions of labour persist, and remain relevant and provocative.

My research tells me that Next Studios is like a digital Disney with hundreds of animators cranking out not just newsreels, but also zombie films, fighting *manga* features, and commercial work for clients. It is a pretty sophisticated corporate production of the entertainment industry and I would guess that most of the workers are hunched over computers all day, rendering figures against backgrounds. I am piggybacking on the resources and investment of the company. I don't take it for granted and it might be useful to compare what I do to a fan edit instead of the more academic trope of appropriation.

Gosse [...] So far we've talked about labour and class, but I wonder if you can speak further to the feminist impulse in your work, and if it relates to the films we are discussing here? Not so much in terms of their literal content (especially since the animated human figures are given only the most basic attributes of gender, such as hairstyle and clothing) but perhaps more in terms of methodology?

Ahwesh I have a tendency to work with trash, discards, and 'worthless' bits of low-status film. Other film-makers working with found footage aim to dismantle masterpieces. To appropriate such masterpieces is a privilege that I won't claim; instead, I adopt the role of the outsider as a position of strength. I'm not sure this is a feminist issue or a class issue, or both.

[…] Another example and one that may be essentialising but comes to mind is this: the *Lessons of War* appropriates the 'cuteness' of the animation in order to reveal an underlying horror, and to render the cute abject – my version thus offers a critical use of cuteness. […]

Gosse Over the past two decades, with the rise of computer-imaging software, digital animation has emerged as a major genre of contemporary art, especially animation that emphasises the violent, uncanny, taboo and grotesque: take, for example, Paul Chan's *Happiness (Finally) After 35,000 Years of Civilization – After Henry Darger and Charles Fourier* (2000–2003). How would you contextualise your work against Chan's work and the 'animated turn' in contemporary art more broadly?

Ahwesh There are many things our work has in common, one being the diminutive scale of the characters – the miniaturisation of the bodies in their tiny settings. Cartoons imply immaturity, I suppose, but my attraction to them, and I assume that of the artists we are talking about, is as a tactic that suppresses 'taste', or at least moves it to the periphery, and opens up a game space of substitutions with avatars and animated figures. I have a long-standing obsession with puppets, as well as souvenirs, miniature books, comics; I find it deeply satisfying to inhabit my tidy subjective world alongside these miniaturised objects.

Chan's video of Darger's Vivian girls is a pageant that contrasts scenes of the girls frolicking in bucolic gardens with brutal battle scenes. It's an intense and dire mash-up of the 'cute' with the brutality of war and violence. Chan describes so clearly that cognitive dissonance one experiences when being mesmerised equally by beauty and violence. In *She Puppet* (2001), our heroine figure 'talks' in voiceover and describes the dilemma of contemporary digital life while trapped inside a video game. This rescaled cartoon world becomes increasingly convincing as we shrink to fit inside it.

Gosse This tension between cuteness and violence in Chan's work brings me back to your earlier, provocative description of your films as a critical use of the cute, or perhaps a *detourning* of cuteness. […]

[Sianne] Ngai [suggests] that the cute is essentially something […] soft, malleable, and thus easily dominated or manipulated.

Her description of an archetypal cute object as an 'undifferentiated blob of soft doughy matter' recalls Sergei Eisenstein's influential theories of animation, particularly his concept of plasmaticness, which he defines as 'a rejection of once-and-forever allotted form, freedom from ossification, the ability to dynamically assume any form'.[1] For Eisenstein, plasmaticness enables animation to behave like 'primal protoplasm, not yet possessing a "stable" form, but capable of assuming any form and which, skipping along the rungs of the evolutionary ladder, attaches itself to any and all forms of animal existence'.[2] Importantly, though, he frames animation's plasmaticness as an expression of its freedom from form rather than its domination by external forces. Accordingly, the formlessness and mutability of animation registers a utopian possibility. Thus, Ngai's cuteness and Eistenstein's plasmaticness represent two competing understandings of animated form, one framed in terms of domination, the other in terms of freedom.

Where do you locate your films in relation to Ngai and Eisenstein's theories?

Ahwesh Eisenstein's dialectical montage is a form of ideological cutting that is in direct opposition to 'cute'. Eisenstein admired Disney animations for their sense of freedom of form and playfulness, and was excited by the instability of those transformations. A different way to think of this aesthetic concept of 'cuteness' might be [Georges] Bataille's theory of the *informe* (formless). With my films, I am scavenging forms and messing with them in a betrayal of their intended logic, shape and meaning – I take forms and render them *informe*.

I am aware of the limitations of 'form' but at the same time I am seduced by the awesome beauty and balance it can attain. My work seeks to upend formal significance. By definition, one aspect of the formless is a base materialism that includes the use of discards, low technologies, found materials, decay, and the marginal. Though generating 'meaning' is typically the professed goal of an artist, I find that we often want to connect on a more fundamental, irrational level of feeling and process, between the push-pull of revulsion and attraction. This impulse is something we recognise easily in sculpture or while moulding shapes out of clay, but I think it is equally operative in moving images.

Cuteness and Agency
Gosse What strikes me about the type of animation that interests you is that in spite of its cuteness, it actually lacks the quality of plasmaticness as Eisenstein describes it. The living creatures that populate these virtual worlds are emphatically *not* protean or changeable – nor are they remotely social. To the contrary, their shapes, movements, and fates are digitally preordained. Like puppets or mannequins, they utterly lack any sense of agency or interiority, and do not act so much as *are acted upon.*

They do not speak or communicate, and when a thought-bubble pops up, it is filled with picture language and emoji. When living beings are threatened or killed, they don't resist or appear to suffer, they merely change colours: red indicates dead. Unlike Lara Croft in *She Puppet*, these figures don't rise to the level of individual avatars or characters, just pawns in an overarching algorithmic narrative. In a more dystopian interpretation, these animations provide a glimpse of how computers view humanity, as toys to be manipulated and controlled rather than individual agents endowed with choice and freedom.

However, if there is a protean sense of mutability (*qua* [Sergei] Eisenstein) available here, it is registered not through the figures themselves but rather through your editing, which injects unpredictability and unruliness, and thus injects some human agency into these virtual worlds.

As editor, you reanimate and remobilise these inert digital narratives, opening up new possibilities for historical revision and new horizons of possibility.

Ahwesh Yes, this word 'mobilised' is a really good descriptor – the figures in the videos are not the totems of so-called primitive cultureanimistic figures of magic with changing temperaments and form.

They are almost the opposite, since they are used in the service of representation – confined by the industry of news production. I hope I return to them to a bit of their shape-shifting potential – allowing for irony, distortions of the real and playful and multiple meanings.

Mick Taussig's *Mimesis and Alterity: A Particular History of the Senses* (1993) is a fantastic text that actually relates to Eisenstein's theory of animation. Taussig describes how native peoples design fetishes and mimetic figures that adopt the likenesses of the colonisers and their alien utilitarian objects, and then use these objects to invert colonial power in the struggle for independence and control over cultural meaning.

To bring something into proximity versus keeping it at a distance – this push-pull constitutes the dynamic of appropriation, in which the original meaning and the revision often move in opposite directions. It creates an eerie friction that gets these multifarious associations all revved up, or in other words, animated.

Cuteness and Control

Gosse Your films go beyond a critiquing cuteness, they weaponise it. I detect a feminist subtext here that, once again, points back to *She Puppet* – like animation, in puppetry, cuteness and control are co-constitutive. In what ways do you think that the cuteness of the animated newsreels, and of animation in general, might provide an opportunity for the deployment of feminised forms and aesthetics (such as cuteness) as a political strategy?

Ahwesh Deep down I have always disparaged the 'cute' and have felt it to be a weakness of femininity and sentimentality, a genteel cover-up of strong emotions. Over the years, most of my work has come from an opposing point of view – one that is raw, direct and improvised. The development of video games in the 1990s was so rapid, their beauty, sophistication and interactivity so amazing, but what was really cool was the constant mutations by users with mods and cheats – play that breaks the rules of the game. I saw gameplay in line with this kind of rule-breaking and improvisation, and started messing around with Tomb Raider, eventually resulting in *She Puppet*. It struck me that there was power in inverting my approach, and discovered that using the game was a shortcut to dismantling this power. I could work with and against femaleness as portrayed in Tomb Raider as an imaginary adventure world designed for the female protagonist's exploits and confrontations. It's a productive mimesis that *detourns* the dominant structures of power and control, allowing for a radical subjectivity to sneak through as a form of redemption.

Regarding the use of cartoons and computer-generated figures as imagery, by me and other artists, I think it's also an attempt to chart the specific reality of who we are right now, how to communicate the complex, deep substrate that is the texture of our present moment. The formal elements an artist chooses are the codes that activate the work, and relay ideas and feelings to make a gestalt within the viewer. The catalogue of old gestures and styles just doesn't work in our new machine world. Using the cartoons in a critical way, or 'weaponising' them as you say, makes visible what is already omnipresent but brings it forward with higher definition. It puts these forms into dialogue with subjective experience in a way that feels real and challenging but also, in some cases, oddly comforting.

1   Sergei Eisenstein, *Eisenstein 3: Eisenstein on Disney*, ed. Jay Leyda (Calcutta: Seagull Books, 1986) 21.

2   Ibid.

Peggy Ahwesh and Johanna Gosse, extracts from 'Cut to Cute: Fact, Form, and Feeling in Digital Animation', in *Experimental and Expanded Animation*, eds. Vicky Smith & Nicky Hamlyn (Cambridge: Palgrave Macmillan, 2018) 183–202, 183–5, 187–8, 191, 197–201.

Mike Kelley
In the Image of Man//1991

In the 1980s, when some artists self-consciously began to produce works that embraced their status as commodities, there arose, simultaneously, the desire in other artists to make works that escaped such commodification.[1] The argument was advanced that an artwork could function analogously to the gift, an object outside of the system of exchange.[2] This is what initially led to my interest in home-made craft items, that is, objects already existing in popular usage that are constructed specifically to be given away. This is not to say that I believe craft gifts themselves harbour utopian sentiments; all things have a price. The hidden burden of the gift is that it calls for payback, but the price is unspecified, repressed. The uncanny aura of the craft item is linked to time. Crafts are the literal embodiment of the Puritan work ethic. They seem to announce that work is its own reward. This is conveyed by the long, labour-intensive hours required to construct them by hand. They speak the language of the wage earner in which there is a one-to-one relationship between time spent and worth. The equation is not between time and money; it is a more obscure relationship drawn between time and commitment, one that results in a kind of emotional usury. The gift operates within an economy of guilt, an endless feeling of indebtedness attends it because of its mysterious worth. And the highly loaded nature of these objects is intensified by their material nature: by the seeming contradiction that their emotional weight far exceeds the worth of the cheap and lowly materials from which they are constructed. However, it isn't proper to speak of the 'junk' status of the craft item; it is in bad taste to comment on the financial worth of a gift. The fine art 'junk sculpture' could be said to have value in spite of its material, while the craft item could be said, like the icon, to have value beyond its material.

In the process of acquiring large numbers of craft items, primarily dolls and stuffed toy animals, I started to become conscious of them for the first time as discrete objects. Beyond thinking of them as mere carriers of 'love hours' (or 'guilt hours'), I became aware that they also had specific forms, and that there must be some connection between these forms and the objects' use. But at the same time that I became conscious of this fact, I also realised that they were extremely limited in a formal sense. The few craft types commonly made can easily be categorised by material and construction techniques. The shift in my interest to the individual craft item led me away from my earlier accumulation works, such as *More Love Hours Than Can Ever Be Repaid* (1987) and *Plush Kundalini and Chakra Set* (1987), into the *Arena* series, which consists of stuffed animals arranged on blankets laid on the floor. Primarily composed of 'autograph hounds', *Arena #10 (Dogs)* (1990) is typical of the series. In these works, I toyed with the viewer's inclination to project into the figures, to construct an inner narrative around them, which I would argue makes viewers less aware of their own physical presence. To counter this tendency, and thus make the viewer more self-conscious, I used extremely worn and soiled craft materials in the construction of these works. The immediate tendency of viewers to be sucked into a narrativising situation was dismantled when they got close enough to the sculptures to recognise the unpleasant tactile qualities of the craft materials. Fear of soiling themselves countered the urge to idealise.

Stuffed toys, especially dolls, lend themselves to invisibility. When you look at a doll, you don't notice its particularities. Rather, you see it in a general way as 'human'. If there are enough suitable cues – head, body, legs, etc. – you can personify it; specific details like facial features, hands and feet are unimportant. In fact, the figure can be stripped down to a simple bag shape and still be accepted as portraying a human being. All of the 'humanoid' details missing in such an object are filled in by the viewer. It is this projective relationship with the doll that allows us to empathise with it. If you were to see the doll as an exact model of a figure, as a portrait statue, empathy would be impossible – it would be seen as a monstrosity.

In my next series, *Empathy Displacement: Humanoid Morphology (2nd and 3rd Remove)* (1990), I concentrated on this process of identification. I take as my starting point the notion that there is a Platonic human archetype, and that individual human beings are at the first remove from it. A three-dimensional doll would be at the second remove; and a two-dimensional depiction of the doll, at the third. These works consist of a human-scaled black-and-white illustrative painting of a doll, presented along with its model concealed in a black box that lies on the floor in front of it. Empathy is problematised in this situation, for the shift in scale makes it difficult to empathise with the painting of the doll, and the viewer is led to empathise instead with the original doll, which they must assume is enclosed in the box. Projection is made complete because the object of empathy can no longer be seen.

My latest work with these materials, *Craft Morphology Flow Chart* (1991), will be presented at the Carnegie International, 1991. This is, I believe, the last of my 'stuffed animal' works. I removed all vestiges of empathy from this piece in order to address the pure 'material nature' of the crafts. Three representational systems are used simultaneously to present the materials. First, the crafts are arranged categorically, according to construction technique and shape, on simple folding tables. Second, every one of these items, accompanied by a ruler to show its true size, has been photographed. And third, one representative grouping of craft items – the collection of 'sock monkeys' – has been rendered in a large black-and-white line drawing reminiscent of archaeological illustration. Through this reiteration, I propose that the psychological baggage that usually attends such objects has been discarded. Of course, by attempting to repress them, these emotional qualities become even more pervasive.

1   Commodity 'readymades', which introduced object-based rather than image-based forms of appropriation, feature in the work of key New York postmodernists such as Jeff Koons and Haim Steinbach. The restaging of mass-produced objects (Steinbach, Koons, Sherrie Levine); of logos, decals and collective image-bites (Ashley Bickerton); or of simulated signs and info systems (Peter Halley, Philip Taaffe) is realigned, as Steinbach put it, in complicity 'with the production of desire' and through the cultivation of an explicit 'pleasure in objects and commodities'. See David Robbins (ed.), 'From Criticism to Complicity,' discussion between Haim Steinbach, Jeff Koons, Sherrie Levine, Philip Taaffe, Peter Halley and Ashley Bickerton (moderated by Peter Nagy), *Flash Art*, no. 129 (Summer 1986) 46–9.

2   Kelley is referring here not so much to recent art-world dialogues with anthropological conceptions of the 'gift' (formulated most notably by Marcel Mauss in his 'Essai sur le Don', 1950) as to ideas of collectivity, collaboration and non-commodity distribution espoused by artists and groups such as the Colab (Collaborative Projects, Inc.) collective in the late 1970s and 80s. He recalls one book in particular that circulated in the art world in the 1980s: Lewis Hyde, *The Gift: Imagination and the Erotic Life of Property* (New York: Vintage, 1979).

Mike Kelley, 'In the Image of Man', artist's statement for 'Craft Morphology Flow Chart' (1991), Carnegie International 1991, in *Mike Kelley: Minor Histories: Statements, Conversations, Proposals*, ed. John C. Welchman (Cambridge, MA: MIT Press, 2004).

Christopher Knight
Charlemagne Palestine: Teddy Bears to the Rescue//2018

A marvellously abundant, even overstuffed installation by artist and composer Charlemagne Palestine fills an industrial warehouse space with tons of plush comfort, kaleidoscopic colour and rhythmic waves of noise. 18,000 stuffed animals have taken up temporary residence in the gallery at 356 S. Mission Road.

Mickey, Minnie, SpongeBob SquarePants, Hello Kitty, plus a much bigger menagerie of anonymous animals (elephants, crocodiles, toucans, lambs, owls, you-name-it) and, most of all, teddy bears cavort among brightly coloured fabric strips, table cloths and yards of inexpensive textiles. The room's big window panes are smeared in bright colours, like finger-painted stained glass for a secular Chartres Cathedral. For good measure, spotlighted and spinning mirror-balls send dots of light gaily skittering around the room.

The plush toys are attached to both sides of nine freestanding walls on wheels. Petals torn from artificial flowers are scattered beneath them on the floor – a traditional wedding symbol of fertility made joyfully secular. Here, creation is artistic.

Other plush toys are loaded inside seven coffins made of plain pine and ranging in size from small child to extra-large adult; piled in great mounds within the cabinets of three baby grand pianos; heaped inside two topsy-turvy rowboats and one small sailboat suspended from the ceiling (the 'Nina,' 'Pinta' and 'Santa Maria'); jammed within hanging bathtubs; strewn along the floor the length of one wide wall; covering the surface of the opposite wall and – here, there and everywhere – hanging from vivaciously colourful fabric parachutes that dangle in the air.

The parachute brigade is like a rescue team arriving to save the day, a Berlin airlift for the beleaguered soul.

The emergency is not topical. Palestine has compared school to a concentration camp and his mother to Margaret Thatcher, the cold-blooded Iron Lady, which gives at least some indication as to why liberation is needed. Soft kiddie toys are cuddly, all purpose talismans of succour and solace.

In the centre of the room, a ceremonial semi-circle has been set up with a makeshift ring of tatty television monitors playing a selection of Palestine's video performances from the past 40 years. In one, the artist runs around a small, plain room, banging into walls as if trapped and unable to break free, yet confirming the protective shelter of the place.

In another, the camera seems adrift at sea. In a third, he swings a lantern on an electrical chord around his head, like a cowboy-shaman with a lariat of light.

Through it all, a soundtrack of rhythmic chanting swells and falls. Sound is integral to Palestine's installation, whose title incorporates letters repeated like resonant sonic vibrations. Buried within 'Ccornuuoorphanossccopiaee Aanorphansshhornoffplentyyy', as the installation is titled, are an orphaned cornucopia and horn of plenty. The gallery, stuffed, becomes its own environmentally scaled stuffed toy.

Palestine's cascades of emotionally loaded plush animals and exuberant explosions of bright commercial gewgaws for children preceded related work by accomplished artists as diverse as Larry Mantello in the 1990s and Mike Kelley in the 1980s. (Palestine taught at CalArts, where Kelley went to school, in the early 1970s, and the current exhibition is sponsored by the Mike Kelley Foundation for the Arts.) The installation is all really just too much – which, in these cruel and emotionally crushing days, means it's almost just enough.

Christopher Knight, 'Charlemagne Palestine: Teddy Bears to the Rescue', *Los Angeles Times* (24 February 2018).

Catherine Grenier
Annette Messager//2000

The Dolls

Annette Messager's working procedure was already clearly established in her earliest ventures: appropriating things and activities that have been devalued, and investing them with supreme value; inventorying the most anodyne private practices and catapulting them into the public sphere: and translating childhood games into the adult world. Feminism she treated less as a cause than as a framework that allowed her to progress onto new things, investigating its territory like, as she has said, 'some ethnologist or art historian specialising in the ethnic arts'. Since many of the practices in which she is engaged are typically 'feminine': the implication might be that her work is primarily autobiographical, though this is a conclusion that she has been careful to neither confirm nor deny. […]

In *Les Pensionnaires* (*The Boarders*, 1971–2), the piece that broke with the early sequences of handmade objects and which saw the beginning of her oeuvre proper, Annette Messager was to seize on a new possibility, which she developed from within a private narrative, whose closest equivalent is a game. Following a request from the Galerie Germain to produce a work using wool (in the context of a show sponsored by Woolmark), one day she came across a sparrow lying dead on the sidewalk. Once back in the studio, she made a mock-up of the bird out of feathers that she then swaddled in wool.

This first sparrow was soon joined by other 'boarders', some stuffed, others simply built up out of feathers. all sporting little coloured cardigans she had knitted for them. They were then christened like human infants. Initially derived from maternal care, the game then developed further: childhood accessories were made – a feather alphabet, a cage, exercise bars, remote-controlled vehicles, toys – which she arranged in various scenarios that were written down in a notebook and recorded in a series of drawings, paintings and photographs. The crucial moments of childhood (the daily walk, various punishments, the afternoon nap) are all there ('mimed', as the artist put it) in a touching yet grotesque manner (Annette Messager has even used the term 'fake' in this connection). [...]

The birds are presented in a vitrine and accompanied by handwritten, disingenuous texts divided into chapters and inscribed in school notebooks. These describe in minute detail everyday situations related in the first person, illustrated with captioned black-and-white photos and even a few colour plates, as well as with little drawings evocative of either the vignettes that appear in picture books or of technical drawings in specialised journals. There are also small-scale painted portraits of each bird. The material is documentary in the sense that materials for a performance are documentary: a few relics to which a growing mass of commentaries are attached: images, and images of images, observations on actions and commentaries on images. The central question revolves around how to record what are after all insignificant activities, and transform them into something legendary, something like the story of a saint's life or an explorer's tale. [...]

It was in this piece that Annette Messager first made use of the image of the doll. The doll is the female archetype par excellence, the one with which women are most often identified: little girls play with dolls, but grown women *turn into* dolls, or at least play at being dolls. The doll is commonly used to refer to the artificiality, the lack of maturity, and even, on a somewhat different level, the malevolence supposedly inherent in the female personality. Some maintain that the predominant trait of females is to be always 'playing at life' – the tendency may be cleverly concealed, but sooner or later, privately, secretly, it will emerge. It is on precisely this feature that Annette Messager's work relies; by deliberately 'playing at life', she turns it into a means of exploring the world through works that stage various 'games of life'. [...] [T]he universe she portrays is populated by dolls, but it is invested with all the powerful experiences of mature womanhood that give all their lost humanity and vulnerability back to the childhood toys.

[...] Annette Messager's toys offer an instrument for measuring life and the body, difference and indifference, for measuring art itself. The action of measuring and of measuring up to art, envisaged as a domestic activity involving recording and weighing, constituted a particular section in Annette Messager's agenda that would be continued over the succeeding months in *The Boarders* project, for which she adopted the ironic sobriquet 'Annette Messager, artist'. [...]

Family Stories

In 1988, preparations began for Annette Messager's debut retrospective to be held at the Musée de Grenoble the following year. The opportunity of revisiting her entire oeuvre, a process that entailed recapitulating earlier works, had a major impact on the more recent *Vows* (1988–91) and *Works* (1987), which harked back to the *Collections*, and, above all, *Mes Petites Effigies* (*My Little Effigies,* 1988). The latter was a new series whose formal approach could be inferred from that of *My Works*, but whose stuffed animals presented in various scenarios clearly echoed *The Boarders*. Although it opened the door to fresh possibilities, the use of toys marked the reappearance of the notion of the doll, as well as of the animal-human metaphor. Pinned and suspended, skewered and flayed, these little figures – closer to the human world than the body-part photos could ever be – were to become a favourite source material for many series to come. [...]

These stuffed toys exemplified a new operative component in Messager's work: the simulacrum. The title of 'effigies' and the humanisation of the toys, some of whom are even dressed in pocket-sized garments, carry connotations of magic. 'In *My Little Effigies,* I hung photos of bits of the body around the necks of ordinary looking cuddly toys on pedestals built up out of words. These ridiculous little creatures thus became disturbing, just like certain voodoo dolls.' 'Ridiculous' and 'disturbing' are specifically human qualities which both – though in very different terms – designate a distance from the norm. Although today magic has lost much of the disquieting appeal it held in former times and in these works has been reduced to little more than an attachment to traditional folklore idioms, a genuine anomaly resides in the importance Annette Messager invests in these worn-out old toys, in the inclusion of their lifeless bodies within a symbolically charged environment. The semantic system stems not so much from the verbal pedestals or from the photographs of ears, eyes or sexual organs hanging round their necks like scarves, than from these animals manqués. Bunny rabbit, Mickey Mouse, Babar the Elephant – each creature conveys a different aspect of the human species, instruments in an anthropological study that taxonomises every last detail of body and soul. Limb after limb, emotion after emotion. Laid out in a continuous line against the wall, the piece resembles a scientist's test bench that can be extended ad infinitum: modern-day fetishes offering a resumé of a humanity severed from its sacred aura. For a show at the Musée d'Art Moderne de la Ville de Paris, they were placed in a vitrine. In the company of a number of

African carvings, where they appeared more paltry than ever, emblems of a world that has lost faith in everything, save in childhood. [...]

Dead Skins

Dissections (Dissections, 1996) and *Dépouilles (Sloughs*, 1997–8) are made out of plush toys which the artist has emptied of the stuffing, flattened out and stretched, inside-out, onto the wall. The exposed loose threads form a haphazard pattern on the surface of firmly symmetrical shapes that are reminiscent of those in Rorschach tests. Although different, these forms all conform to the same structural schema and are used in simple compositions determined by their analogical features. Evocative perhaps of childbirth. a bunch of flowers or a mask, these skins guide the artist's work and condition what viewers see as they scrutinise the figures or hunt for other images. The diversity and inventiveness of these shapes made from simply flattening out a surface or enveloping a body is a source of constant surprise that contrasts with the uneasy sense that one is looking at a hide, a wretched yet comic hunting trophy. It is no longer a body, but the imprint left by a body; but it is not yet an image, rather the embryo of an image. This indeterminate object that turns into a sign, an 'image of naught' (as the Romantics would have had it) that summons up other signs and other images, is typical of the artist's pieces in which stripped and slashed toys, cushions, bolsters or unpicked woollen gloves serve as relays for the imagination, exercising the potential for other images within the form. Two combination works, *Histoire des oreillers (Story of Pillows*, 1995–6) and *Histoires des traversins (Story of Bolsters*, 1996–8), are based on the potential of their chosen raw material – the pillow – to be arranged and reshaped into figurative, meaningful forms without severing connections to its original shape or removing every last trace of its individual history. Like a sloughed skin, a worn old pillow conserves a disturbingly powerful emotional charge, its appropriation being of itself something indecent, like a violation of someone else's private space. Paradoxically, its softness and pliability allow for every reconfiguration the artist demands – decorative figuration in *Story of Pillows*, or as furniture in *Story of Bolsters*.

Little by little, the artist managed to convert her entire vocabulary of solid, regular shapes into an alphabet of soft pliable forms. Progressively, what had had a name became unnameable. *Erection (in Piques)* had been followed by the drooping *Bolsters*, the geometrical *Vows* by the deliquescent 'penetrables' and the scattered unknittings: If some elements from earlier idioms survived, they were for the most part overrun and absorbed by the soft forms, as in the case of the photographs from *Vows* nestling under a heap of bolsters or stuck into folds in pillows. The grimacing children that appear in a number of installations also possess this malleable body, the type of identity that children happily distort. The motif which formed the starting point for the majority of these compositions has become imperceptible, as in *Dependence Independence*, where the installation's large size makes it impossible to fully take in its heart-like shape. One *Story of Bolsters* depicts the kind of domestic interior which the artist had often explored in the past, but in a collapsed version that calls to mind Oldenburg's soft sculptures. This deflation, softening and indetermination exemplifies our contemporary inability to frame certainties, to devise systems, or to forge clear-cut distinctions. The piece echoes a world that may not have fallen when the utopias were overturned, but which has lost much of its solidity, and no longer has the strength to resist the gaze of the viewer. The new environment in which Annette Messager places humanity resembles a cave. Most of her more recent installations are set up within the space of primitive man, from the 'penetrables' to the mixed-media room installations she has created in Venice, Bordeaux and New York, incorporating elements as diverse as bolsters, hangings. netting, wool and soft toys. Human presence is reduced to an allusive hollowed-out being, every element of which harbours a memory. In a period that has been called 'post-human': in which the human is being ousted by the artificial, Annette Messager invites us to slide back into the uterine matrix of the primitive family, to reawaken a nomadic memory from the depths of humanity. [...]

Catherine Grenier, extracts from *Annette Messager*, trans. David Radzinowicz (Paris: Flammarion, 2000) 49–51, 119–20, 156–9 [footnotes omitted].

Friedrich Wolfram Heubach
Remarks That Not Only Have Nothing to Do with the Expanded Concept of Handicrafts...//2011

[...] It is surely unnecessary to emphasise that in [Cosima von Bonin's and Isa Genzken's] common recourse to what I will henceforth (for the sake of brevity) describe as the polymorphously perverse form of things, these two artists nonetheless thematise different aspects of the contemporary object world, in the process developing different 'moves'.

For example, it is impossible to overlook the fact that Bonin's work differs from Genzken's in the important role that softness, smoothness, roundness and plushness, in short the quality of cuddliness, play in the material rhetoric of many of her works. What is the significance of this 'cuddle factor' that so many of her works provide? Does it represent an artistic acting out of something of the child's mania for cuddly things, its totalitarian insistence on cuddliness, just as one might see something of its unbridled enthusiasm for 'materials testing' and its devotion to, and pleasure in, devising ingenious forms of torture in the vandalistic character of Genzken's works?

Or does Bonin's choice of materials reflect a desire to thematise, perhaps in a somewhat cynically sympathetic manner, the commercialisation of the trouble that those who have long since reached chronological maturity clearly still have with that insistence, as evidenced by their demand for 'Kuschelrock' [Trans. note: or 'cuddle-rock', the German term for soft rock], 'chill-out music', 'Diddle Mouse' pendants [Trans. note: a popular German cartoon character], 'Schnuffel' ringtones,[1] and the like? This at any rate is the view of my friend Theo Rettisch, who finds it quite likely that Bonin's forms and materials are a distanced response to the contemporary 'softening' of the world of everyday life, and one that often emphasises the moment of the grotesque.[2] He sees that 'softening' at work in the general trend toward rounder shapes – concretely, for example, in the newly convex fronts of kitchen appliances and the trend toward spongy-body forms in automobile design – and figuratively in the increasing popularity of so-called 'round tables' (= the ideal of a communication that already transcends oppositions and differences in its seating arrangement), in 'all-round carefree packages',[3] and other phenomena that similarly seek to take away life's sharp edges and make it go smoothly.

As usual, my friend Gufo Reale goes one better. He feels that this methodical infantilisation, which in his view is by no means exclusive to the works of these two artists, represents a bold and creative response to the infantilisation that all of us are currently exposed to and that plays an important role in what he calls the 'general dumbing down of society' and never tires of pelting with savage invective. I will leave it to the reader to decide whether what he offers as proof of this infantilisation really does prove it, or whether it merely demonstrates his legendary talent for denunciation, his genius for cultivating suspicion. In any event, he cites the following examples, in addition to many others: the jovially condescending use of the *du*-form that firms like IKEA and Apple have recently begun to permit themselves vis-à-vis the customer, who was once regarded as king, and that imposes a belittling kind of equality on him or her.[4] Just like the toddler in the play group, who isn't anything special yet, or the product on the bargain counter, which has ceased to be anything special, the customer is nothing special either – it's the quantity that counts;

– the public, pet-like fondling by full-grown adults of their Schumi, Poldi, Angie, Schweini, or Depri;[5]

– the rhetoric of safety and security that is currently rampant in the insurance industry, which promises an almost intra-uterine freedom from worry, as in the case of the 'TwinStar Riester-Renie' of the company AXA [Trans. note: a retirement plan], in whose advertising we see a child snuggling up to its young mother and close to her lap as we hear or read: 'remember how it felt when you didn't have to worry about a thing..., when people always helped you..., we give you back that feeling – the AXA feeling!'

– the now universal requirement that one have a little water bottle and a cell phone with one at all times, as a manifestation of the persistence of a desire to nurse that one has actually long since outgrown, or a communicative ideal that was actually over and done with when the umbilical cord was cut;

– and even in the 'New Spirituality' that has received so much attention, Gufo Reale sees a neotenous confusion – a disoriented search for the Meaning of Life that is rooted in a continuing need for a calling as unquestionable as the one that we once received from Daddy and Mommy.

– Etc., etc.

And according to Gufo Reale, who invokes Ernst Kris in support of his view – Kris regards all creative achievements as rooted in the active repetition of something first experienced passively[6] – works like Genzken's and Bonin's seek to effect a liberation from this forced or freely assumed infantilisation by making it active and turning it into an artistic method. So that what happens in these works is something like the conversion of a compensatory regression, which makes it possible to tolerate a condition that is experienced as unsatisfactory into a functional one that innovatively expands or transcends one's given state.

Oh dear... It may well be that my friends have hit on important aspects of Bonin's and Genzken's works. But I doubt very much that their reflections – or mine – have sufficiently highlighted what these works actually say.[7] Any reader who is disappointed that he or she has not been told what these works say is advised to seek consolation by turning to the works themselves. While they won't tell him either, they will show it to him. And it was not my goal in this essay to do more than open up a horizon for understanding what they show us. Or perhaps it was. For my aim was to speak about artworks in such a way that it becomes possible to capture the experiences they stand for in their effect on us, not by appealing to conditions that are pseudologicised in the person of the artist but to conditions that are operative in the viewing of these works – conditions in which they mirror something of the world in which the viewer actually lives.

Readers who come away from this essay with not much more than 'cuddle-mania = Bonin' and 'vandalism = Genzken' are advised to try to see cuddling and breaking things as two different forms of a single effort – the effort to overcome the distance that formed between us and the things of this world when we came to see them as these 'objects' that are always and everywhere and for everyone the same, and when – entering into this world of 'objects' and submitting to its rationality – we finally came to see ourselves as these 'subjects'. That is – looking back to the Latin – as 'subject', or 'subjugated'.

Is this really that necessary?

Whatever else their works may show and whatever Bonin and Genzken may have had on their minds when they did what they did, the fact that they did what they did attests. […]

1   [Footnote 22 in source] [Trans. note: Schnuffel is a German cartoon character used to market a ringtone that was later turned into a popular song called 'Kuschel Song', or 'Cuddle Song'.]

2   [23] My friend Zenzi Belle expresses a similar sense that there is something grotesque in Bonin's work when she associates its world of things with that of Alice's Wonderland.

3   [24] [Trans. note: 'Rundum-Sorglos Pakele', packages or plans in which the company takes care of everything connected with a product or service and everything that could possibly come up or go wrong in the course of using it.]

4   [25] [Trans. note: The familiar form of address instead of the more formal *Sie* – the du form expresses intimacy and is traditionally used when addressing one's family and friends, children, animals, and subordinates. In English, we might say that companies place themselves on a 'first-name basis' or 'intimate footing' with the customer in their advertising.]

5   [26] [Trans. note: *Schumi* = the German race-car driver Michael Schumacher; Poldi and *Schweini* = the soccer players Lukas Podolski and Bastian Schweinsteiger; *Angie* = the German chancellor, Angela Merkel; *Depri* = depression.]

6   [28] See Ernst Kris, *Psychoanalytic Explorations in Art* (2000). Kris refers to the effort 'to repeat actively what one has experienced passively'.

7   [29] I would personally regard as inadequate any discussion of Bonin's works that does not explore sewing as a principle or the textile element as an independent motif and does not consider her assemblies, just as I would any treatment of Genzken's work that does not include her earlier work, which clearly had a very different orientation.

Friedrich Wolfram Heubach, extract from 'Remarks That Not Only Have Nothing to Do with the Expanded Concept of Handicrafts…', trans. James Gussen, in *Cosima von Bonin: 1, 2, 3, 4* (Cologne: DuMont Buchverlag, 2011) 19–20 [some footnotes omitted].

Negar Azimi
The Charming, Disgusting Paintings of Tala Madani//2017

Recently, the Iranian-American artist Tala Madani was sitting in her studio in Los Angeles, tweaking a video in progress. It featured a young girl wearing a bow in her hair and a yellow-gold cardigan, her legs akimbo in a pose that conjured [Gustave] Courbet's *The Origin of the World*. The animated film imagines a sex-education class taught by God. Madani had recently been watching 1970s sex education films from Scandinavia and Britain on YouTube, and was struck by the way they were typically narrated 'from both perspectives, male and female.' In her own film, a pair of men – one thin and boyish, the other tall and pear-shaped – gaze at a projection of the young woman, while the narrator, represented by a pair of disembodied pink lips, wheezily delivers the wisdom of the ages: 'Be present. Find the clit and never let it go.' As the scene unfolds, the girl reaches out of the projector screen, takes hold of the male figures, draws them in, and makes them disappear between her legs. 'I guess I was really interested in exploring female pleasure', Madani told me. 'I wanted to play with the idea of passivity. She's not passive anymore.'

Like her paintings, Madani is alternately droll and punishingly serious. The first time I saw her work, seven years ago, in London, I was struck by a painting of a gaggle of men kneeling on all fours. It was impossible to say whether they were engaged in prayer or in sexual submission. Large parachutes hung limply around their bodies. The men's noses were spewing blood. And yet, somehow, this grotesque group portrait had a sweetness to it as well.

In February, following President Trump's executive order denying the citizens of seven Muslim-majority countries entry into the United States, the Museum of Modern Art exhibited eight works by artists from those countries in its fifth-floor galleries. Among the works on display was a Madani video, from 2007, entitled *Chit Chat*. In the video, which can be seen on YouTube, two men engage in banter that is by turns friendly, argumentative, and literally bilious. It is, like the best of her work, at once charming, thoughtful, and kind of disgusting.

Critics are wont to consider Madani's work through the prism of her Iranian background. Madani is not fond of this manoeuvre. Her work has more in common with the giddy grotesqueries of the Los Angeles artist Paul McCarthy or with Philip Guston's lumpy, comical forms than it does with Islamic calligraphy or Persian miniature painting. And yet, she admitted, 'I probably wouldn't have become a painter if I hadn't been the product of emigration.' Her canvases can be viewed as theatres of cultural encounter, where references from the history of art meld with figures drawn from the Japanese anime that she loves to watch or from the Ladybird children's books that served as her introduction to the English language.

Madani grew up in Tehran, and, as a child, would rise at four in the morning to accompany her grandfather to Mellat Park, one of the traÐc-clogged city's largest green spaces, where he would converse with the shopkeepers and other businessmen who gathered to do their exercises, feed the birds, and munch on fresh bread and cheese. It gave her, she now reflects, a fascination with the secret lives of men. 'I thought I was one of them', she said. At fifteen, she moved with her mother to a tiny, mostly white town in western Oregon. There, as the only Iranian at her public high school, she found her friends in a group that she refers to as 'the Others': a lesbian, an African-American, and a Jehovah's Witness. 'I fit in perfectly', she said. After studying at Oregon State, Yale, and, later, the Rijksakademie, in Holland, she had her first New York solo show, featuring her now fêted 'cake paintings', in which men engage in acrobatic feats of buffoonery in and around sumptuous birthday cakes.

Most of the wildly expressionist works that fill Madani's studio (a former furniture factory) feature these same men: middle-aged, hirsute, and often fully or partially disrobed, the better to display their soft, ladylike hips. Madani tends to capture them with rough, unfinished brushstrokes *in medias res* – pissing, shitting, ejaculating. When I suggested that their buffoonery might feel particularly timely in the Trump era, she strenuously disagreed. She was not mocking her subjects, she insisted. 'They're a little like self-portraits', she explained. Our baseness is 'the most human aspect of our being.' 'The oversocialized aspect of us is so oppressive', she said. 'If we all engaged with our own animal instincts more, we'd be better off.'

The *Sex Ed by God* (2017) animation is one of six of Madani's works featured in this year's Whitney Biennial, which opened last month. (I was an adviser on the show.) The video runs amid a suite of dark, enigmatic paintings. One features a silkscreened image of what appears to be a sunset, overlaid with a tubby man of indeterminate age, bent over so as to expose his anus, which radiates light. (Madani was inspired by the idea of the black sun, which she described as 'a symbol of fertility and death in Mexican mythology'.) Another work in the Biennial shows a man holding aloft a long piece of shit, like a sacred offering or a salami, to four nude men. Light emanates from their anuses, too. In a third piece, a man looks up at two naively drawn Madonnas, his arms outstretched in a gesture of yearning. 'This one is about the missing maternal figure', Madani said. Maternity has been on her mind; Madani and her husband, the English artist Nathaniel Mellors, had a child last year. Madani has been teaching at the

University of Southern California, too. 'My art is about pushing against the taste that you've been brought up with', she said. 'I tell my students sometimes that, if they're making work that their mothers will like, they're in trouble.'

Negar Azimi, 'The Charming, Disgusting Paintings of Tala Madani', *The New Yorker* (28 April 2017).

Elizabeth Legge
When Awe Turns to Awww... //2017

[…] [Jeff Koons's] *Balloon Dog* [1994–2000] has been hard to categorise. While it set a sales record for work by a living artist in a Christies auction in 2013, it has often been dismissed as a glittery consumerist lure without much redeeming intellectual or critical purchase; or, at best, as the *New York Times* reviewer Jed Perl said in response to Koons's huge 2014 retrospective at the Whitney Museum in New York, as 'catnip for intellectuals'. Koons's work raises questions of how far the cute, without the redeeming irony that might signal some critique of art as consumer goods, can be pushed toward conveying a generalised importance or portentousness while remaining cute, and of how much the cute can be compromised by being situated in the context of art and its critical reception – again, while remaining cute.

Balloon Dog's cute features are complicated by its size and its symbolic baggage. Physically, its cuteness begins with its little nose, made of the terminal knot of a balloon, the quintessence of a pert, popular cultural ideal of a child's nose, yearning to be tweaked; and, given the umbilical aspect of the balloon knot, there is something newborn to it – again, cute. That cuteness however is complicated by its keen stance, lean body, and show dog pose. […]. And then, a further complication is its imposing size: 10 feet tall and 12 feet long. Where *Balloon Dog's* cuteness might be thought to be diminished by that size, it arguably amplifies its cuteness, inducing an anthropomorphising sense of valiant overreaching on the part of the plucky little fellow. Given that cuteness has consistently been aligned with smallness […] the enormity of *Balloon Dog* is both surprising and perplexing.[1] Therefore, the pressure of its aspirational size is usefully thought of not so much in terms of the relations implied by 'scale' as in terms of a more naive, less architecturally or art-historically inflected 'bigness', returning us to a childhood perception of our position in the relative scale of things. Seen in this light, the dog is like a giant toy aspiring to be a monument. Further, given its show dog aspect, *Balloon Dog* might claim to be the quintessence of its balloon breed, as if a monumental sculpture of itself the equestrian statue of balloon animals. As such, it is also situated in the tradition of anthropomorphised animals as instrumental symbols and mirrors of human subjectivity, serving human uses as social, political and moral models.

In 2006, *Balloon Dog (Magenta)* was installed on the Grand Canal in Venice in front of the Palazzo Grassi, which housed French businessman François Pinault's art collection, and served as a trophy and emblem of the status of the major collector. At the Chateau de Versailles in 2008, in an exhibition largely funded by Pinault, it resonated with the equestrian statue of Louis XIV in the palace forecourt; and, installed under the baroque ceiling painting of the apotheosis of Hercules in the Sun King's grand chambers, it was as if another hero were waiting to be sucked up into the skies with the gods, fitting right in with the regal inflationary claims and ostentation of kings and collectors. In other words, Koons's political gesture of inflating what we would expect to be diminutive undercuts viewer expectations while destabilising prevailing art hierarchies.

Another key feature of the dog's hybrid putative cuteness is its surface, both in its balloon origins as rubber stretched to tautness, and in its realisation in glossy metal with a jewel-coloured coat. Given the impulse to squeeze or poke or fondle a vulnerable creature, the *Balloon Dog,* insofar as it represents a swollen balloon, induces touch, in the way the giggling 'Poppin' Fresh' Pillsbury Doughboy is always poked in his swelling tummy [...] by a giant finger, and coyly pops right back. A corporate mascot invented in 1965, Poppin' Fresh is one epitome of the cute as marketed to the baby boom generation of which Koons is a member. Some of Poppin' Fresh's cuteness relies partly on the fact that he is made of pure white dough through and through, a perfected form of unfleshly embodiment, as if an immortal child: a modern equivalent of the cherubs and *putti* of art tradition.[2] Moreover, as with dough, prodding a balloon may be gratifying, but poking a balloon past its point of resilience until it pops is a darker gratification. *Balloon Dog* acknowledges the cuteness of poke-able, squeezable rubber objects [...] but insofar as it is made of steel, it resists any such indignity. That armored effect is in turn undermined by the hyper-reflective metal finish, which, paradoxically, creates another impression of vulnerability: the brightly coloured steel looks as breakable as a Christmas ornament. Indeed, Koons played up precisely that illusion of fragility in the giant Easter eggs of his *Celebration* series, which anticipate our knowledge that most chocolate eggs, like cast metal sculptures, are hollow, and that real eggs break. The glittering emptied fragments of very thin steel eggshell in *Cracked Egg* (1994) make the illusion of frangibility explicit. *Balloon Dog,* too, goes back and forth between provoking us to pet it or pop it; that is, whether to pop it – insofar as it is a balloon – or to smash it – insofar as it is not a balloon.

[…] The powerful ambiguity of Koons's cute was fully fledged in the breakout figure in the *Statuary* series, *Rabbit* (1986), a dollar store plastic inflatable bunny embodying a familiar corny cartoon anthropomorphism transmuted to glossy stainless steel.

Once stripped of the lurid colours and the goofy facial features of its original plastic prototype, *Rabbit* emerged as a brilliant challenge to the machine aesthetic modernism of Constantin Brancusi's sleek bronze *Bird in Space* (1928), and could be imagined, again, as ironic postmodern critique of the claims made for MoMA-sanctioned modernist 'masterwork'. *Rabbit* has a baby-like round stomach that invites patting or tickling, and its splayed little legs and vestigial arms suggest a toddler's characteristic side-to-side gait and inept grasp. Only 41 inches tall, it is child size: we imagine we could pick it up. And yet there is an edge to the rabbit. Its strangely sharp pointed ears project like missile launchers, and at the same time are unnervingly fleshy and vulval, deeply grooved within their swelling edges. They set up a visual conversation with the rabbit's carrot as if a goofy phallic lingam and vaginal yoni. The witty coexistence of the cartoonish toy and the gravely abstract artwork; the immature and the sexualised; and the malleable and the armoured submit cultural constructs of the childlike as cuteness to a certain stress. *Rabbit's* cuteness is hybridised with high modernist seriousness. If the *Statuary* and *Banality* works might have seemed jocular postmodern interventions, the *Made in Heaven* series (1989–91), Koons's sexual collaboration with the porn star Ilona Staller in many permutations pressed the cute into a more demanding service. The cutely childlike was Staller's principal sexual selling point – she recorded obscene lyrics to the tunes of children's songs and carried around a teddy bear. Her nickname, 'La Cicciolina', was itself cute, a diminutive term for her pudenda, signifying the pudgily or pinchably cute in Italian. *Made in Heaven* provoked muted to hostile critical response. Koons's white heterosexual condomless narrative seemed tasteless at the height of the AIDS epidemic, and offensive to an art world distraught about the censorship of Robert Mapplethorpe's work and the consequent funding cuts to the National Endowment for the Arts. Using Staller's own sets and costumes, *Made in Heaven* staged a prelapsarian cuteness with giant butterflies, pastel-coloured teddy bears, and wreaths of flowers, along with Koons's chubby putti, shaggy puppies, fluffy cat, and swelling bouquets of flowers in porcelain and polychrome wood. This might be taken as a pretty mockery of Mapplethorpe's sombre cryogenic black-and-white photographs of sexualised flowers and homoerotic fetish practices; a prettiness interrupted by Koons' and Staller's unairbrushed and unwreathed genitals that punctuate the *Made in Heaven* series like a penetration of the Lacanian real into the cute sets of an orgasmic cartoon princess surrounded by adorable attributes. [...]

1 Smallness is consistently aligned with cuteness in most of the literature on the topic. To cite just one example, see [Sianne] Ngai's discussion in *Our Aesthetic Categories* [(Cambridge, MA: Harvard University Press)] of Stein (70), Adorno (102) or, more generally, her assertion that cuteness is an aesthetic organised around smallness and helplessness (78). See also the introduction to this book on Darwinian cuteness and its relationship to diminutive size (27), as well as to design and representation (12; 36).
2 Similarly, Ngai writes that the epitome of cute would be an 'undifferentiated blob of soft doughy matter', and that 'soft contours suggest pliancy or responsiveness to the will of others', in other words, cute objects invite poking, prodding and pinching (Ibid., 64). She further cites Daniel Harris who goes so far as to claim that 'the cute object's exaggerated passivity seems likely to excite the consumer's sadism'. (Ibid., 65).

Elizabeth Legge, extracts from 'When Awe Turns To Awww…: Jeff Koons's Balloon Dog and The Cute Sublime', in *The Aesthetics and Affects of Cuteness*, eds. Joshua Paul Dale, Joyce Goggin, Julia Leyda, Anthony P. McIntyre and Diane Negra (London and New York: Routledge, 2017) 130–31, 132–3, 138.

Lewis Gordon
Disaster Aesthetics: How COVID-19 Made the World 'Cute'//2020

One of the defining images of lockdown, at least in the UK, was that of Captain Tom Moore, diligently, perhaps even a little maniacally, completing laps of his garden to raise money for the National Health Service. As Moore took each step, doctors and nurses were fighting to save the lives of thousands of oxygen-starved COVID-19 patients. Over the course of three weeks, the 100-year-old army veteran went on to secure more than £32 million for the buckling health system, receiving a knighthood and, most recently, a bizarre chair upholstered in a replica World War 2 uniform for his efforts. First and foremost, the friendly-looking and do-gooding elderly man, stooped over his walking frame, was a slowly shuffling embodiment of wartime nostalgia; the Blitz spirit made real. But he was also, crucially, cute – certainly diminutive – and carrying out a task of almost-transcendent wholesomeness.

These two closely related albeit distinct aesthetic sensibilities – the cute and wholesome – seem to have grown ever more present during arguably the most disaster-stricken year in recent memory (and we're yet to experience the full force of the impending economic crisis). […] In this scenario, however, Captain Tom is merely an extension of the now-cutified NHS; a world-leading health service transformed from a highly complex set of systems and services into a non-complex target of pity. There's an obviously sadistic aspect to this metamorphosis instigated by a Conservative government which has arguably underfunded the NHS for a decade, yet seeks to capitalise on its populist fetishisation.

The cutification of the NHS is visible in the physical gestures which have haunted British streets throughout the pandemic. Crude but adorable rainbows painted by home-schooled children appeared as ghost-like apparitions in the windows of homes. In cities, at least, the daily clap for carers reverberated around densely populated concrete spaces, ringing in our ears as front-line workers tried to rest before heading back into the COVID-19 maelstrom (often without the correct protective equipment and at significant risk to their own families). These actions, alongside Captain Tom's, however, hint at […] 'cute' as both the site of a 'static power differential' and a 'surprisingly complex power struggle'; we might treat the NHS as a cute object requiring our sympathy and care but this only reflects our own keenly felt vulnerabilities.

For many, video games have emerged as an embrace, and perhaps a surprisingly committed torchbearer for cute and wholesome aesthetics. […]

In May, Wholesome Direct – an online event designed to plug the gap left by cancelled video game conferences – collected over fifty independent titles under the seemingly in-vogue banner. [These] wholesome counterparts aestheticise self-improvement. This is palpable in Animal Crossing and Ooblets, both of which, alongside outwardly cheerful dispositions, offer a set of interactions to roleplay kindness and consideration. These opportunities for betterment resonate with booming real-world pastimes such as breadmaking; at the height of lockdown, fledgling bakers emptied supermarkets of flour, keen to both learn a new skill and fill their guts with healthy (not to mention cute!) microbacteria.

The purest, and most life-affirming, crystallisation of these cute and wholesome aesthetics arrived via pop artist Charli XCX's *How I'm Feeling Now* (2020), an album recorded entirely during lockdown in dialogue with her fans on social media. The record's intimacy is reflected precisely in its music videos; for the 'forever' promo – a heartfelt pop ballad directed towards her boyfriend Huck Kwong – the British star asked fans to send in their own camera phone footage responding to prompts such as 'your favourite party you want to remember forever'. Rapid-fire cuts of everyday spaces and often cute objects (including cuddly toys) are juxtaposed with images of the singer herself. Charli XCX effectively and self-knowingly transformed herself into an object of cuteness; her hypertextual pop songs were an exercise in lockdown self-improvement; and she deftly captured the everyday qualities of this disaster like no one else.

At their best, these two affable aesthetics – the cute and wholesome – afford us the space to transcend an often bleak-feeling everyday. But there's an inverse, and arguably an impotency to such ostensibly nourishing outlooks. The cute transforms us (and our objects of attention) into both literal and metaphorical vessels of babbling baby-speak, perhaps fatally so in a time when critical facilities are more important than ever. The wholesome, in contrast, is concerned with a different lockdown transformation. It speaks, possibly fundamentally, to a wider belief in the potential for simple, unassuming tasks to make better citizens of us all (and maybe the world). We busy ourselves with these activities, art, and mundane adventures, all while the very fabric of society is being shredded before our eyes.

Lewis Gordon, extracts from 'Disaster Aesthetics: How COVID-19 Made the World "Cute"', *Art Review* (12 August 2020). Available at https://artreview.com/disaster-aesthetics-how-covid-19-made-the-world-cute/

Angelik Vizcarrondo-Laboy
Seriously Cute: Six Artists Harnessing the Power Dichotomy of Cuteness//2020

Cuteness is the first aesthetic most of us encounter in life. We are exposed to it as babies, through consumer goods, even before we are conscious of what we are seeing. Simply defined, a cute object is typically one that resembles a baby human or animal. Anthropomorphism, a strategy used since antiquity to make others, including gods, more relatable to humans, is key to cuteness' effectiveness and requires very little to be successful. The gesture of a face combined with soft textures, rounded forms and cheerful colours produces a tender and vulnerable feeling that inspires the desire to care for and protect. Cute objects are compelling because they are approachable, but, more importantly, because they can be possessed.

We grow up accustomed to the passive comfort of these figures and we witness them come to life through the magic of animation in cartoons and films. Nevertheless, despite its strong association with the infantile, the presence and influence of cuteness in popular culture extend well beyond childhood. [...] Japan's prosperous *kawaii* culture has played a crucial role in catalysing a global phenomenon. In recent years, the aesthetic of cuteness has infiltrated our Instagram feeds and commercial spaces and become integral to the style of some of today's hottest celebrities. Ironically, as our country's political and social landscape becomes increasingly challenging, cute aesthetics, which on the surface appear to be uncomplicated, unthreatening and friendly, are thriving; is this a form of denial or, perhaps, a coping mechanism?

[...] While consumerism is almost inextricable from cuteness, this essay focuses on investigating the complex affective power of the aesthetic through the cultural lens of artists of colour. Historically, the aesthetic of cuteness has been weaponised as a tool to oppress Black, Indigenous and People of Colour (BIPOC) populations. The world of animation, in particular, has been repeatedly guilty of perpetuating negative stereotypes through the dangerously persuasive innocuousness of cuteness.

The work of Brooklyn-based artist Sean-Kierre Lyons is unapologetically cute. Their drawings of fairy-like characters dressed in funky garments composed of colourful and patterned petals are blackface cartoons. Black skin, large rounded red lips and big eyes: simple gestures, in use since at least the 1830s, that signal an extensive history of oppression towards Black people in the US. During the Jim Crow era especially, caricatures were critical tools of white supremacy. Used as propaganda, the imagery grossly misrepresented Black people physically, intellectually and culturally, to construct harmful stereotypes (such as an association with laziness) and to establish the myth that Black servants were happy taking care of white families.

The reality is that while most of us grew up consuming products with packaging that featured a smiling Black person – sometimes as a cute cartoon and perhaps with a catchy jingle in tow – often we are detached from the knowledge and context of what they truly represent. [...] These characters are so compelling that some people passionately defend their continued use, prioritising nostalgia for 'simpler times' (that never existed) over dismantling racist anti-Black practices.

Los Angeles-based artist Alex Anderson, who is Black and Japanese, also uses blackface in his ceramic sculptures. This strategy is particularly poignant in his work when juxtaposed with predominantly white-glazed clay. He says, 'I do not think of the use of this history as a reclamation, but more as the engagement of an imposed birthright...blackface imagery is a visual distillation of a majority perception of my identity, but it also represents how I feel when I enter any white space. An awareness of the assumed truth of Black stereotypes and the feeling of potentially confirming those stereotypes, as the white gaze immediately categorizes me with implicit bias.' This fear directly informs *Pearanoia* (2019), a phonetic play on 'paranoia.' In this work, Anderson represents himself, and Black people generally, through a cutely rendered anthropomorphic pear. The black fruit features gold dots as eyes and the typical red mouth of blackface, twisted into a frown. (Though cuteness is often thought of as optimistic, in actuality it can convey the full range of human emotions, including sadness and anger, without losing its appeal.) The pear hangs, scared, a droplet of sweat on its forehead, while a realistically rendered anonymous white hand reaches towards it and white roses with eyes look on. It is a commentary on the fetishisation, consumption and exploitation of Black bodies and ideas by white people – themes the artist often explores in his practice. 'Blackface in my work is a reflection of the emotional truths of navigating a white world in a black body while framing the entire circumstance as an absurdity.'

The use of cuteness and humour in Anderson's work presents a first line of defence that parallels the code-switching expected of BIPOC communities in the US. He also incorporates Emoji iconography – a universal language that simplifies messages with cute pictographs – which has been especially embraced by Millennials and Gen Z. Anderson harnesses cuteness to create empathy towards the Black American experience and 'invite grace to a subject historically contextualized as abject and other.' These approaches serve as misdirection. The sculptures make you look, draw you in and then hit you with the charged imagery of blackface, which disrupts the comfort and safety that we expect cuteness to offer. Anderson labours to soften the blow and make complex narratives more digestible for his primarily white audience, while providing a platform for dialogue about race in the US.

Lyons similarly uses cuteness subversively. Despite their child-like brightness, the artist's figures are resilient warriors whose regalia acts like the vivid colours used by animals to warn predators that they are poisonous. *Leave That Shit at Home* (2020), for example, depicts one such congenial flower warrior, holding the hood of a beheaded Ku Klux Klan member. Lyons also creates soft sculptures of clouds, ladybugs, children in bunny suits and Murakami-like flowers, which likewise employ blackface. Even cuter because of their tangible softness, it is tempting to want to cuddle them. However, some of the works' titles – *You don't want non of this Smoke* and *Something about this ain't sitting right with me* (2020) – remind us that they are not to be messed with.

Anderson, Lyons and Los Angeles-based artist Alake Shilling are all lovers of animation, which they cite as a significant influence on how cuteness informs their respective practices. The stories of animated characters are proxies for human experiences that help organise and digest information about the world. However, Lyons echoes the feelings of many who are deeply disappointed by representations of Blackness in the medium and brings up renowned actor and comedian Eddie Murphy's roles in animated films as an example. Murphy has voiced two iconic animated characters: the lizard-like spirit dragon Mushu in Disney's *Mulan* and the donkey in DreamWorks' *Shrek*. Both are animals in films otherwise mostly populated by human-like characters. Even Disney's first Black princess, Tiana from *The Princess and the Frog*, spends most of the movie either working for white people or, well, as a frog.[1]

These movies reinforce derogatory messages within the cloak of cuteness and humour; often Black people are not only misrepresented but quite literally dehumanised. This kind of indoctrination – a type of brainwashing – has occurred for generations. Furthermore, with the lack of proper representation, Black children experience childhood very differently than white children do. This is a reminder that representation matters. It has taken Disney's Pixar thirty-four years to produce a Black-centred story. When speaking about the plot of the upcoming release, *Soul*, Lyons expressed their chagrin: 'Why do we need to die to get a movie?' The artist hopes to one day expand their practice into animation, of which we got a glimpse in a recent collaboration with fashion brand Collina Strada. Lyons's 'Flower Warriors' strutted the virtual catwalk for the label's Spring 2021 collection, aptly named *Change is Cute*.[2]

For Los Angeles-based artist Narumi Nekpenekpen, cuteness is a way to process personal experiences. Her sculptures, which she refers to as 'bbs', short for babies, are constructions of many individual pieces of clay that she dresses with an assortment of textures, glazes, patterns and doodles. Small in scale, these 'bbs' feature cutesy faces with big rounded eyes, pretty eyelashes and either an O for a mouth or a heart for pouty lips. They serve as diary entries through which she works intuitively to process complex feelings. Sharing synergy with Nekpenekpen's practice is Los Angeles-based Latinx artist Diana Yesenia Alvarado, who says, 'the fact that looking at something cute has the ability to change our emotions or put us in a state of nostalgia is very powerful'. Alvarado's figures instantly trigger the observer to 'awww' and prompt empathy. She creates ceramic sculptures that combine her experiences with elements from her neighbourhood's architecture and vintage hand-painted advertisements. Her sculptures consist of a series of recurrent figures, including clowns and little devils, that express a range of emotions with simple mark-making. She explains, 'it's a fun challenge to try to capture an expression...the slightest change in line can truly change the entire piece'.

For Alvarado, her work is about creating a balance between vulnerability and strength, which also mirrors cuteness' inherent dichotomy, in which something usually perceived as submissive possesses the power to influence others. Her figures will often feature faux metal studs, to indicate a punk-rock attitude, juxtaposed with the softness of tender, sad eyes in the style of Precious Moments characters. Despite some of her sculptures' tough personas, Alvarado intends to foster connections rather than to intimidate. Similarly seeking to create bonds rather than shock is Alake Shilling. The artist, who is African American, is known for her colourful ceramic sculptures and paintings of a cast of emotive animals, from a sad cowgirl bear to a side-eyeing ladybug. It is easy to see how Hello Kitty and Lisa Frank are essential inspirations for her saturated compositions. She says, 'cute is an indication of life and vitality'. Through this perspective, Shilling's work embodies the limitless potential of youth's pure imagination.

Growing up in Japan, Nekpenekpen, who is of Nigerian and Japanese descent, was surrounded by *kawaii*, but it was not until she moved to the US that she became aware of the magnitude of its reach. Yet, while she appreciates it, she does not cite it directly as a source of inspiration. Rather, Nekpenekpen is deeply influenced by Japanese artist Aya Takano's 2001 book *Hot Banana Fudge*, a staple in her life since high school. Takano is a member of Takashi Murakami's studio and of the Superflat movement; her work uses cuteness to empower women sexually. The depiction of women in cartoons as over-sexualised tropes has also been historically problematic. Some of the most recognisable female cartoons, such as Betty Boop and Jessica Rabbit, feature cute faces and voluptuous bodies and are assigned to the stereotypes of the 'damsel in distress' or the 'femme fatale.' Betty Boop, infamous for her baby voice, is considered the first animated sex symbol; in the words of her theme song, 'she can win you with a wink, ain't she cute?' Today, many have reclaimed this imagery to celebrate female sexuality.

The feminine and the cute are often conflated because they are both labelled as subordinate. Moreover, animated depictions of women reveal that female sexuality is considered threatening. Puerto Rican artist Cristina Tufiño uses cuteness within her sculptural practice as a feminist tool to empower women. She grew up watching the 1980s hit Brazilian children's show *Xou da Xuxa*. In every episode, the eponymous host, Xuxa, landed on stage in a spaceship adorned with full red lips. She often sported no more than a bra and a short skirt. Tufiño cites these images as an influence on a feminist world of her own making.

A recurrent figure in her practice is the sphinx. She transforms the image of the ancient and feared mythological femme creature into a contemporary feminist icon of knowledge and sensuality with fashionable eyewear. Her anthropomorphic sculptural renderings are purposely simplified and painted in pastels, especially in pink, to increase their cuteness and make them less intimidating. The artist's explorations of cuteness have also expanded to her drawing practice. In *Meow 2* (2019), a wild-haired woman performs fellatio on a disembodied phallus, rendered with kitten features. This piece is part of a series focused on a fairy tale in which the heroine experiences conflicting feelings of desire and aggression towards foot fetishes and gender-fluid creatures. The cuteness helps ease the anxiety of otherwise chaotic scenes and softens the taboos around sex and sexuality.

Conversely, working additively, Nekpenekpen downloads nuanced and even conflicting feelings into the clay. The artist says, 'I don't think the cuteness softens these feelings, but actually emphasizes them and allows for them to exist in the way that they do – candidly'. This complexity is paralleled by the layered quality of the sculptures, which wear elaborate outfits inspired by Japanese street style. But, she clarifies 'my pieces do not exist to just be called "cute" and dismissed after that'. This concern stems, in part, from the power struggle inherent to the use of 'cute' in speech. The word features prominently in the lexicon of English speakers; for Millennials and Gen Z, its employment probably verges on overuse. 'That's cute' is a go-to phrase to express approval yet lacks the effusiveness and passion of other adjectives; it can also be dismissive, signalling that something is not worthy of further consideration or merely a conversation filler. In that sense, describing work as cute might even provoke offense.

Nekpenekpen hopes that people engage her work at more than face value, given the intensive process from which her 'bbs' are born, which she describes as 'painful'. On the subject of dismissal, cuteness is also autobiographical for Shilling, whose naturally high voice, full of childish glee, has often been described as cute. She explains that many question the authenticity and, furthermore, the authority of her voice. Feeling a kinship with cartoons whose fictive experiences parallel her way of existing in the world, Shilling's use of cuteness is an extension of her own identity. 'I think it's unnatural to dismiss cute. It's human nature to be attracted to cute…cuteness is the beginning of our existence', she explains.

This selection of artists offers but a limited cross-section of the diversity of applications cuteness has in contemporary creative practices. The wide range of perspectives underscores that cuteness is a compelling aesthetic strategy that should not be underestimated. […] As demonstrated by these artists, cuteness is not a way out of the complicated sociopolitical climate we are living in, but rather a path through it. The next time you encounter the tender gaze of cuteness, dare to discover if there is more than meets the eye.

1   Brooks Barnes, 'Her Prince Has Come. Critics, Too', *The New York Times* (29 May 2009). Available at www.nytimes.com/2009/05/31/fashion/31disney.html

2   Sarah Li, 'Collina Strada Joins Artist Sean-Kierre Lyons for "Change Is Cute" SS21 Collection', *Teen Vogue* (September 2020). Available at www.teenvogue.com/story/collina-strada-change-is-cute-ss21-collection

Angelik Vizcarrondo-Laboy, extracts from 'Seriously Cute: Six Artists Harnessing the Power Dichotomy of Cuteness', *Cultured Magazine* (17 November 2020). Available at www.culturedmag.com/cute-contemporary-art/

Biographical Notes

Theodor Adorno (1903–69) was a German critical theorist of society and culture.

Peggy Ahwesh is an experimental film artist and video-maker based in New York.

Sasha Archibald is a writer, teacher and curator based in Portland, Oregon.

Negar Azimi is a writer and the senior editor of *Bidoun*, an award-winning magazine and curatorial project with a focus on the Middle East and its diasporas.

Roland Barthes (1915–80) was a French cultural and literary critic and theorist of semiology.

Lauren Berlant (1957–2021) was an American scholar, cultural theorist and author, and George M. Pullman Distinguished Service Professor of English at the University of Chicago.

Nayland Blake is an artist based in New York City.

Ian Bogost is a game designer, Professor and Director of the Program in Film & Media Studies and Professor of Computer Science & Engineering at Washington University, St. Louis.

Julia Bryan-Wilson is Doris and Clarence Malo Professor of Modern and Contemporary Art at University of California, Berkeley.

Norman Bryson is Professor of Art History at the University of California, San Diego.

Mary Ann Doane is Chair of Film & Media and Class of 1937 Professor of Film & Media at University of California, Berkeley.

Jennifer Doyle is Professor of English at the University of California, Riverside.

Lee Edelman is a literary critic and Professor of English at Tufts University, Massachusetts.

Adrienne Edwards is a curator, scholar and writer, and Engell Speyer Family Curator and Curator of Performance at the Whitney Museum of American Art, New York.

Alex Fialho is a graduate student in the Combined Ph.D. program in the History of Art and African American Studies, Yale University.

Rosemarie Garland-Thomson is a Professor of English and bioethics at Emory University, Atlanta.

Goutam Ghosh is an artist based in Santiniketan, India.

Lewis Gordon is a writer on technology and culture, based in Glasgow.

Johanna Gosse is Assistant Professor of Art History & Visual Culture at the University of Idaho.

Stephen Jay Gould (1941–2002) was an American palaeontologist, evolutionary biologist and historian of science.

Catherine Grenier is an art historian and Director of the Fondation Giacometti, Paris.

Daniel Harris is an author based in Brooklyn, New York.

Jason Havneraas is an artist based in Oslo.

Friedrich Wolfram Heubach is a psychologist, freelance journalist and writer based in Germany.

Hsuan L. Hsu is Professor of English at University of California, Davis.

Marilyn Ivy is Associate Professor in the Department of Anthropology, Columbia University, New York.

Mike Kelley (1954–2012) was an artist based in Los Angeles.

Sharon Kinsella is Lecturer in Japanese Studies at The University of Manchester, UK.

Christopher Knight is a writer and art critic for the *Los Angeles Times*.

Leigh Claire La Berge is Assistant Professor of English at BMCC, The City University New York.

Elizabeth Legge is Associate Professor in the Department of Art History, University of Toronto.

Wyndham Lewis (1882–1957) was an English writer, artist and critic.

Lori Merish is a Professor of English at Georgetown University, Washington, DC.

William Ian Miller is the Thomas G. Long Professor of Law at the University of Michigan.

Michael Moon is a Professor of Women's, Gender & Sexuality Studies, Emory University, Atlanta.

John Morreall is Doctor of Philosophy and Emeritus Professor of Religious Studies at the College of William and Mary in Williamsburg, Virginia.

Juliane Rebentisch is Professor of Philosophy and Aesthetics, and Vice President at the Hochschule für Gestaltung, Offenbach/Main, Germany, and Visiting Professor at Princeton University.

Frances Richard is a writer, poet and editor based in San Francisco.

Carrie Rickey is a writer and film critic at *The Philadelphia Inquirer*.

David Robbins is an artist and writer based in Wisconsin.

John Roberts is Professor of Art and Aesthetics at the University of Wolverhampton, UK.

Mika Rottenberg is an artist based in New York.

Friedrich Schiller (1759–1805) was a German playwright, poet and philosopher.

Peter Schjeldahl is a writer and art critic at *The New Yorker*.

Kanako Shiokawa is a teacher of Japanese culture, language and folklore.

Kristian Skylstad is an artist based in Oslo.

Angelik Vizcarrondo-Laboy is a curator, writer and arts administrator based between New York and Los Angeles.

Elizabeth Honor Wilder is Editorial Assistant at University of Arizona Press.

Kevin Young is a poet and director of the Smithsonian Institution National Museum of African American History and Culture, Washington, D.C.

Bibliography

Allison, Anne, 'Portable Monsters and Commodity Cuteness: Pokémon as Japan's New Global Power', *Postcolonial Studies*, vol. 6, no. 3 (2003)

Aragón, Oriana R., Margaret S. Clark, Rebecca L. Dyer and John A. Bargh, 'Dimorphous Expressions of Positive Emotion: Displays of Both Care and Aggression in Response to Cute Stimuli', *Psychological Science*, vol. 26, no. 3 (2015)

Azuma, Hiroki, *Otaku: Japan's Database Animals*, trans. Jonathan E. Abel and Shion Kono (Minneapolis: University of Minnesota Press, 2009)

Benjamin, Walter, 'Toys and Play' and 'The Cultural History of Toys', in *Selected Writings. vol. 2, 1927– 1934*, trans. Rodney Livingstone and others, eds. Michael Jennings, Howard Eiland and Gary Smith (Cambridge, MA: Belknap Press, 1999)

Berlant, Lauren, 'Compassion (and Withholding)', in *Compassion: The Culture and Politics of an Emotion*, ed. Lauren Berlant (New York and Abingdon: Routledge, 2004)

Black, Daniel, 'The Virtual Ideal: Virtual Idols, Cute Technology and Unclean Biology', *Continuum: Journal of Media & Cultural Studies*, vol. 22, no. 1 (February 2008) 37–50.

Blom, Ina, 'Dream Work: The Art of Torbjørn Rødland', *Artforum* (September 2015)

Boyle, Jen, and Wan-Chuan Kao (eds.), *The Retro-Futurism of Cuteness* (Brooklyn, NY: Punctum Books, 2017)

Brzozowska-Brywczyska, Maja, 'Monstrous/Cute. Notes on the Ambivalent Nature of Cuteness', in *Monsters and the Monstrous: Myths and Metaphors of Enduring Evil*, ed. Niall Scott (London: Brill/ Roldolpi, 2007)

Burke, Edmund, *A Philosophical Enquiry into the Origin of Our Ideas of the Beautiful and Sublime*, ed. Adam Philips (Oxford: Oxford University Press, 1990)

Caudwell, Catherine Barbara, 'Cute and Monstrous Furbys in Online Fan Production', *M/C Journal*, vol. 17, no. 2 (2014)

Caudwell, Catherine and Cherie, Lacey, 'What Do Home Robots Want? The Ambivalent Power Of Cuteness In Robotic Relationships', *Convergence: The International Journal of Research into New Media Technologies*, vol. 26, no. 4 (2020)

Chan, Paul, 'The Potency of Art', *Social Research: An International Quarterly*, vol. 83, no. 1 (Spring 2016) 149–52.

Cross, Gary, *The Cute and The Cool: Wondrous Innocence and Modern American Children's Culture* (Oxford: Oxford University Press, 2004)

Dale, Joshua Paul, Joyce Goggin, Julia Leyda, Anthony P. McIntyre, and Diane Negra (eds.), *The Aesthetics and Affects of Cuteness* (London and New York: Routledge, 2017)

Dale, Joshua Paul, 'The Appeal of the Cute Object: Desire, Domestication, and Agency', in *The Affects and Aesthetics of Cuteness*, 35–54.

Dale, Joshua Paul , 'Cute studies: An Emerging Field', *East Asian Journal of Popular Culture*, vol. 2, no. 1, 5–13 (2016)

Dale, Joshua Paul, 'The Cute Studies Bibliography' (2013) (https://docs.google. com/document/d/

1qO8qiY8FaFlsMGrBFvH1GRVQqPMFlxp7pEGkldos W1Q/edit?usp=sharing)

Diehl, Travis, 'The Briar and the Tar: Nayland Blake at the ICA LA and Matthew Marks Gallery', *Contemporary Art Review* (3 December 2019)

de Vries, Nadia, 'Under The Yolk Of Consumption: Re-Envisioning the Cute as Consumable', in *The Aesthetics and Affects of Cuteness*, 253–273.

Empson, William, *Some Versions of Pastoral* (London: Chatto & Windus, 1935)

Friis-Hansen, Dana, 'The Meaning of Murakami's "Nonsense": About Japan Itself', in *Takashi Murakami: The Meaning of the Nonsense of the Meaning* (exh. cat.) (Annandale-on-Hudson, NY: Center for Curatorial Studies Museum, Bard College, 1999) 30–41.

Galt, Rosalind, 'Introduction: The Pretty as Troublesome Image', in *Pretty: Film and the Decorative Image* (New York: Columbia University Press, 2011)

Genosko, Gary, 'Natures and Cultures of Cuteness', *Invisible Culture*, no. 9 (2005) (www.rochester.edu/in_visible_culture/Issue_9/genosko.html)

Gombrich, E.H., (with Ernst Kris), 'The Principles of Caricature', *British Journal of Medical Psychology*, vol. 17 (1938) 319–42 [Trapp no.1938A.1].

Gn, Joel, 'Functional/Dysfunctional Beauty: On the Creation and Commodification of Cuteness', in *Cosmetic, Aesthetic, Prophetic: Beyond the Boundaries of Beauty* (Leiden: Brill, 2016) 191–200.

Jackson, Lauren, 'Baby Yoda is what capitalism would look like if an economic system were cute', *Washington Post* (19 December 2019)

Kelley, Mike, 'Interview with John Miller', *BOMB* (21 March 1991). Originally published in *Mike Kelley* (New York: A.R.T Press, 1992)

Kelley, Mike, 'Playing with Dead Things: On the Uncanny', in *Mike Kelley: Foul Perfection*: *Essays and Criticism*, ed. John C. Welchman (Cambridge, MA: MIT Press, 2003).

Keyser, Catherine, 'Ingestion/The White Rabbit And His Colorful Tricks: Breakfast cereal, dietary purity, and race.' *Cabinet*, no. 65 'Knowledge' (Fall 2017–Winter 2018) (www.cabinetmagazine.org/issues/65/keyser.php)

Koestenbaum, Wayne, 'This Usefulness Does Not Dangle in Mid-Air', in *Mika Rottenberg: The Production of Luck*. Published in 2014 by Gregory R. Miller & Co. in association with the Rose Art Museum on the occasion of the exhibition *Mika Rottenberg: Bowls Balls Souls Holes*, 14 February–8 June 2014.

Kümmerling-Meibauer, Bettina and Jörg Meibauer, 'Cuteness and Aggression in Military Picturebooks', *Problemy Wczesnej Edukacji/Issues In Early Education* vol. 3, no. 34 (2016)

Lewis, Wyndham, 'Buy Me an Air-Ball, Please!' ('Sub Persona Infantis'), in *The Art of Being Ruled*, ed. Reed Way Dasenbrock (Santa Rosa: Black Sparrow Press, 1989)

Lloyd, David, *Under Representation: The Racial Regime of Aesthetics* (New York: Fordham University Press, 2019)

Longmore, Paul, '"Heaven's Special Child": The Making of Poster Children', in *The Disability Studies Reader*, ed. Lennard J. Davis (New York: Routledge, 2013)

Lorenz, Karl, *Studies in Animal and Human Behaviour*, vol. 2 (1950), trans. R. Martin (Cambridge, MA: Harvard University Press, 1971)

Lukács, Gabrielle, 'The Labor of Cute: Net Idols in the Digital Economy', in *Invisibility by Design: Women and Labor in Japan's Digital Economy* (Durham, NC and London: Duke University Press, 2020)

McCloud, Scott, 'The Vocabulary of Comics', in *Understanding Comics: The Invisible Art* (New York: William Morrow, 1994)

Mcfarlane, Nicole, 'The Racial Rhetoric of Cuteness as Decorative Decorum' (Clemson University, 2012) (https://tigerprints.clemson.edu/all_dissertations/946)

Messager, Annette, Interview by Natasha Leoff, *Journal of Contemporary Art* (1995) (www.jca-online.com/messager)

Miesler, Linda, Helmut Leder and Andreas Herrmann, 'Isn't It Cute: An Evolutionary Perspective of Baby-Schema Effects in Visual Product Designs', *International Journal of Design*, vol. 5, no. 3 (2011) 17–30.

Miller, Laura, 'Cute Masquerade and the Pimping of Japan', *International Journal of Japanese Sociology* 20.1 (2011)

Milton, Kay, 'Possum Magic, Possum Menace: Wildlife Control and the Demonisation of Cuteness', in *Considering Animals: Contemporary Studies in Human-Animal Relations*, eds. Carol Freeman, Elizabeth Leane and Yvette Watt (New York: Routledge, 2011)

Minamore, Bridget, 'Get Up, Stand Up Now: Q&A With Artist Deborah Roberts' (30 August 2019) (www.somersethouse.org.uk/blog/get-stand-now-qa-artist-deborah-roberts)

Mori, Masahiro, 'The Uncanny Valley', trans. Karl F. MacDorman and Norri Kageki, *IEEE Robotics & Automation Magazine* (June 2012).

Neary, Janet, 'Cotton Babies, Mama's Maybe: Invention, Matter, and Mythology in Kara Walker's *8 Possible Beginnings*', *J19: The Journal of Nineteenth-Century Americanists* vol. 3, no. 1 (Spring 2015)

Norton, Margot, 'Not-So-Easy Pieces', in *Mika Rottenberg: Easypieces*, ed. Margot Norton (New York: New Museum, 2019)

Novina, Alexandra, 'A Swell of Sentiment', in *Pretty Sweet: The Sentimental Image in Contemporary Art* (Lincoln, MA: DeCordova Museum and Sculpture Park, 2005)

Page, Allison, 'This Baby Sloth Will Inspire You To Keep Going: Capital, Labor, and the Affective Power of Cute Animal Videos', in *The Aesthetics and Affects of Cuteness*, 75– 94.

Qiu Zitong, 'Cuteness as a Subtle Strategy: Urban female youth and the online *feizhuliu* culture in contemporary China', *Cultural Studies*, vol. 27, no. 2 (March 2013)

Rickels, Laurence A., 'Silent Reading', in *Larry Johnson*, ed. Scott Watson (Vancouver: Morris and Helen Belkin Art Gallery, University of British Columbia, 1996)

Rundquist, Leisa, *The Power and Fluidity of Girlhood in Henry Darger's Art* (New York: Routledge, 2020)

Rutanen, Eevi, 'Uncanny Dimple: Mapping the Cute and the Uncanny in Human-Robot Interaction' (2019), MFA thesis for Computational Arts at Goldsmiths, University of London (www.eevirutanen.com/wp-content/uploads/2019/09/Uncanny_Dimple_booklet.pdf)

Sawaragi, Noi, 'Dangerously Cute: Noi Sawaragi and Fumio Nanjo Discuss Contemporary Japanese Culture', *Flash Art*, no. 163 (March–April 1992)

Sherman, Gary D. and Jonathan Haidt, 'Cuteness and Disgust: The Humanizing and Dehumanizing Effects of Emotion', *Emotion Review*, vol. 3, no. 3 (July 2011)

Shilling, Alake, Interview by Anthony Valdez (January 2018). Conducted on the occasion of the exhibition 'Alake Shilling: Monsoon Lagoon', 356 Mission, Los Angeles, 23 February–29 April 2018) (www.356mission.com/item/alake-shilling-monsoon-lagoon/?tab=Interview)

Sibley, Frank, 'Aesthetic Concepts', *Philosophical Review*, vol. 68, no. 4 (1959)

Snediker, Michael D., 'Fuzzy Logic', in *Staying Alive*, ed. Eileen A. Joy (Brooklyn, NY: Punctum Books, 2013)

Sousa, Ana Matilde, *Muji Life + Yangire/Yandere* (2015). Presented at the 6th Feira Morta (Lisbon), 20 September 2015.

Sousa, Ana Matilde, *CUTENCYCLOPEDIA: A theoretical-practical investigation on the* kawaii *as an aesthetic category in art and pop culture* [*CUTENCYCLOPEDIA. Uma investigação teórico-prática sobre o* kawaii *como categoria estética na arte e cultural popular*] (2000). Doctoral dissertation in Painting, FBAUL – Faculty of Fine Arts of Lisboa (Faculdade de Belas Artes da Universidade de Lisboa)

Stewart, Susan, 'The Miniature', in *On Longing: Narratives of the Miniature, the Gigantic, the Souvenir, the Collection* (Durham, NC: Duke University Press, 1993) 65–7.

Tiffany, Daniel, *My Silver Planet: A Secret History of Poetry and Kitsch* (Baltimore: Johns Hopkins University Press, 2013)

von Bonin, Cosima, 'Interview with Eleanor Heartney', *Brooklyn Rail* (April 2018)

Wai-hung Yiu and Alex Ching-shing Chan, '"Kawaii" and "Moe" — Gazes, Geeks (Otaku), and Glocalization of Beautiful Girls (Bishōjo) in Hong Kong Youth Culture', *positions: asia critique*, vol. 21, no.4 (2013)

Winnicott, D.W., 'Transitional Objects and Transitional Phenomena', in *Playing and Reality* (London and New York: Routledge, 1971) 1–34.

Yano, Christine R., *Pink Globalization: Hello Kitty's Trek Across The Pacific* (Durham, NC and London: Duke University Pres, 2013)

Young, Damon, 'Sarcastic Cuteness', in *Ironies of Web 2.0* (*Post45*), no.2 'How to Be Now' (February 2019) (https://post45.org/2019/05/ironies-of-web-2-0/)

Zangwill, Nick, 'The Beautiful, the Dainty and the Dumpy', *British Journal of Aesthetics* vol. 35, no. 4 (1995)

Zebrowitz, Leslie A., Sheila Brownlow and Karen Olson, 'Baby Talk To The Babyfaced', *Journal of Nonverbal Behavior* vol. 16, no. 3 (Autumn 1992)

ACKNOWLEDGEMENTS

Editor's acknowledgements

Heartfelt thanks to Lily Scherlis, whose imaginative assistance on this project was essential. This book simply would not exist without the initial inspiration, steady guidance, keen judgment and wit of Commissioning Editor Anthony Iles; I am grateful to him for making working on it a pleasure.

Publisher's acknowledgements

Whitechapel Gallery is grateful to all those who gave their generous permission to reproduce the listed material. Every effort has been made to secure all permissions and we apologise for any inadvertent errors or omissions. If notified, we will endeavour to correct these at the earliest opportunity. We would like to express our thanks to all who contributed to the making of this volume.

Whitechapel Gallery

whitechapelgallery.org

Whitechapel Gallery is supported by

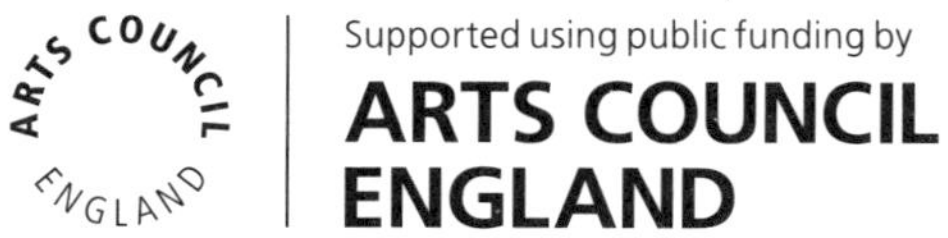